Michael Ahern

Figures in a Clonmel Landscape

by

Michael Ahern

First published in 2006
by
Ardo Books, Melview, Clonmel, Co. Tipperary, Ireland

ISBN: 0-9554477-0-4
ISBN: 978-0-9554477-0-9

Printed by Kilkenny People Printing

This book has received assistance from the Tipperary LEADER Programme which is
financed by the Irish government and part-funded by the E.U. under the National
Development Plan, 2005-2006

for

Deirdre
Niamh
Emer
Gráinne

Contents

List of illustrations

Nos. 1 to 22 are located between pages 93 and 94 and nos. 23 to 49 between pages 242 and 243

List of maps

Acknowledgements

I wish to thank all those whose help and support made this book possible.

I am particularly grateful to Margaret Rossiter for writing such an encouraging foreword.
I am also indebted to Ursula Mullins for her eye-catching cover design.
I would like especially to thank Shay Hurley for his photographic expertise.
My thanks to Niamh Ahern for her drawings and to Maurice Molloy for the genealogical tables.
My gratitude to Dr. Carmel Quinlan, who graciously consented to launch this book.
I must make special mention of Fr. Éanna Condon, Liam Ó Duibhir and Catherine O'Keeffe for their valuable assistance.
I am also indebted to the following:
Dr. Toby Barnard, Marie Boland (Clonmel Library), Evelyn Cody (Waterford County Library), Niamh Cronin (Cork County Library and Arts Service), Terry Crosbie, Mary Guinan Darmody (Tipperary County Library), Micheál Drohan, Pat Holland, Kieran Jordan, Kalene Kennifick, Maud Kerney, Séamus Leahy, Mary McLean (nee Delahunty), Roberta Malcomson, Imelda Malone (nee Patterson), George Mealy, Pat Melody, Jane Thompson Moore, Seán Murphy, Hughie O'Callaghan, Mathúin Ó Caoimh, Michael O'Donnell, Dr. Seán O'Donnell, Sister Louise O'Connell, Frances O'Connor, Paddy O'Keeffe, Mai Patterson, Una Power, Jack Prendergast, Eoin Ryan, Timmy Ryan, Hazel Stapleton, Leslie and William Talbot and the Staff of Tipperary County Museum.

Finally, my wife, Deirdre, who lived with my obsession, accompanied me on my travels in the cause of research and stayed with it to the end.

The right to reproduce photographs and illustrations has been received from the following:

Liam Stapleton (no. 1)
'The Board of Trinity College Dublin' (no. 2)
University of Chicago (no. 3)
Department for the Environment, Heritage and Local Government (nos. 4 and 8)
Shay Hurley (nos. 13 and 29)
National Library of Ireland (no. 22)
Clonmel Borough Council (nos. 23, 24, 25, 26 and 31)
Tipperary County Museum (nos. 30, 32 and 33)

Foreword

Towns are the product of the people who live in them. They influence the physical structure, the ethos, the character and the architecture of the place where circumstances have brought them, whether by birth or work opportunity, affinity or haphazard choice.

Clonmel, the capital, administrative centre, and largest town in the South Riding of Tipperary, is fortunate in its geographical setting, in a valley, on the banks of the River Suir and in the shadow of the Comeragh foothills. It inspires a unique sense of pride in its citizens.

It is a vibrant town which, in the best of times, never allowed that natural pride to descend to arrogance and, in the worst of times, as in the post Cromwellian period, was never entirely defeated nor never lost its will to live and re-build. It was particularly fortunate in having an active Quaker community in the 18/19th centuries. Michael Ahern has already written about some of these Quaker families and their influence on the industrial development and the vernacular architecture and streetscape of the town.

In *Figures in a Clonmel Landscape* he further explores the lives of individuals who have contributed to the many layers which make up the fabric of the town, from the historic and political to the social, artistic and literary life of Clonmel.

Some of the characters in this book have had only a very transient association with this town, yet it was an association which shaped them in some way, but which, in turn, also shaped and influenced the town.

In pursuing the significance of that influence, the author has drawn on a very broad biographical canvas, going back to the initial Anglo Norman foundation of the town itself under the de Burgo hegemony, to the prominence of the 'Old English' Whites in the 17th and the Irish nationalism of Frank Drohan in the 20th centuries.

In his chapters on the builder-architect, William Tinsley, and the cabinet-maker, Thomas Graham, Michael has filled in the background to the rising prosperity and industrialization of Clonmel which accompanied the great Quaker enterprises. Skills and crafts blossomed to accompany and enhance that prosperity and enterprise.

Figures in a Clonmel Landscape is, in essence, a series of biographical studies of famous and notable citizens but, in telling their stories, the author, also tells the story of the town itself through its often turbulent history. It is, too, a reflection of his own sense of place and of his love of that place.

The town of Clonmel is more fortunate than most in how well it has been served by its writers and historians. Within the pages of this book, Michael Ahern has made a further very valuable contribution to that corpus of knowledge and history.

In telling the stories of people who made a difference in the life of a town, he himself has made a difference. This is a book which should not only be in every Clonmel home, but in the hands of every Clonmel-born person, wherever they may be throughout the world.

Margaret Rossiter.

Chapter 1

Founding Fathers

The town of Clonmel lies in a part of the Suir valley in south Tipperary that has attracted settlers for thousands of years. A dolmen in Gurteen wood above Kilsheelan, eight kilometres east and a bronze age settlement at Ballyveelish six kilometres north, overlooking the road to Cashel, indicate a human presence stretching back to pre-historic times. Church ruins and stone crosses mark the arrival of early Christian missionaries. A number of Viking coins discovered some years ago in Marlfield suggest that the Norsemen, in their long boats, may have found their way this far up-river. However, it is the Normans who provide us with the first written evidence of human habitation in Clonmel.

With the blessing of Henry II of England those seasoned adventurers landed on Bannow Strand in County Wexford in 1169. Ostensibly, they came to render assistance in re-instating Diarmuid McMurrough, the deposed king of Leinster, but these land-hungry barons saw this venture as a means of making their fortune. Without much difficulty they seized the Norse towns of Waterford, Wexford and Dublin and overran a large portion of Leinster. Alarmed at the ease of their success, and to curb any notions that they may have entertained of severing their allegiance to the crown, Henry decided to come to Ireland in person. He landed in Waterford in 1171 with his army, assumed control of the newly won towns and received assurances of loyalty from his Norman subjects.

Fourteen years later Henry again found it necessary to intervene in Irish affairs by sending John, his seventeen year old son, to Ireland. By this time Strongbow, Raymond Le Gros and Hugh de Lacy, men who were largely responsible for the success of the initial invasion, were dead. A fresh injection of manpower and a clear-cut policy were needed to hold what was already won and John was willing and ready to supply both. Accompanied by a team of experienced administrators, he landed in the royal town of Waterford which was under threat from the marauding Irish in the surrounding countryside. John took measures to provide a buffer

1

zone for the beleaguered city by building castles at Tibberaughney near Carrick-on-Suir, Lismore and Ardfinnan while, at the same time, making extensive land grants which brought the Normans for the first time on to the plains of Tipperary.

William de Burgo

Among John's followers was William de Burgo, or Burke, as the family was later to become known. William de Burgo has been confused by many historians, including Canon Burke, with William FitzAldelm de Burgo, the steward of Henry II, who was appointed the King's deputy in Ireland in June 1176. Modern research has shown however that William FitzAldelm and William de Burgo were two different persons. As in the case of many of his contemporaries, our knowledge of William de Burgo is scant. No concrete evidence exists of his ancestry or place of birth. He was reputed to have been a native of Norfolk, descended from a family who boasted a proud military tradition. The de Burgos thought very highly of themselves. They claimed descent from the great Charlemagne himself. One member of the family was said to have distinguished himself on the crusades while another, Robert de Burgo, was reputedly with William the Conqueror at the Battle of Hastings and is depicted on the famous Bayeaux tapestry.[1] More objective commentators, however, have dismissed these speculations as 'reckless fabrications'.[2]

William, who was described as Prince John's 'chief trouble-shooter in Munster'[3], was one of the most successful of the new adventurers who 'was soon to show that the road to wealth and power that had been followed by Strongbow ..... and others was still open'.[4] In 1185 John allotted William territory along the Tipperary-Limerick border where the district of Clanwilliam still bears his name. He also received lands in the

---

[1] Eamonn Burke, *Burke: People and Places,* (Galway, 1984, p. 4).

[2] Martin J. Blake, 'William de Burgh' in *Journal of Galway Archaeological and Historica Societyl,* vii (1911-12), p. 92.

[3] C. A. Empey, 'The Norman Period, 1185-1500' in William Nolan and Thomas G. Mc Grath (eds.), *Tipperary: History and Society,* (Dublin, 1985), p. 76.

[4] Robin Frame, *Colonial Ireland 1169-1369* (Dublin, 1981), p. 21.

eastern part of the barony of Iffa and Offa which included the site for the future town of Clonmel. There is very little to be found in the official records to show how or when William made himself master of these lands.

It cannot have been too difficult, for the Irish in their linen tunics and with inferior weaponry could have offered little effective resistance to the chain mail and superior military organisation of their opponents. As happened elsewhere, the invaders may have been aided by those who seized the opportunity to throw off their Gaelic overlords or sought allies to resolve their tribal feuds. Despite their military superiority the Norman colony was small and vulnerable, being surrounded by hostile Irish chiefs waiting for any opportunity to win back their ancestral homelands.

William's greatest threat was Dónal Mór Ó Briain, the powerful king of Thomond and descendant of the illustrious Brian Ború, but this obstacle was overcome when William married Dónal's daughter in 1193. This proved to be a fruitful alliance for both parties. While William's lands enjoyed Dónal's protection, William gave his father-in-law military support against the McCarthys of Desmond, the traditional enemies of the O'Briens. In other respects the marriage had some interesting consequences. William's son, Richard, could claim to be one of the first Gaelic speaking Normans and 'through the marriage with an O'Brien the blood of the great Brian Ború has flowed through the Mortimers and the House of York to the present royal House of England'.[5]

Although William had secured extensive lands in south and west Tipperary William was far from satisfied. He was an ambitious man anxious to increase his holdings and the death of Dónal Mór O Brien in 1194 was to present him with such an opportunity. Dónal's sons needed William's support to protect their inheritance against the ever hostile McCarthys. In return for his help, William was to be allowed to settle in Limerick on McCarthy land. Gathering a huge army and enlisting the assistance of the Normans of Munster he ravaged the lands of Desmond. The annals of Innisfallen record how his 'plundering parties committed great depredations'. Dónal retaliated in 1196 by attacking William's headquarters at Kilfeakle. Despite this setback William and his allies

---

[5] Edmund Curtis, *A History of Ireland* (London, 1936), p. 65.

prevailed, seizing vast areas of west Limerick, while William took control of an area between Limerick city and Lough Derg. In ten short years William had become one of the most powerful Norman barons in Munster. This was reflected, not alone in the lands he had conquered, but in the prestigious appointments he secured. He was made governor of Limerick, appointed the king's representative in Munster and, in 1200, he received a grant of Tibberaughney, the first castle built by King John.

In the same year he founded the largest Augustinian abbey in Ireland at Athassel. It was fashionable for the rich and powerful to provide endowments to establish monasteries. Speaking of this practice, it has been observed that:

> The motivation of the founder was the usual one of having advantages in the next life comparable (at least) to those enjoyed in this life. Specifically of course, such a foundation provided a last resting place for the founder and his descendants: an example of making your wealth work for you long after you are dead.[6]

Its extensive ruins, which can still be seen a few miles south of Golden on the banks of the Suir, give some indication of its former splendour. The abbey was to have close ties with Clonmel when William granted the abbot the tithes of the town. Consequently, the abbot appointed the vicar to the parish church of St. Mary's and gave him one third of the tithes as a salary. The modern locality known as Prior Park is a reminder of this ancient connection.

In 1200 William turned his attention to Connacht. Sometime previously he had received a grant of the province which he was not able to realise because of the existing political situation. His opportunity came when the death of Rory O'Connor, the last high king of Ireland and head of the ruling dynasty in Connacht, plunged the province into civil war. William, supported by an army of mercenaries drawn from the Norman colony, set about destabilising the province still further. The Annals of Loch Cé claimed there was no church from the Shannon westwards that

---

[6] Denis G. Marnane, *Land and Settlement: A History of West Tipperary to 1660,* (Tipperary, 2003), p. 135.

they did not pillage and destroy. William's forces were charged with stripping priests and carrying off women and 'never before was there inflicted on the Connacht men any punishment of famine, nakedness, and plundering, like this'.

The justiciar, Meiler Fitzhenry, who felt that William's ambitious aggression was putting the security of the colony in jeopardy, ordered him, in the name of the king, to withdraw. William was forced to surrender his sons as hostages, give up his lands and to present himself before his majesty to answer the complaints made against him. In response, King John, while allowing him to retain all his lands in Munster revoked his claim to Connacht. Perhaps the king's decision was influenced by William's offer to render him service in Normandy where he was fighting to retain his French territories or he may have felt it inopportune to intervene personally in Ireland. Although there was always the danger that William might be tempted to shake off royal authority, the security and development of the colony was dependent on strong men like him and the king felt that a more prudent course was to check rather than crush him. This was a clear indication of William's importance in maintaining a Norman foothold in Ireland. Shortly after his return to Ireland in the winter of 1205, William died and was buried in his abbey at Athassel.

Richard de Burgo

William's son, Richard, became heir to the family estates. He was born around 1193 and was still a minor when his father died. When he came of age in 1214, King John re-granted him his father's lands in Tipperary and Limerick. During this period Richard appeared to spend a good deal of time abroad. In 1219 he was with King Henry in England while, two years later, he made a pilgrimage to the shrine of Santiago de Compostella in Spain. In 1225 he married Egidia de Lacy, as a result of which he received important estates in Ulster and allied himself with one of the most important Norman families in Ireland. His rising status in the Norman community was reflected in several important appointments. The king made him steward of Munster and gave him the position of custodian of the castle of Limerick. Much of this good fortune could be traced to the influence of his uncle, Hubert de Burgo, who held the position of justiciar in England from 1215 to 1232.

Richard's lifelong goal was to secure the province of Connacht, the prize that had eluded his father. In 1226, through the influence of his uncle Hubert, he received a grant of the province from the king and two years later Richard was appointed justiciar of Ireland. Despite Richard's power, securing his ambition presented numerous difficulties. Numerically, the Normans were not in a position to attempt colonisation on a large scale. The only alternative for Richard was to secure the backing of an Irish king who, in return for Norman support, would accept a reduced kingdom but be strong enough to command the allegiance of his lesser Irish chiefs. The problem now lay in selecting the candidate most likely to accept the terms on offer. And so Richard, like his father before him, decided to act as king-maker in Connacht.[7]

For the next six years, with brief intermissions, Connacht was ravaged and plundered. With Hubert's fall from grace in England in 1232 Richard's ambitions suffered a setback. Shortly afterwards he was ejected from the justiciarship and his grant of Connacht was withdrawn and 'only by virtue of some adroit manoeuvring did he regain it'.[8] Henry III demanded a fine of 3,000 marks from him, increased his annual rent and service to 500 marks and 20 knights, and 'urged him to exert himself strenuously to take possession of the land'.[9]

Richard scarcely needed any encouragement and, in 1235, he invaded Connacht at the head of five hundred knights drawn from all over the land, in what was to be the most ambitious freebooting adventure since the days of Strongbow. King Felim O'Connor was overwhelmed and sued for peace. He gladly accepted the five cantreds of land on offer from the king, while Richard de Burgo received the remaining twenty five and, at last, secured the lordship of Connacht. Richard seems to have set 'the tone with a business-like approach to settlement'. He built a castle in Loughrea

[7] Goddard Henry Orpen, *Ireland under the Normans 1216-1333*, iii, (Oxford, 1920), p. 175.
[8] Robin Frame, *Colonial Ireland, 1169-1369*, (Dublin, 1981), p. 61.
[9] Helen Perros, 'Anglo-Norman settlement in Connacht in the thirteenth century' in *Group for the Study of Irish Historic Settlement*, vii, (Athlone, 1996-7), p. 1.

which became his headquarters in Connacht and established manors in the south:

> These manors were within easy range of the ones he had in Tipperary and Limerick, with Meelick on the Shannon providing a crucial link. Also, both Meelick and his principal manor at Loughrea were on the best agricultural land in Connacht.[10]

He reserved for himself the plains between the Shannon and Loughs Conn, Mask and Corrib which to-day still retain the name Clanrickard and parcelled out the remainder among his followers.

This marks the highpoint of a remarkable career. It has been said that the expansion of English rule in the thirteenth century owed much to the efforts of that one man, Richard de Burgo. His achievements were eulogised in a poem entitled *History of the Burkes* which was translated from the Irish:

> He was king over Shannon, over Suir,
> Over Cong of the murmuring waters;
> Over Moy, over the babbling stream of Bann,
> And over the rivers between them.

Few did more than William and Richard to extend the Norman occupation of Ireland and, by so doing, incurred the enmity of the Gaelic lords they deposed. William was a man who provoked strong passions. Even his death was controversial. It was stated that he died of a loathsome disease 'too shameful to be described', the wishful thinking of an injured party perhaps. His ambition knew no bounds. His lifelong goal was to secure as much land as possible and to use every opportunity to do so. For William the end always justified the means. Treachery, deceit, murder and a willingness to go to war as the occasion demanded were the hallmarks of his turbulent career. In Ireland, he was undoubtedly one of the great military leaders of his day, displaying personal bravery, extraordinary

---

[10] *Ibid*, p. 2.

energy and making a series of astute alliances with both the Normans and Irish.

William's inability to secure Connacht was perhaps his one failure. Although he was known as William the Conqueror Burke because of his exploits in Connacht, Orpen said it is to 'Richard de Burgh, rather than to his father, that critical history will give the title of 'conqueror of Connacht'.[11] William was an able administrator, capable of holding down widely dispersed lands which were to provide his successors with a firm base for further expansion. Richard proved himself to be just as ambitious and ruthless as his father. He was more than capable of seizing the opportunities which presented themselves and displayed a similar fondness for battle and intrigue.

The Infant Town

In 1184, the year before William de Burgo was granted the lands on which Clonmel now stands, the Welsh historian, Giraldus Cambrensis, describing the progress of the river Suir from Ardfinnan to Tibberaghney makes no reference to Clonmel, so we may assume that it was not in existence before that date and that the founders of the future town were none other than the de Burgos. Although William and Richard were involved in almost continual warfare, they did not neglect what they had already won. On the contrary, these methodical Normans showed their customary flair for organisation and planning. The division of their newly won lands into administrative units known as manors marked the first stage in the colonisation and settlement of the conquered lands, and it was through this process that we find the origins of the town of Clonmel.

Although the colony had been established through the efforts of a military aristocracy it could only be maintained and economically developed by the skills and contributions of farmers who were needed to cultivate the manorial land and tradesmen who were needed to provide various services. While the farming community was scattered throughout the manor, the tradesmen, consisting of millers, masons, thatchers, weavers,

---

[11] Orpen, iii, p. 189.

8

bakers, brewers, smiths and others were accommodated in a specially designed manorial village.

The creation and development of manorial villages, such as Clonmel, 'was part of a much more extensive development of European towns during the twelfth and thirteenth centuries' at a time when 'the chartered borough was one of the standard methods of economic development employed throughout medieval Europe'.[12] The necessary tradesmen, generally recruited in the Lord's homeland, were given specific inducements to settle in the new manorial villages. Such rights and privileges guaranteed by the lord were set out in a charter. This form of urban constitution conferred borough status on the infant settlement and its occupants were collectively known as burgesses.

The foundation charter of liberties for the borough of Clonmel is missing, as is the case in many other towns, but we may surmise that it contained the same basic elements common to other charters in the Ireland of this period. Each burgess was provided with a plot of borough ground or site for a house at an annual rent of one shilling, and also enjoyed an allotment of land in the burgagery lands and access to the commons. The burgesses were mainly engaged in craft and commercial activities, but since they held a certain amount of land in the town fields outside the village they were also involved in agriculture. Gradually however, they took on an exclusively urban role as Clonmel developed into a market town.

Other liberties included the right to marry without the lord's permission, leave the manor and sell their burgess lands. They were entitled to be tried in the town court, called the hundred court, which dealt with commercial disputes and breaches of the peace, and was presided over by their fellow burgesses. The court also determined prices, wages and issued by-laws. The burgesses received certain trading concessions, including the freedom to trade everywhere on the lord's lands and they had an exemption from the tolls that were levied on outsiders.

In return for these privileges, the lord, as founder of the manor, received revenue from his investment in the form of rents from the burgage lots and market tolls. The tenants were obliged to grind their corn at the

---

[12] B. J. Graham, 'Urbanisation in the middle ages' in T. Barry (ed.), *History of settlement in Ireland*, (London, 2000), pp. 127,128.

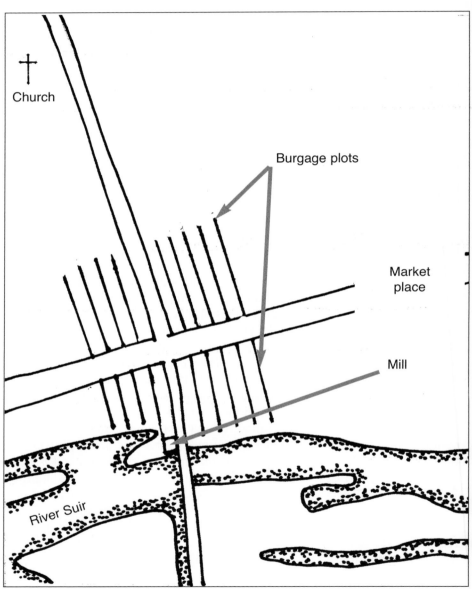

Map 1. Manorial village of Clonmel.

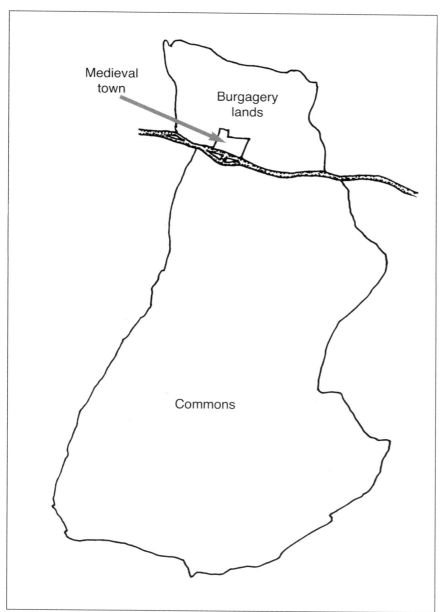

Medieval town

Burgagery lands

Commons

Map 2. The medieval manor of Clonmel

lord's mill and pay for the service. Other lucrative sources of income were the fines derived from the manor court, which settled disputes that occurred among the occupants of the manor outside the manorial village.

The manor of Clonmel consisted of the manorial village which was built on the north bank of the river Suir and the burgagery lands, surrounding the village which, in time, became part of the expanding borough. The most extensive portion of the manor was the commons which extended south of the river into the county Waterford. It stretched for a distance of approximately eight kilometres, almost reaching the Nire valley, and was approximately five kilometres in width.[13]

By planning the layout of Clonmel, the de Burgos effectively shaped the structure of the town for centuries to come. We can still detect reminders of the original concept in the linear street pattern and in traces of the medieval urban design. Two grassy intersecting trackways, which today have developed into O'Connell Street, Bridge Street and Mary Street, formed the nucleus of the embryonic town. This cruciform design was typical of Norman towns elsewhere.

Stretching back from either side of O'Connell Street, which formed the east-west axis, the remnants of the original burgage plots may still be seen. Surviving Norman charters for towns in south-east Ireland show that the burgage plots measured approximately twenty feet or 6.1 metres wide and had a length to width ratio of approximately 5:1. Nineteenth century maps of the town indicate that the original burgage plots in Clonmel had similar dimensions. These long, narrow burgage plots were so designed as to allow the maximum number of dwellings to enjoy a street frontage. Today however, few, if any, retain their original proportions. Dwellings, being obliged to conform to the limitations of the site, had their gables facing the streets. The shop occupied the ground floor, with living quarters upstairs, while the outhouses, stores and gardens were placed to the rear. A series of laneways were created to provide access from the street to the backyard and also helped to light the interior of the houses. Through the centuries many of these laneways have disappeared by becoming incorporated into the adjacent dwellings.

---

[13] Burke, *History of Clonmel*, (Waterford, 1907), pp. 232, 233.

Provision was also made for a market place, which was situated at the east end of the present O'Connell Street where the Main Guard now stands. Its central feature was the market cross, an indication, perhaps, of God's watchful eye being trained on the transactions. Bargains were sealed by each party placing a foot on the stone base or 'nail' as a mark of good faith. It was this custom that gave rise to the expression 'to pay on the nail'. Although the cross has long since vanished, its base is preserved in the gable of Mc Mahon's shoe shop at the top of Sarsfield Street.

Along the north-south axis was the manor mill, situated in the present Bridge Street. The parish church occupied a site in Mary Street where the present church still stands. The original church was in existence in 1228 when Stephen of Lexington preached there and the record of that occasion gives the church the distinction of being the first building in Clonmel referred to in written records of the town.

A most significant mark of the borough's growing economic importance was the grant Richard de Burgo got from the king in 1225 allowing the town to hold an annual fair beginning on the feast of All Saints and lasting seven days. In 1242 the fair was transferred to the feast of St. Magdalen which fell on the twenty-first of July. The fair created an important focus for commercial activity, attracting merchants from far and near. Clonmel's advantageous location enhanced its trading potential. Surrounded by fertile lands and built on the bank of a navigable river which provided a direct link to the port of Waterford were significant factors in turning Clonmel into a thriving market town.

On the death of Richard de Burgo in 1243, an 'inquest' into his property showed that he received a total burgage rent of £19 6s. [14] At one shilling a burgage this would imply a total of 386 burgages attached to the borough of Clonmel. Using a multiple of five for each household suggests a population of approximately 2,000. Although these figures are no more than an estimate, they indicate that at this early date Clonmel had established itself as a successful trading centre.

Richard de Burgo died in Bordeaux in 1243 on the way to help his king, Henry III, in the French wars. It was said that his death was the result

---

[14] *Ibid*, p. 12.

of hardships endured at sea. Richard's son, another Richard, was given his father's land in 1247 but he died the following year without issue. Walter, Richard's second son, was a minor and did not obtain his father's lands until 1250. As a result of his marriage in 1264 to the de Lacy heiress, Walter received extensive estates in Ulster and was created earl of Ulster, the first Norman in Ireland to be so ennobled. His elevation and acquisition of Ulster lands resulted in his being forced to surrender the manor of Clonmel, thus ending the de Burgo connection with the town.

Chapter 2

The Knight from beyond the Seas

The next owner of Clonmel manor, following the departure of the de Burgos, was one of the most fascinating and colourful characters of his day. His life was the stuff of legend. As a trusted advisor to Edward I of England, his duties took him to the four corners of Europe where he mixed with royalty, was present at the elevation of five popes and went on two crusades. In an age when travel was both a hazardous and arduous undertaking, he lived to a remarkable ninety years.

Otho de Grandison, who was born in 1238, came from the town of Grandison on the shores of Lake Neuchatel in Switzerland. He was the eldest son of Peter, Lord Grandison, and his wife, Agnes, one of a family of six boys and six girls. His childhood was spent behind the grey walls and conical towers of Castle Grandison, where his family had lived for two and a half centuries. It was said that a sage who was present at his birth predicted that the newborn infant would be famous and powerful. If this were true then the prediction was certainly fulfilled, for he was one of the most extraordinary men of his day. Legend has it that the sage then took a brand from the fire and declared that the boy would live only as long as it lasted but that he might live the longer if the brand was placed in an alcove high up in the wall. The boy lived, grew to manhood, and to old age, with ever increasing honour until, at last, weary of life through the burden of his years, he ordered the brand taken from the wall and cast into the fire. No sooner had it been consumed by the flames than the good knight expired.[1]

The family was fortunate in having the patronage of the powerful Duke of Savoy, who was also grand-uncle of Eleanor, wife of the future king, Edward I of England. When Otho's father died in 1258, the Duke brought Otho and his brothers, Gerard, Edward and William to England. He had Otho placed in the service of Prince Edward and during the next fifty

---

[1] C. L. Kingsford, 'Sir Otho de Grandison 1238-1328' in *Transactions of the Royal Historical Society*, series, iii, (1909), p. 126.

years, a close bond developed between the two men as Otho travelled throughout the length and breadth of Europe as his ambassador.

In his early years at court we catch glimpses of the man who was destined to play such a prominent role in the affairs of his adopted country. He first came to notice during the Barons' War. Led by Simon de Monfort, the nobles rebelled against Henry III in an unsuccessful attempt to extend their privileges. When Edward rallied to his father's support, Otho served under the prince's banner at Lewes and at the decisive battle of Evesham.

Having proved himself a trusted friend of Edward he was generously rewarded. From this time on he appears as Sir Otho in the records and becomes a permanent part of the prince's household. He also received the lands of William le Blund, one of the king's enemies who perished at Lewes in 1263. More significantly, he secured a grant for life of extensive property in Tipperary, which included the manors of Clonmel, Kilsheelan and Kilfeakle. In 1281 Edward, who had succeeded his father as king in 1272, made a permanent grant of these properties to Otho and his descendants.

We know relatively little of Otho's activities in Ireland, apart from the fact that he was Sheriff of Tipperary from 1267 to 1269[2]. In the latter year he introduced the Franciscans to Clonmel. They received a plot of ground enclosed by the present Sarsfield and Mitchel Streets, Dowd's Lane and the River Suir. There is no evidence that Otho ever set foot in the town and, if he did so, it could have been no more than a fleeting visit before he was off on his travels again. In 1267 when the pope called for a crusade to rescue the Holy Land from the infidel, Edward answered the papal plea. Shortly afterwards Otho joined his prince in taking the cross at Northampton. Before leaving Ireland, he made arrangements to secure his properties, leasing some and appointing his relatives to take charge of others.[3]

Otho's crusading pledge, although not taken lightly, was scarcely a difficult decision for a devout Christian. He said 'I have taken the cross, and because of what I hope to achieve, I trust the Blessed Virgin and St. John will intercede for me, so that once I have put off this garment of flesh,

---

[2] William Burke, *History of Clonmel*, (Waterford, 1907), p. 13.
[3] Paul J. Flynn, *The book of the Galtees*, (Dublin, 1926), pp. 61-63.

I shall rest in Abraham's bosom'.[4] In 1270 the army was equipped, supplies procured, transport arrangements made and the crusaders sailed from Portsmouth with all the pageantry the occasion demanded. From Bordeaux they went overland through the Spanish Pyrenees, crossed the Mediterranean to Tunis, where Edward hoped to join the crusading expedition of King Louis of France. They landed to find that Louis had died of fever some days previously. Although his force was too small to accomplish much in military terms, Edward continued the crusade and landed in Italy. They spent Christmas in Palermo and the following year reached Acre in the Holy Land.

Acre may have been in the Holy Land but there was nothing holy about it. In this sordid trading town, where Christians traded with the enemy, the arrival of an English prince was an unwelcome intrusion. The forces at Edward's disposal prevented him from undertaking more than a handful of raids and skirmishes, but the Ottomans decided to prevent him making a further nuisance of himself. The Emir of Joppa was chosen to carry out the task. He was a member of a subversive force known as The Assassins. He gained access to Edward's tent and stabbed him in the arm with a poisoned dagger, before Edward managed to kill him. After some days the king's arm began to fester. The Flemish historian, John of Ypres, said that Otho 'dared to suck the venom from the wound' and because of this, 'the lord of Grandison and his family were raised to honours at the English court'.[5] More significantly, when Edward made his will a few days after the attack, he named Otho as one of his executors, a further indication of the esteem in which he was held.

On his way home from the crusade, Prince Edward received word that his father had died in his absence, and for the next thirty years we find Otho at the centre of every important event throughout Edward's reign. The king employed him not merely in delicate, personal matters but also in complex affairs of state. We hear of him being sent abroad to purchase horses for the king's use or to negotiate a loan on his behalf with the merchants of Florence. He was a familiar figure at the courts of Europe, concluding peace treaties or arranging matrimonial alliances for Edward's

---

[4] Esther Roland Clifford, *A knight of great renown*, (Chicago, 1971), p. 270.
[5] Kingsford, p. 126.

offspring. He proved he was capable of dealing with everybody, from ambitious kings to conniving moneylenders and from haughty popes to scheming officials. In Edward's own words, 'there was no one about him who could do his will better; nay, it could not be better done if he were to attend to it in person'.[6]

The Duchy of Gascony which lay between the Pyrenees and the Gascons in the south-west corner of France was all that remained of the once vast French possessions of the English king. In the eleventh century it became united with the Duchy of Aquitaine and Edward enjoyed the title, Duke of Aquitaine. In 1275, he appointed Otho to administer the affairs of the Duchy and, in October of that year, Otho made the first of many trips to this region where he appointed officials, made grants, settled disputes and dispensed justice. It was a difficult and time-consuming mission.

The demands of administration would have kept Otho shuttling indefinitely between England and France had not more pressing matters demanded his services at home. Llewellyn, Prince of Wales and Edward's vassal, disobeyed the royal summons to come to England to pay homage. In the early months of 1277 Otho took a leading part in spearheading the invasion into Wales. With John de Vescey and a force of two thousand men, he landed on the island of Anglesey, which had been blockaded by the English fleet. They forced Llewellyn to surrender and Otho was one of those charged with drawing up the terms of the subsequent treaty.

With the Welsh question settled Otho paid a visit to his homeland where for the first and only time, he flirted with the idea of matrimony. The lady in question was a daughter of Count Othon IV of Burgundy but Otho, for reasons unknown, decided against marriage and remained single for the rest of his life. In 1280 he embarked on his first mission to the papal court to persuade the Pope to accept Edward's brother, Edmund, as leader of the next crusade. Edward felt that political problems would prevent him from keeping his crusading vow and, in a letter written to Pope John XXI in 1276, he said that if he were unable to fulfil his promise he would send his brother in his place. John's successor, the French pope, Martin V, had little sympathy for Edward's predicament and turned down his request.

---

[6] *Ibid*, p. 129.

Otho was still on the continent when, in March 1282, Llewellyn rebelled once more. He hurried back to England, where he assumed his old command in Anglesey. By securing the island and command of the sea, Otho was able to safeguard the king's triumphal advance. With the fall of Llewellyn in battle and the execution of his brother, David, the rebellion was suppressed and Wales was annexed to the crown. Otho was appointed justiciar of Wales and given the responsibility of consolidating the English victory.

This was to be achieved by the construction of a string of castles, the most impressive of which can still be seen at Carnarvon. The architect was a Savoyard by the name of George St. James but it is said that the influence of Otho can be seen in that some of the features of these new castles reflect those of his ancestral home at Grandison. Although he held the position of justiciarship or King's Representative until 1295, the duties of office were for a large part filled by a deputy since Otho's talents were in constant demand elsewhere.

With the situation in Wales under control, Otho was dispatched to Sicily where Edward was most anxious to arrange peace between the rival claimants to the Sicilian throne. Among the reasons for Edward's intervention was that any war in Europe would jeopardise the cause dearest to his heart, the prospect of a further crusade. In the course of negotiations, Edward had not only to provide funds but also to hand over a number of hostages, including his closest friend, Otho. Having spent seven months in semi-captivity in Saragossa beyond the Pyrenees, he was released in May 1289.

Hostilities having re-commenced, Otho was sent to Rome where he pointed out to the pope the folly of stirring up strife among Christians at a time when the Saracen advance made the necessity of a crusade more urgent. In a surprise move, the Pope appointed Otho papal envoy with instructions to conclude a new truce. He persuaded the various combatants to lay down arms, giving Edward the breathing space he badly needed to make preparations for the forthcoming crusade.

Arriving home in England for the first time in four years, Otho found that plans for a new crusade were well advanced. He was instructed to proceed to Acre to make preparations for the king's arrival. Before he left England for the Holy Land in the summer of 1290, he put his affairs in order. He signed over the manors of Clonmel, Kilsheelan and Kilfeakle to his brother, William, but continued to use his influence to promote his brother's interests in Clonmel by securing permission from the king to build walls around the town. In 1298, on the insistence of Otho, Edward I authorised the citizens of Clonmel to levy tolls on goods passing through the town for ten years in order to raise money to undertake this work. In the following year, certain burgesses of Clonmel were ordered to appear before the king's courts, a step which ignored the jurisdiction of the manor courts. Otho, determined to protect the rights of his brother and those of his tenants, petitioned the king and had the proceedings quashed.

In the subsequent siege of Acre, Otho was one of the eight commanders appointed to defend the city. He fought bravely, leading many successful sorties outside the walls and inflicting heavy losses on the enemy. He held out until all hope was lost before making good his escape to Cyprus. For Otho it had proved a costly venture. He lost everything. Like many of his crusading colleagues, all he owned had been pledged to fight the infidel and to pay for the contingencies that followed. Friends in England had to send out a horse, some clothes and other necessities for his personal use. On his way home from the Holy Land he received a gift of 7,000 marks from an old friend of his, the newly elected Pope Boniface VIII, in recognition of the sacrifices that he had made and in compensation for the losses sustained.

Otho remained in Cyprus for over three years attempting to make peace among the warring Christian factions in the east. He also paid a visit to King Hayton of Armenia in response to that king's request for assistance in settling the affairs of his kingdom which was threatened by the Saracens from without and by dissention within. His efforts won the praise of an Armenian historian who described him as that 'wise and noble lord, Otho de Grandison'.[7] Otho also took the opportunity of getting Hayton to accept Edward's request that Armenian ports be used as a future base of operation against the Ottomans in the Holy Land. Little did they realise that six centuries would pass before a Christian commander would capture

---

[7] *Ibid*, p. 151.

Jerusalem. Before returning home to England from Cyprus, Otho made a pilgrimage to Jerusalem to pray for those who fell at Acre.

In the spring of 1296 Otho set foot on English soil for the first time in six years, only to find Edward at war on two fronts. The quarrel that had been brewing between England and France broke out into open warfare in 1294 when Philip IV of France confiscated Gascony. At home the news was equally bad. Edward, claiming the suzerainty of Scotland, had pushed the Scots into revolt and when Edward marched on Scotland on 28 March 1296 Otho was at his side. With Scottish resistance crushed, Otho was sent to the continent to conclude a treaty with Philip. He spent the next seven years on such a bewildering series of missions that it is almost impossible to keep track of his comings and goings.

His travels took him to Paris, the Low Countries, Germany, Rome and to virtually every duchy and kingdom from the Rhine to the Rhone, besides fitting in numerous fleeting visits to England to report on progress. Part of Otho's strategy in his efforts to find a lasting peace was to isolate Philip. He concluded a series of alliances with the nobles of Burgundy, the Duke of Lorraine and others who were willing to serve the English cause. He was responsible for negotiating the truce of Tournai on 31 January 1298 when the warring parties agreed to refer the whole dispute to the arbitration of Pope Boniface VIII, but five more years of tedious negotiations were needed before peace was finally secured. Otho was a member of the English delegation when the case was heard before the Roman Curia and he was largely responsible for drawing up the treaty which brought the war to an end. After ten years of strife, the Treaty of Paris in 1303 saw Gascony back in English hands once more.

With the resurgence of Robert Bruce in Scotland, Edward was forced to gather an army and march north. When Otho met Edward for the first time in four years at Lanercost in the autumn of 1306, he found him extremely ill. Otho was back in London waiting to set off on another mission to France when he received news of Edward's death. After the funeral Otho left England, never to return. For the next ten years he served at the papal court in Avignon as the permanent ambassador of Edward II.

In January 1312, when another crusade was declared, Otho again took the cross and by summer was preparing to leave for the Holy Land. On his way to Avignon to receive the papal blessing, he was attacked and robbed of 20,500 gold florins. Pope Clement, who was outraged by this attack on one of his principal knights, condemned it in the strongest possible terms to the Archbishop of Lyons. He decreed that, unless the offender made retribution within two weeks, he would be excommunicated and his lands put under interdict. Whether the money was returned or not we do not know but Otho's crusading plans were deferred for the time being. Time was running out for the gallant old knight and seven years later he made a payment of 10,000 gold sovereigns to be released from his crusading pledge.

All official documents refer to him as 'staying beyond the seas'[8], and the last ten years of his life were spent in his ancestral home by the shores of Lake Neuchatel. He spent his time organising his estates, as well as endowing and building churches. He erected a church for the Franciscans at Grandison and secured permission to found a monastery for thirteen Carthusian monks at La Lance. He provided favours for the Abbey of Lac Joux over twenty miles from Grandison, where the bodies of his ancestors were buried, and he had an altar dedicated to St. George built in the cathedral of Lausanne. Though it could be said that such acts were the fashionable way for the powerful to seek reconciliation with the almighty, the papal registers estimation of him as being 'deeply religious' may mean that he did not merely seek to buy his way to paradise.

It was said of him that 'he was a good and holy man'. The chronicler of Vale Abbey in England, where Otho laid one of the foundation stones, tells how the abbot offered him 'a not inconsiderable quantity of gold and silver', but professed that he preferred to be 'rewarded by God rather than by man, and he held earthly riches as vanities'.[9] He was also given permission by Pope Honorius I to have a portable altar for himself and his household, on which mass could be celebrated by his own chaplain, and he was further allowed the liberty of choosing any discreet priest as his own confessor.

As a man of wealth and influence, he never lost an opportunity to promote the interests of his family and friends. He secured profitable

---

[8] Clifford, p. 257.
[9] *Ibid*, p. 271.

employment and received papal favours for his nephews and cousins. The most famous of these, who owed his clerical advancement to the influence of his famous uncle, was John, son of his brother William who later became bishop of Exeter. Otho successfully requested that other relatives might enjoy plural benefices and be granted the next vacant living or prebend in a specified diocese. He also used his influence for those less fortunate. 'Dover boatmen in trouble with the authorities over a rented house, old servants, and men fined for killing the king's deer or outlawed for killing the king's subjects, all turned to him for a way out of their difficulties'.[10]

On 5 April 1328, fifty miles from his home at the house of Prior Barthelemy at Aigle on the road that leads to the passes of Italy, he died at the advanced age of ninety years. The precise instructions and careful planning surrounding his funeral arrangements reflect a career where attention to detail was of vital importance. According to the terms of his will:

> He had a tomb with his effigy on top placed in the cathedral of Lausanne. Two mounted men were to precede the cortege to the cathedral both wearing his colours and one carrying his pennon; the horses on which they rode to be magnificent beasts, for each was worth 100 livres lausannois; they were to have trappings bearing his arms, and both horses, with their accoutrements, were to be given to the cathedral chapter.[11]

He set aside a considerable amount of money for masses and left vestments, plate, chalices, crosses and golden cloths for the adornment of the high altar.

Otho was a man of inexhaustible physical endurance. To live to be ninety in the thirteenth century was something of a phenomenon in itself, but to succeed in doing so when it seems as though half his life had been spent on the road suggests considerable stamina. Travel was still at a stage when a pilgrimage could be imposed as a penance, and it can hardly have

---

[10] *Ibid*, p. 182.
[11] *Ibid*, p. 276.

been conducive to longevity when, apart from the most obvious dangers, the mere business of getting from one place to another entailed a multiplicity of hardships. The countryside was infested with robbers, accommodation was primitive and the roads, dusty and rough in good weather, were impassable in winter. To make a daily journey of twenty miles or so took a determined effort, to do it day after day demanded physical energy and dogged perseverance almost unimaginable today. His travels took him from the north of Scotland to the southern tip of Italy, from the mountains of Wales to far-off Armenia, to Paris and Rome and over the Alps to Acre and back again.

Apart from his natural vitality he obviously possessed the qualities of a successful diplomat and administrator. His attention to detail, his perseverance and infinite tact, allied to his diplomatic skills won for him the respect and trust of his royal master. There is an epic quality in the story of his life. The son of a simple knight, he rose to become the leading diplomat of Europe. Despite his pivotal role on the European stage for over half a century, there is no description of him in any contemporary chronicles. The only image we have is a marble effigy of a medieval knight which stands in the doorway of Lausanne Cathedral in Switzerland, showing a man with a short, determined nose, a long upper lip and a firm chin. To what extent the artist captured the essence of his subject we cannot say.[12]

It is not known whether Otho ever set foot in Clonmel. However, we do know that he made a lasting contribution to the welfare of its citizens by securing a grant for defensive walls, and by inviting the Franciscans to minister to their spiritual needs. William de Grandison, like his illustrious brother, may have been another absentee, but we do know that at least one member of the family came to Clonmel. In 1326 on the morning of the vigil of Michaelmas 'the noble squire Theobald de Grandison', a nephew of Otho died in Clonmel. The records of the previous year stated that he had been acting as Otho's attorney in Ireland. William, like his eldest brother Otho, died at a very advanced age in 1335. Three years later the de Grandison connection with Clonmel came to an end when Maurice

---

[12] *Ibid*, p. xi.

fitzThomas, first earl of Desmond, bought Clonmel, Kilsheelan and Kilfeakle manors from Peter, William's son and heir, for one thousand one hundred marks.

Chapter 3

The Fight of the Earls

It has often been said that it was Ireland's tragedy was that it was never fully conquered. The fact that the Normans never came in sufficient numbers to complete the task job left vast areas in native hands. Local resistance was strong and Gaelic chiefs awaited the opportunity to pounce from forest and mountain to win back what was rightfully theirs. By 1300 the tide was turning against the Normans. Harassed by the marauding Irish and further undermined by the Bruce invasion and the migration of Anglo-Norman families back to England, the colony was considerably weakened. Ireland became a patchwork of semi-independent lordships, varying in size and influence, which threatened English rule in Ireland. In an effort to restore order to an unruly colony, the crown was obliged to elicit the support of powerful Norman families such as the Butlers and Fitzgeralds.

Origins of the Feud

It could be said that Henry II was the founder of the Butler family fortunes. The king, in his repentance for his complicity in the murder of Thomas a Beckett, Archbishop of Canterbury, conferred valuable favours on the churchman's relations. He appointed Theobald Butler, who was descended from the prelate's sister, to an office of the highest authority by making him his chief butler. In 1185 Prince John granted Theobald extensive lands in north Tipperary, where Nenagh became the principal seat of the family. The territorial losses which the Butler family suffered at the hands of the resurgent native Irish in the late thirteenth and early fourteenth centuries were more than offset by the number of prestigious appointments they received. In 1328 James Butler was created earl of Ormond and endowed with jurisdiction over or palatinate of Tipperary. The palatinate consisted of the lands within the county held directly from the crown or its agents but excluded church lands and districts under native control where neither 'earl's nor king's writ ran'. Clonmel was selected as caput or headquarters of the palatinate, an indication of its growing importance. This

26

appointment made the earl of Ormond the most influential and politically powerful figure in the county by transferring to him the responsibilities of government virtually immune from royal interference. Ironically, the creation of the palatinate did little to pacify the county but instead became a source of conflict between Ormond and their great provincial rivals, the neighbouring Fitzgeralds of Desmond.

The Fitzgeralds, whom Macauley considered to be 'the greatest and proudest subjects that any sovereign of Europe ever had', were of Italian origin. Dominus Otho, a member of this Florentine family, the Gherardini, accompanied William the Conqueror when he launched his successful invasion of Britain. He was awarded substantial estates and his son, Walter FitzOtho, was appointed first constable of the newly built Windsor Castle. Walter's son, Gerald, married Nesta, daughter of Rhys, prince of south Wales, and their children became known as Fitzgerald or the Geraldines.[1] One of them, Maurice, was to become the founder of the family's fortunes in Ireland.

Maurice came to Ireland in 1170, one year after the first Normans landed. His descendants established themselves in Kildare, while another branch of the family, who became known as the Desmonds, secured territory in Cork, Limerick, Kerry and West Waterford. In 1328, the family received honours similar to that of the Butlers when Maurice fitzThomas Fitzgerald was created earl of Desmond and lord of the liberty of Kerry.

The origins of the quarrel between the two families lay in the purchase of the manors of Kilfeakle, Kilsheelan and Clonmel by Maurice Fitzgerald from the de Grandison family in 1338, which extended 'their dominion beyond its natural frontier, the river Suir, into the heart of the Ormond palatinate'.[2] This made Maurice lord of the manor of Clonmel which was also part of the newly created palatinate of Tipperary and thus part of the Butler domain. With both families claiming control over the town, Clonmel became one of the flashpoints of a feud marked by raids, reprisals and bouts of open warfare for the next two hundred and fifty years

---

[1] Brian Fitzgerald, *The Geraldines* (London, 1951), p. 15.
[2] George Butler, 'The Battle of Affane' in *Butler Society Journal*, v, (1972-74), p. 320.

and, 'Clonmel accordingly soon began to share the varying fortunes of the two lords'.[3]

<h2 style="text-align:center">The Feud</h2>

It is not known precisely when hostilities began between the Desmonds and the Ormonds, but what is certain is that the activities of Maurice, 1st earl of Desmond, irrevocably damaged relations between his successors and the people of Clonmel. The earl was a ruthless and unscrupulous man who harboured ambitions of becoming king of Ireland. He embarked on an incredible career of rebellion, treason and crime. Instead of exercising his manorial responsibilities by safeguarding the interests of Clonmel's inhabitants, not alone did he demand and collect 'protection money' but he even allowed the town to be pillaged by his followers. Following his death in 1356, the people of Clonmel looked to the Ormonds, the 'most loyal' of all Anglo-Norman families, for protection. Unfortunately, the Ormonds were not always in a position to provide it.

The rivalry between the two earldoms was marked by periodic raids and skirmishes, which several marriages between the families failed to bring to an end. The career of the 3rd earl of Desmond (1359-98) was punctuated by very damaging feuds with his father-in-law, the earl of Ormond. The disruptive activities of the two lords were such that in the course of a requiem mass in Dublin Castle in 1380 the celebrant, Richard Wye, Bishop of Cloyne, remarked that 'there are two in Munster who destroy us and our goods, namely the Earl of Ormond and the Earl of Desmond with their followers, whom in the end the Lord will destroy'. A contemporary observer stated that, 'both these noblemen laboured with tooth and naile to overcrow and consequently to overthrow one another. And so much were they in honour peeres, they wroughte by hooke and by crooke to be in authoritie superioures'.[4]

Throughout much of the fourteenth and fifteenth centuries the English crown was too distracted by more pressing domestic matters to

---

[3] William Burke, *History of Clonmel*, p. 15.
[4] *Chronicles of Raphael Holinshend*, i, (London, 1875), p. 52. The earls in question were James, 2nd earl of Ormond and Gerald, 3rd earl of Desmond.

devote much attention to Ireland. From 1337, the Hundred Years War in France took up much of England's energy. With the monarchy unable to intervene directly in Irish affairs and recognising that such towns as Clonmel were the bulwark of the English colony, successive kings issued a series of charters in support of their hard-pressed allies. The loyalty of the townspeople was recognised by Henry V who declared that 'Clonmel is inhabited by English merchants and burgesses ... who are observing English law and are a great succour to the government'.[5]

The preamble to Edward III's charter of 1371 stated that Clonmel was 'in need of ampler and more powerful government' at a time when its loyal citizens were being 'seriously and openly threatened by malefactors and robbers'. Permission was given to appoint a sovereign 'to make liberal provision' for its 'safety and defence'.[6] In 1385 it was found that the people of Clonmel had been unable 'to repair the bridge, tower and fortifications' because 'of harassment by Irish and English rebels'[7], the latter being a reference to the Fitzgeralds. Richard III granted the townspeople permission to set the rate of taxes for themselves and to the enjoyment of the market tolls, measures which helped to finance the town's defences.

The general lawlessness in the surrounding countryside and the sporadic outbursts of violence between the two lordships kept the burgers of Clonmel in a constant state of vigilance. Outside the walls, 'they and all that they had were at the mercy of every enemy whom they were not strong enough to resist or fortunate enough to escape'.[8] Within, all able bodied men were expected to do guard duty on the walls and practise their archery at the butts. To strengthen the defences of the town the parish church of St. Mary's was re-constructed, resulting in a building which resembled a 'half-church, half fortress'.

The conflict between the Butlers and Fitzgeralds was halted by periodic efforts to secure peace. In 1400 James, son of Gerard, 3rd earl of Desmond, was drowned at Ardfinnan crossing the Suir. He had been returning from negotiations in Inishlounaght with James, 3rd earl of

---

[5] Burke, *History of Clonmel*, p. 18.

[6] *Ibid*, p. 16.

[7] *Ibid*, p. 264.

[8] *Ibid*, p. 18.

Ormond. Hostilities between the two families were renewed in 1404 when James, 4th earl of Ormond, or the 'White Earl' as he was known succeeded to the lordship, and they continued sporadically until his death in 1452.

The quarrel between the two families intensified when they became involved in the War of the Roses (1445-1485), with Ormond supporting the Lancastrians and Desmond on the side of the Yorkists. In 1461, after the Yorkist victory at Towton in Yorkshire, James, 5th earl of Ormond was captured and executed and his head displayed on London Bridge. His brother, John, 6th earl of Ormond, returned to Ireland to rally support for the Lancastrian cause. According to the *Annals of the Four Masters* he was accompanied 'with a powerful host of Englishmen and a great war arose between the earls of Ormond and Desmond'. Ormond summoned the Butler towns of Kilkenny and Clonmel to arms, only to be defeated at Piltown by Thomas, 8th earl of Desmond. Edmund Mac Richard Butler was taken prisoner. Two books, the *Psalter of Cashel* and the *Book of Carrick* had to be handed over to secure his release. The loyalty of Clonmel to the Lancastrian cause earned the tribute '*Fidelis in Aeternum*' – Faithful Forever – which was later incorporated into the town's coat of arms.

The battle at Piltown had the distinction of being the only engagement in the War of the Roses fought on Irish soil and also had considerable consequences for the rival families. Five years later, the victorious earl of Desmond who, like his ancestor Maurice, had entertained ambitions of becoming king of Ireland, was hanged by the lord deputy at Drogheda. This incident caused a permanent rift between the Desmonds and the crown. In 1533, an English observer in Ireland remarked that the earls of Desmond 'have such cankered malicious rebellion rooted in them ever since the putting to execution of Thomas, earl of Desmond, at Drogheda that they be far separate from the knowledge of any allegiance ... as the Turk is to believe in Christ'.

Desmond alienation from the crown had been compounded by their continued involvement in internal English politics. In 1485, the War of the Roses came to an end when Richard III was slain at Bosworth and Henry Tudor ascended the throne of England. For the next twelve years Ireland became the base for successive attempts against the new Tudor monarchy. In 1487 the Pretender, Lambert Simnel, was crowned Edward VI of

England in Dublin. While Simnel enjoyed the support of Desmond and the majority of the Anglo-Irish lords, the Butler towns and the city of Waterford remained loyal to Henry. A well-equipped force was assembled in Clonmel and successfully prevented Simnel and his supporters from landing in Waterford. The following month the plot was crushed on the battlefield of Stoke and Simnel ended his days as a scullion in the royal kitchens.

As relations between the House of Desmond and the crown continued to deteriorate, the Butler lordship was plunged into a state of anarchy. John Butler, who had been defeated at Piltown, and his brother, Thomas, departed for England leaving their territories without effective leadership. The security of the earldom was left to junior branches of the family whose constant feuding reduced the Butler lordship to chaos. In 1501 Thomas White, the Recorder of Waterford, wrote to earl Thomas informing him about the plight of Clonmel. The letter stated that Edmund Butler of Cahir was compelling the burgesses of Clonmel to contribute to the cost of supplying fighting men to make private war. As a consequence the burgesses felt so threatened and oppressed that they intended to leave the town, thus destroying it as the commercial centre that it was.[9]

The decline of the Butler family fortunes was halted by Piers Butler. In 1515, he was declared heir to the family estates and immediately set about asserting control over his inheritance. Clonmel, to the annoyance of the burgesses, was being held by the Cahir Butlers against government wishes. Piers enlisted the support of the Lord Deputy, earl of Kildare, who was his brother-in-law, and in 1517, they besieged and captured Clonmel. It was said that a truce between Sir Piers Butler and his Butler cousins at Cahir was sworn upon a relic of the true cross which had been brought to the town.

As Piers Butler set about revitalising the Butler lordship, the family's feud with the Desmonds was about to enter its final phase. With the marriage of Joan Fitzgerald, daughter of the 10th earl of Desmond and James Butler, son of Piers and 9th earl of Ormond in 1532, it looked as if the quarrel between the two great houses was at an end. As part of the

---

[9] Cited in Patrick C. Power, *History of Tipperary,* (Cork, 1989), p. 38.

marriage settlement, the manor of Clonmel and other disputed properties over which so much blood had been spilled, were to be settled on Ormond.

When James Butler died in mysterious circumstances at a banquet at Ely House in London fourteen years later, he was succeeded by his young son, Thomas, 10th earl of Ormond or Black Tom, as he became known. In 1550 Black Tom's widowed mother, Joan, married Gerald Fitzgerald, 14th earl of Desmond. Consequently, Gerald became Black Tom's stepfather. Although Joan was twenty years Desmond's senior she was powerless to control the rivalry between her husband and son. It was these two young men who would play out the last act of the feud between their two families.

The Final Chapter

Gerald Fitzgerald and Thomas Butler were two of the most powerful Norman-Irish leaders in the country. Both inherited extensive lordships, one no less impressive than the other. In addition to their extensive territories in county Tipperary the third earl of Ormond bought the city of Kilkenny in 1392 which became the principal seat of the family, making them the dominant power in the Suir-Nore-Barrow basin. The earldom largely comprised the counties of Tipperary and Kilkenny, but also extended into the adjoining counties of Wexford, Carlow and Laois. The Desmond lordship encompassed 800,000 acres and six hundred castles, stretching from Kerry to west Waterford and taking in large areas of counties Cork and Limerick. However, the two lordships showed distinct differences. Butler lands were more centralised and most of the landowners were of old English origin, whereas Desmond lands were scattered and the principal tenants were of Gaelic stock.

The contrast between Black Tom and Gerald Fitzgerald could not have been more striking. Gerald was raised a Catholic among his own kinsmen, whereas Thomas Butler had been born in England and brought up a Protestant. He had grown up with Elizabeth and was educated with her half-brother, Edward, both of whom were to occupy the English throne. It was said that his loyalty to Elizabeth 'was woven out of the strands of young affections and alliances'. Blessed with a powerful physique, handsome, charming and cultured he had all the attributes of the courtier. Black Tom's loyalty to Elizabeth lasted throughout her long reign. Her reference to him as 'her black husband' gave rise to much speculation as to the nature of their relationship. Building a magnificent manor house in Carrick-on-Suir where he hoped to entertain his beloved queen did little to dispel such rumours. After years of eclipse by the Fitzgeralds, the Butlers, under the leadership of Black Tom, re-emerged as champions of the crown in Ireland. On the other hand, the Catholicism and gaelic ways of Desmond were viewed by the autocratic Elizabeth as the great barrier to the proselytising and subjugation of southern Ireland.

Gerald lacked personal connections at the English court. He had received little formal education and his upbringing was that of a warrior prince. Proud and ambitious, he was melancholic and inordinately vain. His volatile temperament led many of his contemporaries to doubt his sanity, referring to him as 'the brain-sick earl', 'the weak-brained' and 'the faint-brained earl'. Rash and incapable, he embarked upon a course of action which was to have disastrous consequences both for himself and the earldom of Desmond.

In 1560, a disagreement arose between the two noblemen. Gerald claimed the rents from Clonmel, Kilfeakle and Kilsheelan manors as part of his wife Joan's dowry, but Black Tom refused to pay. Gerald responded by leading an army into South Tipperary but was confronted on the road to Kilfeakle by Black Tom. Like the knights of old they decided to settle their differences in battle on a given day. Outside Cashel, Desmond with an army of 4,000 foot and 750 horse was faced by Ormond with an equal force supported by some cannon. Following fourteen days of constant pleading by Countess Joan with both husband and son the two armies withdrew without a blow being struck.

The conflict led to the two earls being summoned to London by Elizabeth. Desmond delayed for a month before complying. When he finally decided to present himself at court he was accompanied by a large retinue, including bards and harpers. His provocative behaviour infuriated the Queen, who decided to detain him. After two years, growing impatient at his confinement, Desmond promised to keep the peace, to pay the Queen her feudal dues and to suppress Gaelic practices within his territories. At the same time, she issued an order confirming Ormond's right to Clonmel and the other manors in question, a decision Desmond adamantly refused to accept.

Hostilities recommenced when Gerald laid claim to the rents of the Decies from Sir Maurice Fitzgerald. When Maurice refused, Gerald crossed into his domain with a large army and Fitzgerald appealed to Ormond for assistance. Black Tom responded by assembling an army at Knocklofty, outside Clonmel, before marching to meet Gerald at the ford of Affane, below Lismore. The ensuing encounter was to be the last pitched battle fought by two private armies on these islands.

In the affray three hundred of Desmond's followers perished, many being drowned when attempting to escape by swimming the Blackwater. Gerard had his thigh broken by a pistol shot and was taken as prisoner to Clonmel where he was lodged in the jail at the end of Middle Row in Main Street. The story is told that when Desmond was being carried off the battlefield he was asked by some of Butler's soldiers, 'now where is the great earl of Desmond?' To which he replied 'riding on the backs of the Butlers, where he wished to be'. Angered by the behaviour of both earls, Elizabeth once more ordered them to London. Gerald was imprisoned in the tower, while Black Tom was left at large and subsequently was allowed return to Ireland.

In Gerald's absence, his cousin, James Fitzmaurice, who felt that the independence of the Desmond lordship was threatened, rebelled. To undermine this threat, Elizabeth ordered Desmond's release. Following six years confinement he returned to Ireland but, in the meantime, Fitzmaurice had submitted and was allowed to leave for the continent. Six years later, he returned from Europe with papal backing and promises of aid from Spain, proclaiming holy war against a heretic queen. Although he was killed a few weeks later in a skirmish, Elizabeth was thoroughly alarmed and decided that disloyal subjects like the Desmonds would have to be crushed once and for all.

The English authorities adopted a policy of goading Gerald into rebellion. Continual raids and incursions into his territories made his position increasingly untenable. Askeaton Abbey was desecrated by English troops. They broke open the tombs of his ancestors and scattered their remains along the river bank in full view of his castle walls. He was forced to witness the grave of his late wife torn apart and her bones flung out with the rest.

Desmond wrote to Butler telling him that his mother's grave had been 'broken and burnt', but more than the violation of her tomb was required to sway his allegiance. Desmond was then ordered to surrender his two chief strongholds or be charged with high treason. When this demand was greeted by a blunt refusal he was proclaimed a traitor. Reluctantly forced into taking up arms, he was accused of waging a religious war in Ireland with the assistance of foreign powers and sworn enemies of the crown. A reward of £1,000 and a pension of £40 a year was pledged for his capture, and half these sums offered to anyone who would kill him. Elizabeth appointed her favourite 'Black Tom', Lord General of Munster, to suppress the rebellion. He landed in Waterford in January 1583 with a force of 1,000 men. He set up headquarters in Clonmel where his soldiers were billeted and provisioned.

From there Ormond moved on Gerald's stronghold in the Glen of Aherlow, driving him westwards to Kerry. On 11 November 1583 Desmond was treacherously seized by some of his own people, the Moriartys, near Tralee. They struck off his head and had it conveyed to Ormond. He sent it as a trophy to the Queen who had it set up on a spike on London Bridge. Ormond then ordered a search for the earl's body, but a number of Desmond's followers concealed it and later it was interred in a small chapel at Kilnamagh, near Castleisland. The fall of the house of Desmond was complete. As Bagwell remarked, 'with the earl's death the mediaeval history of Munster closes'. Rebellion was followed by confiscation and plantation. Ormond was rewarded with 3,000 acres in Tipperary and an extensive area of poor land in Kerry.

In 1594, when Hugh O'Neill rose in arms to maintain the independence of Ulster in the face of Tudor aggression, Ormond was called on once more to serve his Queen. During the subsequent seven years war he briefly assumed command of all English forces in Ireland. In the course of the campaign he suffered the indignity of being kidnapped and ransomed. His main contribution lay in protecting the towns within his territories from the rebel forces. Once again he received the assistance of the people of Clonmel who placed 'their goods and their money' at his disposal. By the time Gaelic resistance was brought to an end at the battle of Kinsale 1601, Ormond had departed from the national stage.

At the height of his career, he was regarded as 'the most influential subject in the kingdom of Ireland'.[10] He held land in three provinces embracing twenty three counties, in addition to three counties in England. With an annual income in excess of £8,000 he was among the twenty richest men in these islands. He died in 1613, at the age of eighty-three, following a lifetime's service to the crown but the Butler connection with Clonmel, was however, to last a further century.

---

[10] Ciaran Brady (ed.), *Worsted in the Game: Losers in Irish History, (Dublin, 1989)*, p. 49.

Chapter 4

Distinguished Jesuits

Throughout the Middle Ages towns were often governed and controlled by small groups of prosperous merchant families, who exercised power through monopolising urban office. One such family was the Whites. Before 1608, seven of the eleven sovereigns of Clonmel known to have held office were members of the White family. After that date they continued to exercise the same dominance over the mayoralty until John White, in 1650, had the unenviable task of surrendering the keys of the town to the victorious Cromwell.

The Whites, originally called by the French name Le Blunde, were among the first Norman settlers in Tipperary. The family's earliest known connection with Clonmel occurs in 1215 with the mention of Thomas White as a vassal of Richard de Burgo. By the seventeenth century the Whites had become so numerous that it order to identify them it became necessary to append the Christian names of the fathers to the sons, so that the Mayor of Clonmel in 1608 was called John White fitzGeoffry – John, son of Geoffry.

Many deceased members of the White family were interred in the vault beneath the south aisle of Old St. Mary's, then the Catholic parish church. In 1622 Barbara White, widow of Nicholas White, and their son Henry, had a mortuary chapel built outside the church adjoining the south-west corner. When it fell into ruin around the beginning of the nineteenth century, a number of the mortuary slabs were removed to the church at St. Patrick's Well, outside the town, where they can still be seen.

It has been said of the Whites that they 'have always clung steadfastly to the faith', and that 'it is beyond all doubt that there are more priests of this one family than of any other Irish name'.[1] Their loyalty was exemplified by Victor White who, in 1585, was prepared to suffer the loss

---

[1] Rev. E. Hogan, 'Father Thomas White' in *Distinguished Irishmen of the sixteenth century,* (London, 1894), pp. 49, 50.

of his property, liberty, and life rather than betray, the fugitive priest, Fr. McKenraghty.[2]

Two members of this leading Catholic family who won fame and renown in the service of the church were the brothers, Thomas and Stephen White. They were the sons of Pierce White, who lived in a large house, described as a castle, which was situated at the western end of town. The young Whites grew up at a time when efforts were being made to introduce the reformation into Ireland, an event that was to have a marked impact on Clonmel. In March 1539, the Lord Chancellor Alen arrived to receive the surrender of the religious houses from their respective heads. Members of the Franciscan community led by Robert Travers, the guardian, left their monastery and a fortnight later the Cistercian Abbey at Inislounaght was handed over. With the suppression of the monasteries the provision of education was left to private individuals, priests and laymen, who established schools at various centres throughout the country.

Thomas White (1556–1622)

Thomas White, who was born in Clonmel in 1556, received his early education at Peter White's school in Waterford. Peter, a relative of his, was the most outstanding schoolmaster of his day whose teaching attracted students from all over Ireland. His school was regarded as the 'Trojan horse' of the Counter-Reformation[3], for his pupils received a sound classical education which was a considerable advantage to those who wished to enter the priesthood. It meant that the students arrived at their chosen seminary with a working knowledge of Latin, the language in which courses were conducted.

With opportunities for higher education becoming increasingly limited, young Irishmen, who were anxious to continue their studies, were flocking to Spain, which at that time had more connections with Ireland than any other continental country. They enjoyed a shared religion and close commercial ties, and not only was King Philip II the leading

---

[2] The story of Fr. Mc Kenraghty is featured in chapter seven.

[3] John S. Silke, 'Irish scholarship and the Renaissance 1580-1673' in *Studies in the Renaissance*, xx, (1973), p. 183.

protagonist of the counter-reformation but he also sent military assistance to Ireland during the Desmond revolts.

Dr. Walter McDonald, a nineteenth century rector in Salamanca, gives a vivid description of the privations endured by these young students travelling from Ireland:

> The heroism of these devoted children ... cannot be conceived in these days of mail steamers, express trains and comfortable stage coaches. They first braved detention and consequent imprisonment; then they embarked in frail open boats, in which no traveller would embark to-day, to cross one of the most treacherous seas in the world, and be set down without friends, but such as Providence might provide, at some port in a foreign land, with whose tongue they were wholly unacquainted.[4]

Among them were aspirants to the priesthood who, in many cases, came from families 'so reduced by wars and spoilings as to be able to afford them very little support, if any at all'. There was an urgent need 'to unite the candidates for the priesthood in colleges where they would live without care as to maintenance and expenses, and where they would enjoy a special training for their future mission'.[5] The man who took up this daunting challenge was Thomas White of Clonmel who, in 1582, was resident in the Spanish city of Valladolid where he had gone to pursue his theological studies. White was so appalled and touched by the misery of his fellow countrymen in Valladolid that 'he made the establishment and maintenance of Irish seminaries his life-long aim'.[6]

He gathered the Irish students together and set up a hostel which he financed both from his own pocket and through collections obtained from the wealthy citizens of Valladolid. He struggled on for ten years, praying that God would provide a regular foundation with adequate

---

[4] Cited in Daniel Murphy, *A History of Irish Emigration and Missionary Education,* (Dublin, 2000), p. 99.
[5] D. J. O'Doherty, 'Fr. Thomas White, Founder of the Irish College, Salamanca' in *Irish Ecclesiastical Record*, xxix, (1922), pp. 578, 579.
[6] *Ibid.*

educational facilities and sufficient revenue to survive. His prayers were answered in 1592 when Philip II paid a visit to Valladolid. White presented his students to the king who responded by providing a large sum of money. Feeling that this was not adequate to accommodate the growing number of Irish youths who needed to be looked after, he continued to plead with the king until they received a fully established college where they could live and study. Philip agreed to transfer White and his nine students to the University of Salamanca where they were housed and incorporated as a distinct Irish college under the patronage of the crown.

A royal charter dated 3 August 1592 instructed the chancellor of the University of Salamanca to admit the Irish students to the university's degree courses. In his address the king stated that:

> They have left their own country and all they possessed in it for the service of Our Lord God, and for the preservation of the Catholic faith, and as they undertake to go back to preach in that country and to suffer martyrdom should needs be, they should get in the university the reception they have a right to expect.

Irish students could now lead an organised collegiate life and pursue their studies to prepare them for their future ministries. This Irish seminary, named St. Patrick's College, was one of twenty-five colleges affiliated to the university. At that time, Salamanca University was one of the largest in Europe with almost seven thousand students and was renowned for its work in the fields of theology, medicine and law.[7] Thomas White was placed in charge of the students, assisted by two Jesuits, Fathers Richard Conway, a native of New Ross and James Archer from Kilkenny.

White was then a secular priest and since the king decreed that the new foundation was to be a Jesuit run college, he decided to become a Jesuit and duly entered the order on 11 June 1593. On completion of a year's novitiate at Villagarcia in Castile, he spent some time at the Irish college in Lisbon, which had been founded the previous year.

---

[7] Murphy, *A History of Irish Emigration etc.*, pp. 93.94.

Two years later he returned to Salamanca and on 1 December 1596, he set out from there on the first of many fund-raising journeys, or questing expeditions as they were called, which he undertook on behalf of the college. His first expedition lasted six months, returning to Salamanca in the following May. The book of receipts gives a list of the places visited and the amounts contributed by each person. In that time he covered an area considerably greater than twice the size of Ireland and raised a total of over 5,000 reales, sufficient to keep seven students for a year.

In the absence of Fr. Archer, who was then on a mission to Ireland, White was appointed acting rector of Salamanca from October 1597 to December 1604. Apart from his financial and administrative responsibilities, White found himself faced with problems from another quarter. In 1602, his rectorship at Salamanca was criticised by Florence Conroy, later Franciscan archbishop of Tuam, who protested to King Philip III that White maintained a rigid Munster monopoly that excluded students from other parts of Ireland. In defence of this policy it was stated that:

White's bias towards his native province can, however, be accounted for by missionary requirements. He had to prepare students for mission; it is obvious that he tried to make this venture as safe as possible in an area where he and they had personal connections.[8]

This regionalism was not exclusive to Salamanca. Similar problems existed in other Irish colleges such as Lille which favoured students from Meath and Leinster. Charge and counter-charge followed which led to White being removed from office. In deference to the King's wishes Spanish rectors were appointed, three of them in succession. This decision was revoked in 1609 when Father Conway, White's former colleague at Salamanca, became superior.

The upheaval at Salamanca in no way reflected adversely on White's standing within the Jesuit order for he was immediately appointed rector of Lisbon College in 1606, a position he held until 1609. In that year he commenced another series of questing missions to raise funds for his

---

[8] Helga Hammerstein, 'Aspects of the continental education of Irish students in the reign of Elizabeth I' in *Historical Studies*, viii, (1971), p. 149.

beloved Salamanca. His subsequent travels took him all over the Iberian peninsula and into Italy going as far south as Sicily, undertakings that mark him out as a man of extraordinary zeal and energy.

In 1606, White was among those who made representations to the Pope on behalf of the students at Lisbon and Salamanca. The Pope responded in 1610 by granting permission to fishermen in the surrounding districts to fish on six Sundays or festivals every year, on condition that a proportion of their catch was sold for the benefit of the two colleges. Early in 1610 White returned once more to Salamanca where he succeeded Fr. Conway as rector and continued in charge until 1619.

During that time he was asked to resolve the growing dissatisfaction in the Irish college at Santiago de Compostella. The rector had admitted the young sons of Irish exiles who were not destined for the priesthood, giving the college a semi-lay character, contrary to the aims of its founders. In 1611, representations were made to King Philip that remedial measures needed to be taken. This resulted in a royal directive being issued to the Jesuit provincial and in 1613, Thomas White, with the assistance of two colleagues, took over Santiago college from the secular clergy who had been in charge since its foundation in 1606. The Jesuits insisted that all students entering the college should take an oath that once ordained they would return to the Irish mission. Some of those already in residence in the college refused to comply. Most of those joined other religious communities and new students were taken in their place.

In 1618 White set off once more on another fund-raising tour. He was in Rome when he was informed of student unrest and poor administration within the Irish college of Seville and was asked to use his influence to get the college placed under the care of the Jesuit fathers. White enlisted the support of the Superior General of the order and that of the King and, on 25 July 1519, Seville received its first Jesuit rector.

The monopolizing of the Irish seminaries in the peninsula by the Jesuits evoked a storm of criticism. In addition to their colleges at Salamanca and Lisbon, they took over Santiago and Seville, which had been founded by secular priests, leading to accusations of 'ambition and self-interest'. In their defence Fr. O'Doherty felt that 'they were actuated by high motives, and no doubt believed that the interests of religion could

42

be better served by themselves than by others' and with regard to Fr. White said that 'whatever we may think of his politics and of his conduct on certain occasions, we have no doubt that he acted according to his lights, and therefore we cannot deny him the meed of praise that is due to a great pioneer and indefatigable worker.[9]

In 1519 White resigned his position as superior in Salamanca to take up appointment as Superior of Santiago which he held up to his death two years later. His passing was recorded by a Spanish Jesuit, Ferdinand de Castro:

> This day, Sunday, the 28th of May, 1622, at seven o'clock in the morning, Father Thomas White was called to receive the rewards of his great labours and merit. He died of fever. He was sixty-four years of age, and had spent thirty-four years in the Society, during which time he laboured apostolically in the service of God and of the Catholic faith, which through the means of the colleges he founded in Spain has been preserved in his native land.[10]

His portrait which hangs in Salamanca, painted apparently in his fiftieth year, represents him as an exceedingly mild, ascetic man. It shows him to have been of medium height, with a large nose, well set eyes, high cheek bones and square forehead. His hands are long and tapering, the right resting on the breast, the left holding the book of discipline of the Jesuit order. A translation of the Spanish inscription reads, 'The Venerable Father Thomas White of the Society of Jesus, a native of Clonmel in Ireland, Missionary Apostolic and first Jesuit of the Irish seminarists in Spain. He died a holy death in Santiago de Galicia the 28th of May, 1622'.

Thomas White was one of the pioneers of the Irish college movement. He has been regarded as 'the outstanding figure in the constructive work for Irish education, done by the Irish Jesuits within the century 1540-1640, either within Ireland or abroad'.[11] For over thirty years he devoted himself to organising Irish student life at Valladolid,

---

[9] O'Doherty, 'Fr. Thomas White etc., pp. 596, 597.

[10] T. J. Corcoran, 'Early Irish Jesuit educators' in *Studies*, xxix, (1940), p. 545.

[11] *Ibid.*

Salamanca, Lisbon, Santiago and Seville. These seminaries produced a zealous and learned clergy who became a thorn in the side of the authorities, making Ireland the only country in Europe where the counter-reformation succeeded against the will of the head of state. This is borne out by a report from the Irish privy council to James I in 1608 which stated that:

> Priests land here secretly in every port and creek of the realm and afterwards disperse themselves into several quarters in such sort that every town and country is full of them and most men's minds are infected with their doctrine and seditious persuasions.[12]

Salamanca was undoubtedly the most famous of all the Irish colleges and a fitting tribute to the efforts of Thomas White. In the first two hundred years of its existence, 'at least from the point of view of numbers and revenues, was more successful during the period of Father White's connection with it'. In an introduction to a list of students dated April 1611, White wrote:

> Without including numerous visitors, bishops, friars, priests and laymen, 208 students have been inmates of the College. Of these, thirty have met holy deaths in Ireland after martyrdom, torments, persecutions and labours. Sixty-eight are actually working in the vineyard of the Lord in Ireland. Twenty-two died in Salamanca, and eighty-one entered various religious orders.[13]

Salamanca was to have a long and illustrious history. Up to the outbreak of World War II in 1939 it was still educating Irish students. The last vestige of Irish educational activity in Spain disappeared in 1951 with the sale of the college at Salamanca to the Spanish government. The ancient building, so full of Irish memories, is now part of the medical school of the university.

---

[12] Margaret Mc Curtain, *Tudor and Stuart Ireland,* (Dublin, 1972), p. 118.
[13] Cited in O'Doherty, 'Fr. Thomas White etc.', pp. 596, 597.

Thomas White was an unassuming man with modest needs, 'most simple in dress and manners; his usual food every day was a little bread and cheese which he ate along the road. He practised great mortification and, in spite of his years, kept the hair shirt and the discipline which he took daily'. In the opinion of Fr. O'Doherty:

> What we know of Father White does not lead us to regard him as a very learned man. Spanish, the language which he apparently used in correspondence with fellow-Irishmen, he wrote neither eloquently nor correctly.

Thomas White was a man of considerable energy and extraordinary organisational ability who spent most of his time putting the colleges with which he was involved on a firm footing. He was an inveterate traveller, enduring long journeys on foot seeking finance through preaching tours and coaxing 'alms and gifts from prelates and princes'. In the process he built up an extensive network of important and influential contacts. White also found support among the Irish merchant community in Balboa and other Spanish ports where they had established trading bases. He made time to meet incoming emigrants from the boats, many of whom were helpless teenagers with little money and no Spanish. Lonely and bewildered, without friends or contacts, they were dependent on White for their welfare.

Dr. Walter McDonald, one of White's successors at Salamanca, said in tribute:

> He did more for the preservation of the faith in his native land than any other Irishman ever did, during the terrible ordeal through which the Church of Ireland passed in two or three centuries of persecution. To him is due the idea of establishing Irish Colleges in foreign lands, in order to educate priests for the trying and dangerous Irish mission. Clonmel may well be proud of having been the birthplace of this saviour of the faith of Ireland. Such a man is in every way worthy of a national monument; and I hope to see the day when the Irish

Church will, in gratitude to his memory, raise one in the capital of the kingdom, and another in his native town.[14]

Stephen White (1574-c1646)

Stephen White was the younger brother of Thomas. He received his first education in Clonmel at a school kept by one Derby Mc Thomas and at the age of twelve, like his brother Thomas, he was sent to his uncle's academy, Dr. Peter White, who was now operating in Kilkenny. Prior to this Peter had been a dean of the diocese of Waterford but was expelled in 1570 because he refused to conform to the Protestant religion. When Stephen was in his eighteenth year, Trinity College was founded by Elizabeth I and Stephen was one of three foundation students enrolled there. It is said that his stay was short-lived because it became mandatory for all students to take the Oath of Supremacy, acknowledging Elizabeth as head of the church.

Sometime later, Stephen was smuggled on board a ship leaving Waterford for the Spanish port of Corunna. In 1595 he enrolled in the college of Salamanca, and was the first student of the college to become a Jesuit. He secured the degree, bachelor of arts and, by 1600, he was lecturing in philosophy and theology at the college. During this time he acquired a doctorate in theology and collaborated with William Bathe, the spiritual director of the college, in publishing a treatise called *Janua Linguarum* which was regarded as a pioneer work in the scientific teaching of languages. While priests generally returned home on completion of their studies, White was one of a select few 'whose scholarly distinctions qualified them for influential positions in continental universities'.[15]

White's reputation as a lecturer reached the ears of the father general of the Jesuit order and he was sent to teach in Germany. In 1606 he was appointed to the chair of scholastic theology at Ingoldstadt, one of the country's leading universities. Three years later, he became professor of sacred scripture at the University of Dilingen, situated on the Danube, some

---

[14] Cited in Burke, p. 468.
[15] Helga Hammerstein, '*Aspects etc.*', p. 143.

eighty kilometres above Ingoldstadt, where he taught for the next sixteen years.

Before he took his final vows in 1613 he made his will and he gave permission to his superior to dispose of the contents as he saw fit. He appeared to have been reasonably well off as he had in his possession such items as horses, swords, boots, spurs, ivory watches, gold watches, a silver ring, a gold ring and other objects, most of which he had received from his father. Despite his poor health and onerous professional duties, he became the author of a number of theological treatises which earned him a growing reputation for learning and scholarship. Contemporaries said of him that 'Stephen White is a most accomplished theologian' and that 'amid his unwearied labour at Dilingen, he is the wonder of Germany'.[16] Unfortunately, most of these works are lost

Around 1611, according to his own account, White found time to devote himself to a subject which had always been close to his heart, the study of Ireland's past. This took place at a critical time in his country's history. After 1603 there was a widely held view that the conquest of Ireland would be accompanied by the disappearance of Gaelic civilisation. Traditional lore, which had been handed down from generation to generation, was in danger of being lost. Certain scholars made a heroic attempt to preserve historical manuscripts and antiquities from destruction by gathering together the surviving remnants of old Irish learning.

Irish priests and friars on the Continent were foremost in safeguarding their country's literature and antiquities and in defending Irish culture. Among them were the Franciscans in Louvain, who were responsible for preserving much material on Irish history and on the saints in particular.[17] White's interest in Irish history and antiquities became a lifelong passion and led him to discover many valuable Irish manuscripts.

Among White's students at Dilingen were about one hundred and fifty religious from fifty different abbeys and monasteries throughout Germany. He wrote to the fifty abbots concerned and most of them gave him permission to visit their monasteries, examine their libraries, inspect

---

[16] Cited in Burke, p. 459.

[17] Patrick Conlon (Fr.), *St. Anthony's College of the Irish Franciscans, Louvain,* (Dublin, 1977), p. 20.

their manuscripts and find if there was anything of interest concerning Ireland. In this way White was the first to open up the mine of Irish texts in German libraries, often unearthing material that contemporary scholars did not even know existed. On one occasion he found a life of St. Columba in a chest in a library in Schaffhausen.

Having copied what manuscripts he found by hand he sent them back to Ireland to men like the Four Masters who were collecting similar material around Ireland. Commending White's achievement in bringing such sources to light, Dr. Reeves, in a paper read before the Irish Academy in 1861, stated that he 'opened that rich mine of Irish literature on the continent, which has ever since yielded such valuable returns, and still continues unexhausted'.[18]

White wished to show that Ireland was worthy of a place of honour among the nations of Europe. He said that 'the sole purpose of my writing is to defend the injured reputation of the old Irish with whom I, and my fathers for four hundred years, have shared a common fatherland'.[19] Consequently, he felt obliged to refute the attacks on his native land from English antiquarians who were anti-popish and anti-gaelic in character. Stephen White was outraged when an English Catholic called Campion published the work of Giraldus Cambrensis or Gerald Barry, a Welsh historian who accompanied the early Norman invaders to Ireland, and who wrote with a very prejudiced and jaundiced view of the Irish. White set out to debunk these charges in a notable work, begun in 1611, which he called *Apologia Hibernia adversis Cambri calumnies*.

White's historical researches were constrained by the fact that he had no access to original documents held in Ireland and in a letter to the Franciscan historian, Father John Colgan, he admitted, 'I keep working as well as I can, though not with as much success as I should wish on account of my age and the want of a good library'. Despite these disadvantages the Reverend M. Kelly, who edited White's *Apologia* in 1849, said 'this work will be found as free from error as most of them written on new subjects. To some of his arguments the research of subsequent writers has been able

---

[18] Rev. Dr. Reeves, 'Memoir of Stephen White' in *Proceedings of the Royal Irish Academy,* vol. viii, (MDCCCLXIV, Dublin), p. 29.
[19] Burke, p. 460.

to add very little'. This was but one of many of his historical works, some of which are lost, while others have survived in manuscript form.

In 1623, White left Germany for the province of Champagne, spending four years at Pont-a-Mousson and a further three at Metz. Following many requests by the head of the Jesuit order in Ireland for Stephen to return to his native land, the superior general reluctantly parted with his 'great jewel', adding that 'the Irish were the most intelligent people on the continent of Europe and of them Stephen White himself was the supreme one'. He was to take up a professorship in a university which his order was building in Dublin but by the time he arrived the ruling body of Trinity College, viewing the new institution as a threat, prevailed on the authorities to have it suppressed.

It would appear that White never returned to the continent. He was to spend the remaining years of his life 'for the most part teaching a few boys by stealth'. He spent some time in the Clonmel ministry where he made contact with historian and kindred spirit, Fr. Geoffry Keating. At the time of the outbreak of war of 1641 broke out we find Stephen in Dublin. From there, accompanied by a few friends, he made his way to Galway. It would appear that he died shortly afterwards for the last reference to him in the archives of the order is in 1646. It is thought that he died the following year.

White never sought glory for himself but, considering the honour of his country more important, generously shared his knowledge with others. Among those indebted to him was, James Ussher, Protestant primate of Armagh, with whom White formed a firm friendship when they were students together at Trinity College. Ussher was a great admirer of White, a man he respected for his learning and for his vast knowledge of Irish history. He wrote of him as 'a man of exquisite knowledge in the antiquities not alone of Ireland but also of other nations'.[20] They corresponded regularly and White sent him a transcript of the life of St. Erherd. Stephen was made welcome in Armagh where the bishop placed his library at his disposal.

---

[20] Louis McRedmond, *To the greater glory. A History of the Irish Jesuits,* (Dublin, 1991), p. 83.

White copied the life of St. Colman, which he had discovered in a Swiss monastery for the Franciscan Fr. Hugh Ward, founder of the school of Irish history at Louvain. Not alone did he send a life of St. Patrick to Fr. John Colgan, Ward's successor, who was researching the lives of Irish saints, but wrote to him praising and encouraging his efforts:

> I congratulate our country on finding one so gifted by God as you, to win, to extend and to proclaim her glory. Have courage, continue as you began, go on cheerfully ….. your memory shall live forever in benediction among all the good men of our race as long as it survives.[21]

Stephen White will be remembered for the efforts he made in preserving our national literature and antiquities and in defending the glories of his native land. Burke said of him that 'one of the strongest claims which White has to the gratitude of his country is that he was the first to demonstrate the great part which Ireland played in the history of Europe from the seventh to the tenth century'.[22]

It has been stated that Stephen White was one of the three or four most learned men that Ireland has ever produced.[23] Referred to by Reverend Lynch, archbishop of Tuam, as 'a walking library', he had the title of polyhistor conferred on him by contemporaries, in deference to the vast extent and great variety of his learning. These were some of the tributes paid to a man regarded as one of the greatest European scholars of his time. The Whites, like the Barons and others who came after them, were to find fame in places far from Clonmel. However, they deserve to be remembered, not alone for the contribution they made to the reputation of their country but for the credit they reflect on their birthplace.

---

[21] Burke, p. 463.

[22] *Ibid*, p. 462.

[23] Edmund Hogan (Fr.), 'Life of Father White, S.J.' in *Journal of the Waterford and South East of Ireland Antiquarian Society*, iii, no. xii (April, 1897), p. 55.

Chapter 5

Under Siege

One of the most outstanding episodes in the history of Clonmel was the heroic defence of the town during the siege of 1650. Although it lasted little more than three weeks it was one of the defining moments in a war which began nine years earlier. The siege was marked by courage and defiance, bravery and treachery, plague and famine. The leading protagonists were Hugh Dubh O'Neill and Oliver Cromwell. Subsidiary roles were filled by the Duke of Ormonde, who viewed the proceedings from a safe distance, the sinister Major Edward Fennell and John White, mayor of Clonmel, who epitomised the bravery of the townspeople. The war in Ireland was part of a broader conflict fought out in England between king and parliament and it occurred at a time when Europe was torn apart in the name of religion, with monarchs fighting subjects who differed in their 'method of devotion'.

In October 1641, the native Irish in Ulster, who had never accepted the plantation of 1607 as final, rose in rebellion against those settlers who occupied their ancestral lands. The Old English, as the descendants of the original Norman conquerors were called, also felt threatened. As Catholics, they were finding it increasingly difficult to practise their religion. In addition, they were being excluded from public office and feared their estates would be confiscated. They were also alarmed at the political situation in England where the power struggle between king and a Puritan-dominated parliament was coming to a head.

Representatives of both Native Irish and Old English met in Kilkenny on 24 October 1642 and formed what proved to be an uneasy alliance known as the Confederation of Kilkenny. Both parties demanded full freedom of Catholic worship and a guarantee that Catholic landowners should enjoy undisputed title to their lands. These objectives were to be attained through a mixture of force and diplomacy. The most prominent of the Old English rebels in the Clonmel area was Richard Butler of Kilcash, brother to James Butler, earl of Ormonde, who had been appointed to look after the king's interests in Ireland. In the beginning of January 1642, the

Mayor of Clonmel handed him over the keys of the town. The citizens, while strongly insisting on their allegiance to the king, proclaimed that their purpose was to defend themselves against a parliament equally hostile to the sovereign and themselves. Ireland's destiny was ultimately to be decided by the unfolding political situation in England, and on the day before the Confederation met in Kilkenny, the Battle of Edgehill signalled the outbreak of civil war in England between King Charles I and Parliament.

The cause of the Confederacy was hampered by a divided military command. The Ulster rebels took the initiative of recruiting Owen Roe O'Neill, who had seen service in the Netherlands and Spain, to command their army, while Colonel Thomas Preston, another veteran from the Spanish campaigns, took over the leadership of the Old English in Leinster. Unfortunately, O'Neill and Preston were rivals since their days of service in Spain and refused to co-operate. For the next eight years, the war in Ireland dragged on, punctuated by protracted negotiations, changing alliances and indecisive military engagements. By 1649, the king had been executed and the parliamentary armies were triumphant in England. In Ireland the Confederation was in disarray and the country braced itself to face the might of Cromwell.

James Butler

James Butler came from a strong Catholic family; his grandfather was the pious 'Walter of the Rosaries', while two of his sisters became cloistered nuns. He was born at Clerkenwell in London on 19 October 1610. When, at the age of nine, his father died in a drowning accident, he was made a ward of court. He was sent to England where he was educated by the Archbishop of Canterbury and subsequently emerged a confirmed Protestant. His devotion to the established church and his loyalty to the crown were the hallmarks of his long career. In 1633, on the death of his grandfather, James became 12th earl of Ormonde.

In a very short time, Ormonde rose to become the leading royalist in Ireland. His advancement was due to his friendship with Thomas Wentworth, who had been appointed Lord Deputy in 1633. Ormonde quickly proved himself a trusted and useful ally, enthusiastically supporting the deputy's attempts to raise finance to equip the Irish army. Impressed by Ormonde's zeal, Wentworth recommended that such efforts be rewarded. Following the rebellion of 1641, Charles I appointed Ormonde commander of the royalist forces in Ireland with instructions to defend the king's interests and to ensure that Ireland did not fall into the hands of the Parliamentarians while, at the same time, containing the forces of the Confederacy.

An indifferent military leader, he adopted the expedient of entering into negotiations with the Confederacy hoping 'to buy time' for his royal master. By 1647, with the king's cause almost lost, Ormonde decided to surrender Dublin to the forces of Parliament, preferring as he said, 'English rebels to Irish rebels'. He left for England where he was allowed to see the king, now a prisoner of parliament. In March 1648, he left for France, where he joined the exiled queen in Paris. He returned to Ireland in September where he attempted to gather all the royalist elements under his leadership. News of the imminent execution of the king in January 1649 precipitated an agreement with the confederates. Ormonde was re-appointed Lord Lieutenant by the exiled king, Charles II, but his abortive attempt to recover Dublin cleared the way for the safe arrival of Cromwell.

Hugh Dubh O'Neill

After the defeat of Gaelic Ulster, many members of the O'Neill clan left for Europe in 1607 in what became known as the Flight of the Earls. Among them was Art Oge O'Neill, who found fame in the army of Spain. His son, Hugh Dubh, was born in Brussels about 1611, where his father, Art Oge O'Neill, was serving at the time. Hugh Dubh's military pedigree was impeccable. His father was Eoghan Roe's youngest brother and he was the great-nephew of the great Hugh O'Neill.

He received his early military training in the Spanish army and was mentioned as one of the 'brave warriors and prime captains', who came to Ireland with Eoghan Roe O'Neill in 1642. When the Irish forces were defeated by Sir Robert Stewart at the Battle of Clones in June 1643, he was captured and imprisoned at Derry. He was released in an exchange of prisoners after the success of Eoghan Roe and the Confederacy forces at the battle of Benburb in 1646. During the subsequent illness of Owen Roe, Hugh Dubh was given command of the Ulster army.

On the death of Owen Roe, Hugh Dubh entertained ideas of being chosen as commander of the Confederate forces. Daniel O'Neill considered him an ideal choice 'being a man who knew the ways Owen Roe O'Neill took to manage people', and having spent sixteen years under his command. The author of a contemporary work *The Aphorismical Discovery* speaks of him as a 'tried, wise, faithful, successful officer, unsurpassed in courage, valiant, industrious, zealous for religion, loyal to the king, faithful to his country, constant in his principles'. Unfortunately, he fell victim to the jealousies and rivalries within the Confederation, so that he had to be satisfied with the command of a section of the Ulster army which, at the invitation of the Earl of Ormonde, undertook the task of defending Clonmel.

We must rely on Eoghan Roe's biographer, Gilbert, for our only description of Hugh Dubh O'Neill who was, he said:

> of middle height and rather corpulent. He was about fifty years at this time. Dressed in a blue tunic and a dark blue breeches, with black high top boots and an Irish black glengarry with a gay feather; he had mail breast-plate and back plates. He looked a resplendent figure. He was a wise, cautious, far seeing commander – well trained in his profession and well beloved by his troops.[1]

This 'old, surly, Spanish soldier' was to prove a worthy opponent for Oliver Cromwell.

Oliver Cromwell

Hugh Dubh O'Neill and Oliver Cromwell were the products of two different worlds. While O'Neill was a born soldier, Cromwell, on the other hand, did not leave the obscurity of rural England until his involvement in

[1] Colonel Patrick Dineen (Col.), 'The siege of Clonmel' in P. O'Connell & W. C. Darmody (eds.), *Tercentenary Souvenir Record* (Clonmel, 1950), p. 12.

the Puritan revolution revealed him to be one of the greatest military geniuses of all time. While comparatively little is known of the life of O'Neill, Cromwell, one of the most controversial historical figures in these islands, is the subject of countless books and articles.

Oliver Cromwell's early life showed no intimations of greatness. He was born at Huntingdon on 25 April 1599 to Robert and Elizabeth Cromwell of comfortable farming stock. His two brothers, one older and one younger, died very young, leaving Oliver to be brought up as the only son and heir in a household of seven daughters. He seemed a normal enough youth, playing truant, gambling and drinking a bit, a boy whose worst crime was stealing birds from a dovecote. He was described as a man of average height, physically strong, somewhat 'rough hewn' in appearance, blunt in his manner, apt to take offence easily, and inclined to be quarrelsome.[2] Some contemporary portraits show the celebrated warts on his chin, forehead and by his left eye. He was a lover of dogs and horses, of hunting and hawking, a man who enjoyed his pipe of tobacco and small ale. Although no intellectual, he showed a keen interest in music and singing. His sartorial defects led a contemporary to remark that 'his plain cloth suit, seemed to have been made by an ill country tailor'.

Having spent a year at Cambridge University, the death of his father compelled him to return home. He briefly studied law at Lincoln Inn before marrying Elizabeth Bouchier, daughter of a wealthy fur dealer, who had done well enough to be knighted and buy a country estate in Essex. Cromwell settled down to married life in Huntingdon, sharing the house with his widowed mother and unmarried sisters. The marriage was blessed with five children and Oliver proved a devoted husband and family man.

The defining moment of his life occurred around this time when he underwent a severe spiritual crisis. He became identified with the Puritan element within the reformed church which felt that the Protestant Reformation had not gone far enough in sweeping away Catholic beliefs, forms and practices. They objected to the retention of certain holy days, to elaborate ceremonies in many church services and to ornate decorations within church buildings. Puritans saw it as their duty to put pressure on the

---

[2] Pauline Gregg, *Oliver Cromwell*, (London, 1988), p. 13.

establishment to abolish such practices. From this time on Cromwell displayed all the convert's enthusiasm which is evident from the intense religious language of his letters and political speeches.[3] He attributed his success at Marston Moor to his being a chosen instrument of the Lord. He wrote 'it had all the evidence of an absolute victory obtained by the Lord's blessing upon the Godly party principally'.[4]

These religious beliefs were to shape Cromwell's political views. In 1640, when Charles decided to call another parliament, Cromwell was invited to stand for the neighbouring town of Cambridge and was duly elected. He and other Puritans, increasingly alarmed by the church practices of Charles I who favoured the ceremonial rites of Catholicism, became an outspoken critic of the king's religious policies. As the situation worsened, a clash between the king and a Puritan dominated parliament was imminent because of the king's obduracy in refusing to recall parliament and the religious revolt in Scotland.

At forty-one years of age, this Cambridgeshire farmer was only at the beginning of a political career of which he could have scarcely dreamed. Soon the Civil War was to make him the most powerful man in England. On 22 August 1642, when the king gave the signal for the beginning of hostilities by raising his standard at Nottingham, Cromwell was already an active and committed officer of the parliamentary army. As captain, he had raised a troop of sixty horses at Huntingdon. The following year he was promoted to colonel and given command of his own cavalry regiment. Their presence proved decisive at the battles of Marston Moor and Naseby, winning for their commander, lieutenant-general Colonel Oliver Cromwell, the name 'Old Ironsides'. By the end of the decade, he had become commander-in-chief of the parliamentary army, a truly remarkable achievement for a man with no previous military experience or training.

Although Cromwell consistently attributed his success to God's will, he proved himself to be a born leader of men and a soldier of genius.

---

[3] W. C. Abbott, *Writings and speeches of Oliver Cromwell,* i, (Massachusetts, 1937-47), p. 287.

[4] Cited in Antonia Fraser, *Cromwell: Our Chief of Men,* (Hertfordshire, 1976), p. 129.

He had all the qualities necessary for success. He was confident and decisive. He instinctively knew what needed to be done and then carried it out. He had a flair for organisation. He inspired by example and was willing to share the hardships of his men. It was said of him that, 'No man knew more of men'. Historians point to his personal courage and skill, to his care in training and providing the best equipment available for his men and to the tight discipline he imposed on and off the battlefield. He played a vital role in planning the campaigns in the major battles. He was a genius at handling cavalry, and though neither a military innovator nor a brilliant tactician, he had an extraordinary ability to instil self-belief into his men. He shared with them his own utter conviction that God was with them and willing them to victory, while also ensuring that they were better paid and fed than were other armies.

When it came to recruitment, his approach was original. The men he selected were religious men who were prepared to fight as a matter of conscience. 'Truly I think', he declared, 'he that prays best will fight best'. He applied the same standards to his officers, who up to now had come from the ranks of the landed gentry. Instead Cromwell looked for men with commitment. As he said himself, 'I had rather have a plain russet coated captain that knows what he fights for than what you call a gentleman and nothing else. If you choose goodly men to be captains of horse, honest men will follow them. A few honest men are better than numbers'.[5] Discipline was strict. Every soldier was expected to keep his arms and mount in top condition. Plunder was not permitted. Any man who swore had to pay a fine of twelve pence and, if found drunk, was put in the stocks or worse. On one occasion, two troopers who tried to desert were whipped in the market place at Huntingdon.

It was this formidable fighting machine that landed in Dublin on 15 August 1649 under the command of a man who had never known defeat. A sea journey, which made him violently sea sick, did nothing to shake his belief in divine providence, 'God hath brought me thither in safety', he declared. He said that his intention was to deal with 'the barbarous and bloodthirsty Irish' who had been responsible for the atrocities which

---

[5] Cited in Christopher Hill, *God's Own Englishman*, (Reading, 1970), p. 64.

followed the 1641 rebellion. While several thousand Protestants had indeed perished, these numbers were inflated with unrestrained exaggeration in England and were used to justify Cromwell's harsh treatment of his Irish enemies.

Cromwell's campaigns were as much a religious crusade as a military necessity. 'I fought with the bible in one hand and the sword in the other', he once said. In Dublin, he told his troops that they 'were the Israelites about to enter Canaan to extirpate its idolatrous inhabitants'. At New Ross, he made his anti-Catholic intentions clear to the governor: 'But if by liberty of conscience you mean the liberty of exercising the mass, I judge it best to use plain dealing, to let you know, where the Parliament of England have power that will not be allowed of'. Liberty of conscience was to be for those who agreed with him. It was clear that victory for the forces of Cromwell would mean victory for the forces of intolerance.

Cromwell had 12,000 highly experienced and well equipped troops under his command. He first moved north on Drogheda and the wholesale slaughter that accompanied its capture came to be recognised as the greatest atrocity in Irish history. One eyewitness account of the massacre, where 3,500 soldiers and civilians perished, wrote: 'To none was mercy shown; not to the women; nor to the aged; nor to the young'. Cromwell viewed this as 'a righteous judgement of God upon these barbarous wretches'. At Wexford, he gloated that 'our forces put all to the sword that came our way'. He justified this by saying that he hoped to frighten other towns into speedy submission, thus avoiding long and costly sieges, preventing what he called 'an effusion of blood'. In this he was partly successful. The carnage of Drogheda and Wexford inspired such fear that many towns surrendered without firing a shot, including Youghal, where Cromwell set up winter quarters.

Preparations

The townspeople of Clonmel had remained faithful to the Confederacy throughout a decade of warfare but soon that loyalty was to be put to its sternest test. As 1649 drew to a close, news filtered through of the advance of the Cromwellian forces. The realisation that Clonmel too might share the fate of Drogheda and Wexford made the decision to resist all the more courageous. Following the execution of king Charles the previous January, the Royalist sympathisers in the Confederacy had placed their forces under the command of Ormonde and it was to him that Mayor John White looked for assistance in facing Cromwell's parliamentary army. In response to this request, Clonmel received a force of 1,500 under the command of Hugh Dubh O'Neill, who arrived in the town in November.

The prospect facing O'Neill was a daunting one. Clonmel was a town suffering the strain of a decade of warfare and its citizens were struggling to pay the weekly levies of money and corn to assist the war effort. For some, this was more than they could bear and many of the poorer inhabitants had deserted the town. Now, as an additional burden, they had to endure having over one and a half thousand soldiers in addition to their wives and children billeted in their homes. In spite of these difficulties, O'Neill, a professional soldier of the highest order, lost no time in 'building brauve works for the defence of the towne'. To overcome the shortage of weapons, he set up a foundry to make munitions. In these endeavours he had the wholehearted support of Mayor John White and the inhabitants, which reflected the spirit of the townspeople and their confidence in O'Neill.

The mild winter enabled Cromwell to renew his campaign earlier than expected. He left Youghal in January and, twelve days later, reached Clogheen. So impressed was he with Tipperary's verdant acres that he reputedly remarked, 'that this indeed was a land worth fighting for'. Surrounded by a ring of castles, Clonmel appeared to be in no imminent danger but Cromwell was not long in dismantling them. He received the surrender of Fethard and Cashel before moving on to Kilkenny. He left his son-in-law, Ireton, to complete the operation. Ardfinnan Castle fell to him after eight or nine shots. His capture of Cahir, Kiltinan, Kilcash, Ballydine and Ballyneale quickly followed. With the betrayal of Kilkenny, Cromwell was now in a position to devote his full attention to Clonmel. Before the end of February the first Cromwellian troops appeared before its walls.

O'Neill had some 1,500 seasoned troops at his disposal, consisting of two regiments of foot, of whom 700 were armed with muskets, 600 with pikes and the rest with assorted weapons. In addition to these, there were

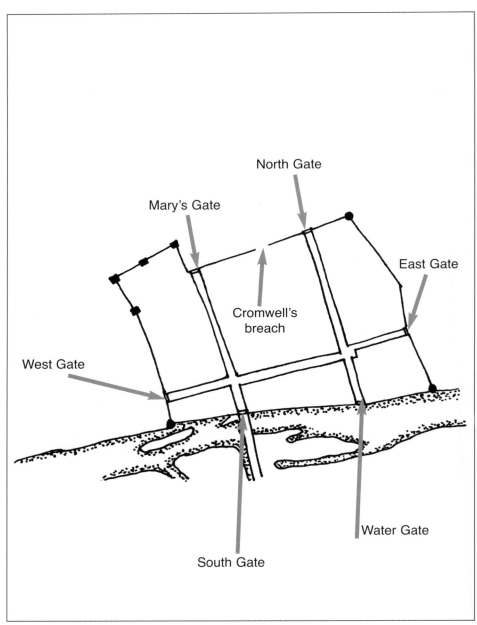

North Gate

Mary's Gate

East Gate

Cromwell's
breach

West Gate

Water Gate

South Gate

Map 3. Clonmel in 1650

100 horse under the command of the untrustworthy Major Edward Fennell, whom Eoghan Roe O'Neill referred to as 'that terrible cock with a feather in a cap'. Cromwell had the cream of the Model Army under his command. It included a force of 12,000 with 600 horse, 25 field guns, a battery of howitzers and four siege guns, all led by an invincible general. Despite the overwhelming odds, O'Neill was to prove himself an astute and resourceful commander. The sustained defence of Clonmel was a tribute to his tenacity and military skill.

Siege

With the appearance of the first Cromwellian troops before the town walls, O'Neill wrote an urgent letter to Ormonde seeking assistance. In his reply, dated 3 March 1650, Ormonde informed O'Neill that if he could hold out for ten days, in the meantime he 'would have drawn all the forces of the kingdom into a body for its relief' and that he himself 'would be in readiness to advance'.[6] On March 19 Cromwell arrived. He made the customary demand for the surrender of the town. O'Neill told him that he had no intention of giving up and challenged Cromwell to do his worst.[7] These were brave words, considering the fate of Drogheda and Wexford.

Cromwell proceeded with preparations for the siege and planted his cannon on the high ground overlooking the north wall. O'Neill took the offensive and launched a series of attacks under cover of darkness. He sent out raiding parties to ambush the enemy, bringing back much needed food supplies. It is said that one such foray resulted in 500 Cromwellians being killed.

Cromwell was equally resourceful and attempted to take the town by treachery. He was well served by the unscrupulous Colonel Fennell who agreed, for a sum of £500, to open the North Gate. O'Neill had every reason to distrust him. During the Battle of Clones where O'Neill himself had been taken prisoner, Fennell, though he had a strong brigade of horse under his command at the time, showed great inactivity, while some of O'Neill's kinsmen were cut down before his face. Others say he deserted at

---

[6] William Burke (Rev.), *History of Clonmel*, p. 71.
[7] *Ibid*, p. 72.

the height of battle. The vigilant O'Neill, on inspecting the guard in Clonmel, was quick to see that his own men had been replaced by Fennell's. The traitor was arrested and on the promise of his life, revealed all. Cleverly, O'Neill turned the situation to his advantage. He admitted five hundred Cromwellians at the appointed hour and put them to the sword.

On 27 April O'Neill made a final plea to Ormonde for assistance, telling him that he would defend the town for as long as possible but nonetheless he was anxious to 'prevent any bloody tragedy'. Ormonde managed to raise a small force under Lord Roche for the relief of Clonmel but, unfortunately on 10 May, it was destroyed by the parliamentary commander, Lord Broghill, near Macroom.

Ormonde's critics claimed that he abandoned Clonmel to its fate by refusing to help during the subsequent siege, and that the frequent requests he received from the commander of the garrison, Hugh Dubh O'Neill, were met with empty promises and free advice. In his defence, it could be argued that Ormonde's military supplies were severely limited, and that the garrison he sent to the town was more than the population could tolerate. This was emphasised by Mayor White's complaint that 'a multiplicity of soldiers' was proving an intolerable burden for the people. On the other hand throughout the campaign Ormonde showed a distinct reluctance to engage Cromwell in pitched battle. Perhaps, he found the challenge too daunting, or he may have entertained the idea of keeping his army intact, until a more favourable opportunity should present itself.

On 16 May, the town wall was breached at a point west of the North Gate. O'Neill lost no time preparing a hot reception for the invaders. With the assistance of the townspeople he constructed a passageway stretching from the breach in the wall into the town. It was said to be about fifty metres long and was constructed of mortar, stone and timber. At the end the defenders dug a ditch and placed two concealed cannon above it, directly facing the breach. At either side of this passageway and in the houses overlooking it, O'Neill's soldiers lay in wait.

When the hymn singing, unwitting Cromwellians entered the breech they were cut to pieces. The ferocity shown by the defenders was such that Cromwell's foot soldiers mutinied when he called for another onslaught. The Model Army had been finally humbled and it was left to the cavalry to redeem its reputation. They entered unchallenged and, when they found themselves in a cul de sac, the order 'to halt' was given. Those at the rear thought this was directed at the fleeing Irish and continued to advance. With the laneway crammed with Cromwellian cavalry O'Neill's men sealed the breech and fell on those trapped within. Over 1,000 of Cromwell's elite troops lay dead, while their leader was waiting to be admitted at the North Gate. This rebuff, according to one British officer, 'left him as much vexed as ever he was since he first put on a helmet against the King for such a repulse he did not usually meet with'.[8]

O'Neill's victory however was a pyrrhic one. With virtually no ammunition left, many of his men sick or wounded, typhus rampant and the townspeople exhausted, he had no option but to withdraw. A colourful anecdote tells that Cromwell too considered giving up the fight but the finding of a silver bullet in the grass revealed O'Neill's predicament. Having consulted with the mayor, John White, O'Neill led his troops under cover of darkness over the Old Bridge to safety. He advised the mayor to request an audience with Cromwell to 'seek conditions for the town' but not to inform him of the departure of the garrison.

That night the mayor met Cromwell and surrender terms were agreed. Cromwell then asked mayor White was O'Neill aware that he had come out to meet him. When he was told that O'Neill had left some hours previously Cromwell demanded to know why he had not been so informed. To which the Mayor replied that 'if his Excellency had demanded the question he would tell him'. Cromwell then asked the mayor who was this Hugh Dubh O'Neill, and when the mayor said that he was an 'oversea soldier' born in Spain, Cromwell thundered: 'God damn you and your oversea. By God I will follow that Hugh Dubh O'Neill wherever he goes'. Angered that O'Neill and his troops had escaped, he dispatched some of his soldiers to follow them. They overtook some stragglers, mainly camp followers, and put them to the sword. Although Cromwell had promised to spare the lives of the citizens and their property, it would appear that he did not keep his promise for when his army entered the town 'the inhabitants

---

[8] *Ibid*, p. 77.

were pillaged, rifled and plundered without respect of persons or mercy or degree'.[9]

Clonmel, proud in defeat, had offered the greatest challenge to Cromwell during his entire campaign in Ireland. It had been three months since the enemy first appeared before its walls and there had been three weeks of intense fighting in which Cromwell lost between 2,000 and 2,500 men. The finest tribute that could be paid to the heroism of the defenders came from those on the opposing side. Whitlocke, a Cromwellian soldier at the siege, said that 'they found in Clonmel the stoutest enemy that ever was found by the army in Ireland, and that there was never seen so hot a storm of so long continuance, and so gallantly defended, neither in England or Ireland'. John Milton, secretary to Cromwell, but best remembered for his poetical endeavours, spoke about 'that sore breach made up by the Lord upon us at Clonmel, which was the heaviest we ever underwent either in England or here'.[10]

Cromwell's Return to England

Shortly after the siege Cromwell sailed for England, leaving his son-in-law Ireton to complete the conquest. Cromwell devoted his energies to the great problem of the future government of England, but he did not achieve the same success in the political arena as he had on the battlefield. Cromwell's last years were marked with conspiracies and failing health. He was seized with a fever and died on 3 September 1658 in his sixtieth year.

In Ireland, Cromwell's character has long been the subject of passionate and prejudiced discussion. One commentator said that 'unknowingly, Cromwell became the midwife of modern Irish nationalism'. He spent a mere nine months in this country and in that short time succeeded in making himself one of the most hated figures in Irish history. The carnage of Drogheda and Wexford, and his virulent hatred of Roman Catholicism are the greatest stain on his reputation. Like all villains, his vices have been exaggerated and, among other things, we are

---

[9] P. O'Connell, 'The defenders of Clonmel' in P. O'Connell & W. C. Darmody (eds.), *Tercentenary of the Siege of Clonmel,* (Clonmel, 1950), p. 32.
[10] *Ibid*, p. 33.

led to believe that most churches of that period stabled his horses. He was an ogre that haunted future generations and to the Irish peasant 'The Curse of Cromwell' was a frightening imprecation. This detestation transcended the social classes and, in 1889, an Irish member of the House of Lords saw fit to defeat a proposal to have a statue of Cromwell erected in the Houses of Parliament.

In England he has been no less controversial. He has been regarded by some as 'the greatest hero of the century' or as 'a man of piety and a great champion for the liberties of the nation'. He is seen at the true republican who challenged the absolutism of the Stuarts. Others have considered him 'the most corrupt and selfish being that ever disgraced a human form' and 'one of the most notorious tyrants and usurpers that the world ever beheld'. In 1661, on the instructions of parliament, his coffin was dragged to Tyburn where his mummified corpse was pulled out, hanged from the gallows for several hours and then decapitated. The head became an undignified collector's item until it was finally buried in his old Cambridge college in 1960, while the body presumably lies somewhere beneath London's urban sprawl. In 1969, the following commemorative notice appeared in The Times newspaper: 'Cromwell. To the eternal condemnation of Oliver; sodomite, traitor, regicide, racialist, proto fascist and blasphemous bigot, God save England from the like'. What kind of man could arouse such passionate hatred, three centuries after his death? How would the man, who wished to be painted 'warts and all', have reacted to all of this?

O'Neill Fights On

Although Cromwell's nine months campaign had been ruthlessly efficient, the war in Ireland was not yet over. Important centres, like the cities of Waterford and Limerick, had yet to be taken. After the surrender of Clonmel O'Neill retreated to Waterford only to be refused admittance by Preston, the governor. From there he proceeded to Limerick where Ormonde appointed him military governor of that city. Limerick, together with Athlone, was one of the two strategic gateways to Connacht. Ireton made him 'offers to great preferment, to induce him to surrender' but

O'Neill refused to 'betray the trust reposed in him'. In an uncompromising reply he wrote:

> No such threats are able to daunt my resolutions, seeing I am no stranger to the like. Sir, I am entrusted with this place from my lord lieutenant to maintain it for the use of his majesty King Charles, which I resolve by God's assistance to perform, notwithstanding any power shall offer against me, even to the effusion of the last drop of my blood.[11]

Despite these brave words, Limerick was a divided city, with one faction wanting to surrender and the other refusing to yield. O'Neill defended the city valiantly. The siege began in June and dragged on into October. O'Neill, as he had done in Clonmel, conducted a number of successful sallies outside the walls, while contending with a rampant plague, food shortages and the increasing demands of those who wished to surrender. In order to diminish the ordeal of starvation, O'Neill 'tried to get rid as many useless mouths as possible by expelling them'. Ireton countered 'by sending them back with a letter to O'Neill saying that any more persons sent out would be severely dealt with. O'Neill would not let them in and sent out some more to join them'.[12] Ireton, true to his word, gave orders to attack these misfortunates which led to a number of them being killed.

O'Neill managed to hold out for three months, until the city was betrayed by none other than Colonel Edward Fennell. He admitted two hundred English soldiers into the gate tower of St. John's Castle and threatened to turn their guns on the city unless the garrison capitulated. Further resistance was futile. The most surprising thing about Fennell, is that in spite of his cowardice and treachery, he seems to have been allowed to continue in positions of trust. After Clonmel, he surrendered Cappoquin without striking a blow. He abandoned Killaloe, and allowed Ireton to

---

[11] J. T. Gilbert (ed.), *A contemporary history of affairs in Ireland from 1641 to 1652,* iii, (Dublin, 1879/80), p. 180.
[12] J. G. Simms, 'Hugh Dubh O'Neill's defence of Limerick, 1650-1651' in *The Irish Sword,* iii, (1957-58), p. 119.

attack Limerick on the Clare side. Eventually, in December 1652, he was taken to Cork where he was found guilty of two capital charges and executed.[13]

O'Neill, having met Ireton at the city gate and handed over the keys of the city was held prisoner, while his troops were allowed to march out. The victors were of the opinion that O'Neill's letters and actions showed that he was responsible for the city's stubborn resistance, while he maintained that he had only done his duty. In a letter addressed to Ireton, dated 30 October, he wrote, 'I endeavoured the surrender of this place, being satisfied in all humane reason and policy (from the beginning) that it could not withstand your power' and that 'he was guilty of no base or dishonourable act, having only discharged the duty of a soldier subject to a superior power to which I must have been accountable'. He went on to say that 'I shall therefore humbly entreat your honour to take my condition into your serious consideration that I be not otherwise dealt with than the justice or injustice of my case requireth'.[14] Ireton, proposing to execute O'Neill, put him on trial twice. On the first occasion he was sentenced to death on the grounds that he had been responsible for the killing of many English soldiers but, at the second trial, Ireton's officers prevailed on him to spare his life.

A few days later, Ireton fell victim to the plague. On his deathbed he instructed Ludlow, his lieutenant-general, to show his vanquished opponent every courtesy. He even went so far as to request that O'Neill might accompany his body to England and in fact O'Neill was present at Ireton's burial in Westminster Abbey. O'Neill arrived in London on 10 January 1652 and was duly committed to the tower. The following July, the Spanish Ambassador requested the Council of State to release O'Neill. His request was granted on the understanding that he would take no further part in fighting against England. Cromwell, who was anxious to preserve friendly relations with Spain, consented.

After his release, O'Neill went to Belgium and from there to Spain. For the next seven years he served with distinction in the Spanish army as a

---

[13] Thomas Fitzpatrick, *Waterford during the Civil War 1641-1653* (Waterford, 1912).

[14]. Simms, p. 122.

general of artillery in Catalonia. In 1660 he proceeded to petition Charles II and the Duke of Ormonde in the vain hope of having his family estates restored and, as rightful heir, assuming the title Earl of Tyrone. He died not long after. Some claim he was on active service in the war with Portugal but more convincing evidence suggests that he was incapacitated by his failing health.

The man who served Clonmel so well lies under the sunny skies of Spain, far from his ancestral lands in Ulster. What finer tribute could be paid than that of his former adversary, Oliver Cromwell, who 'commended him for a brave soldier and accused his own retrograde fortune at not being able to win one petty town or wrest it by fine force out of the hands of one single man so long a time without relief'.[15]

James Butler, 1st duke of Ormonde

A little over a month after O'Neill had been put on trial by Ireton in Limerick, Ormonde set sail from Galway for France on 11 December 1650. His departure marked the final collapse of the royalist cause in Ireland. Ten years later, on the 25 May 1660, when Charles II landed in Dover to reclaim his throne, Ormonde was at his side. The numerous titles and offices that the king now conferred upon him reflected his gratitude for past services. These newly won honours included the office of Lord Steward of England, a rank never before attained by an Irishman, and advancement to the Dukedom of Ormonde. He was also appointed to serve two further terms as lord lieutenant. All the estates he held at the outbreak of the insurrection in 1641 were restored to him. In addition, he received a grant of almost the entire town of Clonmel and the palatinate rights of Tipperary, formerly enjoyed by the Ormondes but confiscated by James I in 1621, were restored to the family.

The physical improvement and economic recovery of Clonmel after 1660 owed much to the patronage of Ormonde. After the siege of 1650 the town 'presented a scene of awful desolation'. Sixteen years later, the principal streets still contained 'waste tenements', 'a house slated

---

[15] P. O'Connell, 'The Defenders of Clonmel', p. 22.

ruinous', 'a house and back side waste' and 'a decayed castle'. In a flight of fancy Burke said it 'had become in great part the habitation of the bat and the owl'.[16] Ormonde set out to beautify 'this borough with such public and most useful structures as are not to be paralleled through this whole kingdom, and by a lasting fixation of several fairs within our walls and of the regality courts at our very doors'.[17] He started by providing a new courthouse to serve the palatinate, which had been revived after a lapse of forty years. This building, which was erected in 1675, is now known as the Main Guard. Although much altered over the years it has been recently restored to its original splendour. In 1677 he had plans drawn up for a new town gaol and, two years later, he advanced proposals for 'erecting good houses without Kilsheelan Gate (on the east of the town)'. He provided land for a free school, built in Mary Street in 1681, on a site now occupied by the Sisters of Charity primary school.

He also attempted to promote the woollen industry in Clonmel. The venture was launched in 1674 when Edward Nelthorpe, a London merchant, proposed to Ormonde that a serge and cloth industry be established in the town. A capital stock of over £20,000 was to be made available, and families skilled in cloth making were to come over from England. About 500 families of French and Walloon extraction resident at Canterbury were involved in the scheme and houses were provided for them in what became known as Weaver's Row, the present Bolton Street. There are no records as to how successful this initiative was or how long it continued in operation.

The First Duke of Ormonde died in July 1688 and was laid to rest beside his beloved wife in Westminster Abbey. Throughout his life he was a dedicated Royalist, earning Macauley's tribute as being 'the most illustrious Cavalier of the great Civil War'. On hearing of the execution of Charles I he exclaimed, 'The world hath not seen the like since the Crucifixion of the Saviour'. His unswerving loyalty won him the distrust of many of his countrymen who felt that in serving his king well he served his country badly. He once stated that 'Ireland must, if need be, suffer for the

---

[16] Burke, p. 89.

[17] Cited in T. P. Power, *Land, politics, and society in eighteenth century Tipperary,* (October, 1993), p. 20.

sake of the monarchy'. His loyalty to the crown was only exceeded by his loyalty to his religion. He once said that if the king should command anything contrary to the interests of religion he could 'only obey by suffering'. For a half century James Butler, 1st Duke of Ormonde, was the most prominent figure in Irish politics. An indifferent soldier, he displayed a remarkable gift for survival in a volatile political situation. Despite personal danger and the financial drain on his resources, he clung consistently to his principles.

Clonmel faces the new order

The siege of Clonmel was one of the defining incidents in the history of the town, bringing to an end the Catholic world of medieval Clonmel. The Cromwellian administration introduced what nowadays would be called a policy of ethnic cleansing. Under the terms of the subsequent settlement, the old burger families like the Whites, Brennocks, Brays and others, who had controlled the commerce of the town for centuries, were uprooted and transported to Connacht. Among them may have been John White, the former mayor, who had served his town well, distinguishing himself by his bravery and integrity.

These old families were replaced by adventurers who had lent money for the reduction of the Irish, ex-soldiers who received lands in lieu of pay and by various officials of the new regime. On their heels came the merchants and traders who were to become leaders of the new economic order. In time, their mercantile wealth allowed some of them to acquire extensive estates in the surrounding area and to dominate the political and social life of Clonmel for the next two hundred years.

Chapter 6

The Baron Brothers

Old St. Mary's Church in Clonmel contains an impressive grave slab leaning against the outer wall of the north aisle dedicated to the memory of Geoffrey Baron and his wife, Ellen White. Its size and elaborate designs indicate that they were people of some standing in the community. Their son Laurence Baron, who lived in Mary Street, became a successful wine merchant.

Geoffrey Baron (1607-1651)

Geoffrey Baron, born in 1607, was the eldest of four boys born to Laurence Baron and his first wife, Maria Butler, sister of Fr. Luke Wadding, the famous Waterford-born Franciscan. He also had a half-sister, Katherine Butler, from his mother's first marriage. His mother, Maria, died when he was nine years old and, shortly afterwards, his father married Catherine White of Waterford by whom he had a daughter called Bess. Being still a minor when his father died in 1622, Geoffrey was made a ward of court.

Although Geoffrey inherited seventeen mortgages valued at £1,304, and various lands and houses, he was far from financially secure. In a letter to his uncle Father Luke Wadding, dated 2 December 1626[1], he wrote of being 'deeply vexed in worldly troubles' which his father's death had brought upon his 'green head'. His father left him with debts totalling £1,900 which he was 'daily labouring to pay'. Under the terms of his will Geoffrey had to give his mother £300 and an annual jointure of £30. Bess was to receive £200 when she married and be provided with an annual jointure of £10. The remaining three family members were each to receive £100 'when they could manage it'.

Circumstances cannot have been easy for young Geoffrey, who obviously took his responsibilities seriously. He went on to describe how

---

[1] Cited in Burke's *History of Clonmel*, pp. 469, 470.

he had been acting *in loco parentis* to his siblings since his father's death. His sister, Katherine, aged seventeen, was still unmarried and his step-sister, Bess, was a mere six and a half at the time. He had maintained his two brothers at school, Bartholmew, who two months previously had entered the Franciscans and Michael who was still a student. His youngest brother Luke, 'a sickly boy' had died, aged thirteen, the previous year.

Around 1628 Geoffrey married Dorothy, daughter of Nicholas Wyse of Waterford and niece of Sir Arthur Wyse, Grand Prior in England of the Order of St. John of Malta. Unfortunately, she died after a few months and there is no indication that Geoffrey re-married. Two years later he went to London to study law. Father Thomas Strange, O.F.M., who shared accommodation with Geoffrey at the time, gave a glowing account of him to his uncle, Luke Wadding. He said that Geoffrey was a man of great promise and virtue and felt he would make an excellent lawyer. He went on to say that he was very popular and, in character, the essence of goodness, like his late mother.[2]

In 1632 he was admitted to the bar in London and quickly began to establish a reputation for himself. Apart from his legal skills, Geoffrey was considered a highly educated man. In his early years, he collected a great variety of books and formed his own private library' and was said to have written 'some works on literature', though none have survived.[3] In 1634, he was elected a member of parliament for Clonmel. At that time, the Catholic representatives were hoping to obtain concessions known as the 'graces' from king Charles I, which would remove the obstacles that had been placed on their freedom of worship. When it was discovered that it was the king's intention to introduce further restrictive measures, Geoffrey Baron led the opposition by the Catholic members. The fact that they choose a twenty seven year old as their leader was both a reflection on his ability and the regard in which he was held by his colleagues.

Baron, as leader of the opposition, incurred the wrath of Thomas Wentworth, the Lord Deputy, who was charged with pushing this legislation through parliament. He scathingly described Baron as 'a kind of

---

[2] *Ibid*, p. 470.
[3] Father Athanasius, O.F.M., 'Geoffry Baron' in *Tercentenary Commemoration of the Siege of Limerick,* (Limerick, 1951), p. 51.

petty chapman's son, who by peddling, left him some two hundred pounds a year, of all others the most mutinous and bold'. Wentworth engineered his expulsion from the Irish House of Commons and Geoffrey found himself detained for eight days in Dublin Castle. It was said that a bout of ill health led to his early release. He was escorted to the House of Commons where he was forced to make an abject apology on his knees for his behaviour. Although his parliamentary career was at end, he continued to involve himself in the political affairs of his country.

Following the outbreak of rebellion in 1641, he joined the ranks of the Old English who, frustrated with the king's refusal to grant religious tolerance, had sided with the native rebels. United by a common religious bond, they formed an uneasy alliance known as the Confederation of Kilkenny. For the next ten years, Geoffrey Baron was to play a leading part in the affairs of the Catholic confederation. In a letter to his uncle he said that he had taken up arms in defence of his religion, his king and to protect the liberties of his oppressed country.[4] A few days after Clonmel had declared for the Confederation, he accompanied Richard Butler, brother of the earl of Ormond, to Waterford where he persuaded the city fathers to join the cause.

He was selected as one of Clonmel's representatives to the Confederate parliament. Then, in March 1642, because of his linguistic skills, he was sent to the continent with Matthew O'Hartegan, S.J., as a confederate agent to procure arms and money. The two sailed on different ships to lessen the chance of capture by Parliament vessels. Both arrived safely. Geoffrey was taken aback at the lack of support from Catholic Spain, while he found the continuous waiting for the promised help from the French and the Papal Nuncio frustrating. To add to his troubles he fell sick once more. 'I brook not my health well heare, and am now the fifth day troubled with a continued headache, and a distemper of all my body'.[5]

Despite these setbacks, Baron doggedly persevered and in September 1642 he set sail for Ireland. He was accompanied by Colonel Preston, together with three hundred officers who had served in the Spanish forces and were now pledged to the Confederate cause. The six ships which

---

[4] Burke, p. 472
[5] *Ibid.*

brought them were laden with supplies of French muskets and powder. After an adventurous crossing from France, pursued by three cruisers under the command of the Earl of Warwick, they landed safely.

O'Hartegan was so impressed by his colleague's diplomatic skills, that he wrote to the Council of the Confederacy proposing Baron for the position of Secretary of State, a proposition that the Council did not entertain. This was hardly surprising in an organisation divided by racial origins and historical differences. Baron, who sprang from old-English stock and yet constantly sided with the native Irish, would have been seen by many as a controversial figure, resented by one side and distrusted by the other. The observation of a contemporary, who also described him as 'a difficult man' is also significant.

Nonetheless, because of the successful outcome of his mission, the Council decided to appoint Baron and Hartegan as joint ambassadors to the French court. A few days after Christmas in 1642 Baron again set out for France. Unfortunately, he was captured at sea and held at Dunkirk. He was released, following representations to the French court and he finally reached Paris in April. Following four months of fruitless negotiations with Louis XIV's advisor, Cardinal Mazarin, the Confederation granted him permission to return to Ireland.

Baron's high standing within the ranks of the Confederacy was reflected by his appointment as treasurer of accounts. He was also selected to act as negotiator with the Earl of Glamorgan, an Englishman and a Catholic, who was sent to Ireland by the king in an attempt to broker a treaty with the Confederacy. Meanwhile, following complaints of Hartegan's mismanagement of his mission at the French court, Baron replaced him as permanent ambassador, a position he held from 1645 to 1647.

On his way to take up his appointment, Baron met Cardinal Rinuccini at La Rochelle, who was making his way to Ireland as Papal Nuncio. Baron made a favourable impression on the nuncio, who remarked on his 'fine appearance' and 'very polished manners'. He became a firm supporter of the nuncio whom he admired for 'his particular zeal'. He also supported him in his opposition to all peace proposals that failed to guarantee full restoration of Catholic rights.

Baron returned to Ireland on 11 March 1647 having, once again, failed to secure large scale assistance for the Confederate cause. Five days later he gave a report of his mission to the Assembly in Kilkenny. He suggested that his lack of success could be attributed to French reluctance to antagonise the English parliament, and consequently, despite royal promises, he admitted that no aid was forthcoming. All he could procure was a mere 12,000 livres from Cardinal Mazarin.

He took part in the protracted peace negotiations between the Confederacy and Ormond, the king's representative, who had returned to Ireland in September 1648 to rally support for the King's cause. Whatever their political differences, Ormond regarded Baron as one of the most competent of the Confederation lawyers. Baron was all too aware that Ormond was not in a position to offer concessions to the Irish Catholics, for to do so would have incurred the wrath of the king's Protestant supporters in England. But as Burke put it, 'religion apart, Baron was a trained diplomatist, and he knew that in King Charles and Ormond he had to deal with men practised in sham negotiations, whose faith was limited by the exigencies of English politics'.[6]

By January 1649, the news that the king was to be put on trial precipitated an agreement and the Confederacy was dissolved. The treaty was rejected by Rinuccini, and in the following month he left Ireland, while diehards like Baron resolved to carry on the struggle to the bitter end. By the end of January the king had been executed and in the following August Cromwell landed in Ireland.

In 1650, Baron was in Waterford when it was besieged by the Cromwellian forces under Ireton. He opposed the wishes of the Waterford corporation who advocated the speedy surrender of the city. Following the city's capitulation he was one of those, who on behalf of the defenders, signed the terms of submission. After the fall of Waterford Baron set out for Limerick. Once again, he adamantly opposed surrender and was 'one of the leaders, who, amidst plague and dissention and great suffering, tirelessly urged those within the walls to continue the fight rather that accept the terms of the besieging forces'.[7] Finally, when further resistance

---

[6] *Ibid*, p. 477.
[7] Athanasius, p. 52.

became futile, he was a member of the group of officers who negotiated terms with Ireton on 27 October 1651.

Ireton, all too aware of Baron's implacable resistance and staunch Catholicism, refused to spare him. Baron did not plead for mercy and remained defiant in the face of death. The day before he was executed he made his will, bequeathing his soul to God and the bulk of his property to his cousin, Thomas Baron fitz Richard of Clonmel, and the remainder to his servant, Geoffrey Baron fitz Nicholas, with specific instructions that his debts be honoured.

On the day of his execution, he asked and was granted permission to return to his lodgings. Under the eye of the guard, he broke open his trunk and proceeded to dress himself in his suit of scarlet and white, symbolic colours of martyrdom and innocence, similar to the manner of St. Thomas More who donned a suit of Camelot-silk before he walked to the gallows. Baron's merry manner astounded his executioners. When asked to account for his strange behaviour he said that if he were to be married he would have done no less and since he was about to face his maker he felt that he should likewise prepare himself for his heavenly nuptials.

As he walked to the scaffold he held his rosary beads in his hands. It was said that he was followed by a huge multitude anxious to hear the last words of this brave man. It was said that Ireton promised to spare him if he renounced the Pope and dissociate himself from the Catholic cause in Ireland. It was an offer that, needless to say, Baron rejected.

On mounting the gallows he addressed the crowd:

> At last I have come to meet my death, a thing difficult and displeasing to others but sweet to me ..... I declare that I was always loyal to the Catholic, Apostolic and Roman faith, in which I now die, and also to my king as opposed to Cromwell and his Parliament.

His body was quartered and his head cut off and spiked on one of the gates of the city. Many of his garments were taken away and cherished as relics. His burial place is unknown, but presumably it lies somewhere in Limerick city.

This brave and committed patriot was, in the opinion of Burke, an heroic figure:

> The passion for a creed or a cause, which ennobles a man, was his. The sacrifice which gives up talents, fortune, life itself for an ideal, he freely made, and in him a character clean, candid, unselfish, left wanting no element of greatness.[8]

Fr. Bonaventure Baron (1610-1696)

Bartholomew or Bonaventure, as he was known in religion, was Geoffrey's younger brother and one of the foremost scholars of his day. Unfortunately, his unpublished autobiography is missing. The manuscript had been in the archives of St. Isadore's College in Rome until, in 1872, it was transferred to the Franciscan friary in Merchants Quay, Dublin. It was given on loan to Father C. P. Meehan, who was compiling a history of the Franciscan monasteries in Ireland, but was never returned. Despite, the loss of this valuable source a surprising amount is known about his life.

Baron tells us that he was an unwilling schoolboy and according to his own account he was:

> a lad of high spirits, who did not take well to the drudgery of learning. He preferred to play truant from school, excuses for his absence being glibly made, even those that were not in accord with strict truth. He was wayward and held out little promise of making good.[9]

Despite this unpromising start, he had exceptional ability and 'profited well' from the education he received at Robert Saul's school in Clonmel and later under the tutelage of the renowned professor, John Flahy in Waterford.

---

[8] Burke, p. 479.

[9] Thomas Wall, 'A Distinguished Irish humanist' in *Irish Ecclesiastical Record*, lxvii, (February, 1946), p. 94.

Flahy seems to have been well established as a professor of classics by 1603, and from that date to 1617 no name appears more frequently than his as the preceptor of Irish students entering the Irish college at Salamanca.[10] In the years young Baron spent under Flahy's roof as a boarder and student, he received a love and knowledge of the classics that shaped the rest of his life. He later admitted that his writings were a monument to his excellent knowledge of Latin which he acquired in Ireland.[11]

In 1626, his older brother, Geoffry, sent him to study philosophy at the Franciscan Abbey at Timoleague in County Cork and, in October of that year, he entered the Franciscan order. His superiors, impressed by his scholastic ability, decided to send him to St. Isadore's in Rome where his uncle, Luke Wadding, was guardian. It was a source of pride to Baron that his celebrated uncle had the distinction of receiving a number of votes in a conclave for the papacy.

Before he left for Rome, Baron recalled an occasion when he got an opportunity to display his classical knowledge. In 1629 Falkland, the king's deputy in Ireland, paid a visit to Clonmel. It was customary at the time to greet distinguished visitors with an address in prose or verse, written in Latin or Greek. Baron was entrusted with the task of composing one and was given the additional honour of reading it. The earl of Cork, who accompanied the deputy, was so impressed that he was about to offer him a job as his secretary but quickly changed his mind when he discovered that Baron was not only a Catholic, but a Franciscan. We can imagine the chagrin Falkland felt about this display of oratory from the product of a Catholic school, since one of the deputy's first proclamations in Ireland advocated the suppression of such schools. One observer suggested 'that those bold and very Catholic burgers derived some little disloyal joy from discomfiting their truculent rulers by displays of Latin oratory of this kind, which may even have taken the form of protestations of loyalty'.[12]

---

[10] Thomas Wall, 'Parnassus in Waterford' in *Irish Ecclesiastical Record,* 5th series, lxix (August, 1947), p. 710.

[11] Benignus Millet, 'Irish Literature in Latin, 1500-1700' in T. W. Moody, F. X. Martin and F. J. Byrne (eds.), *A New History of Ireland,* iii, (Oxford, 1976), p. 565

[12] Thomas Wall, 'Parnassus in Waterford', p. 713.

Baron left Ireland in the Spring of 1629 but did not reach Rome until several years later, having first completed his studies in philosophy at the Franciscan college in Louvain. In a letter to his brother Michael, who was about to set out for Lille, he described his journeys and the places he had visited on his way to Rome. He advised him to make the best of the opportunities that travel presented, condemning those 'who grow hoary in their cradles'

He arrived at St. Isidore's on 8 January 1633 where he enrolled as a student of theology and, on 3 September of the following year, he was ordained to the priesthood, taking the name 'Bonaventure' in religion. Two years later he was appointed lecturer at the college and remained there as professor of philosophy and later theology for more than thirty years. During this time he produced a series of scholarly works. The first of these, published in Rome in 1643, consisted of a series of essays in praise of eloquence, abstinence and some sacred subjects. It was dedicated to his native town of Clonmel. This was followed two years later by a collection of verse, dedicated to his mother's town, Waterford. One composition recalled fond memories of his mother who, as has been stated, had died when he was six years old. It was translated from the Latin by the nineteenth century Anglo-Irish poet, Sir Samuel Ferguson:

Dear mother mine, with what a thumb of haste
Impelled, fate's scissors have your threads unlaced!
You Nature nothing, fortune nought denied,
Parent well parented on either side,
Still ruddy-cheeked, still robed with tresses wrought,
Round grave brow garnered with the wealth of thought,
Crowned with all the chaplets of a genial life,
Maid's, widow's, happy mother, happy wife,
Most honoured! And you leave us. Be it so.
Heaven's pledge from alien earth should early go.

Perhaps, it has lost something in translation!

In 1651 he published a book of essays on matters relating to education, some of which offer glimpses into his own life. In that same year his brother, Geoffrey's life ended on a Limerick scaffold. In contrast, Bonaventure's life was a peaceful one. Cut off from the events of the outside world he wrote of his enjoyment of the serenity of the cloistered academic life 'in an age of great political and theological bustle'. As a relaxation from teaching he often composed a poem or essay, and his friends and the people he admired most were literary men like himself.[13]

While his early writings are marked with memories of Clonmel and Waterford and other references to Ireland, he later devoted himself to producing a series of large volumes on theological matters, a number of which were published in Rome. He arrived at Schwaz in the Tyrol in late 1661 where he spent some time preparing other theological writings for publication. From there he appears to have travelled extensively. He was present in Cologne in June 1663 and, five months later, we find him at the Franciscan Abbey in Salzburg. He is also reputed to have spent time in Paris and then at Wurtzburg, which housed a magnificent library. It was here that a list of his writings was first published.

In 1668, his name was put forward as a suitable candidate for the vacant archbishopric of Cashel and Emly, an honour he declined. The life of the humble scholar appealed more to him than the eminence of ecclesiastical life. In his own words, he said that 'though nominated by the lay folks and bishops' he 'did not rise to the occasion, and so ceased to be troubled with similar loads and lands'.[14] In 1669, he was appointed professor of humanities and theology at St. Bonaventure's Friary in Lyons. From there he went to Milan and later to Florence in 1676, where Cosmo III, Grand Duke of Tuscany, made him his official biographer and theologian.

During his stay in Florence a contemporary writer who met him was deeply impressed by his erudition and piety:

> It certainly causes no small wonder how this excellent, most learned and holy priest, while living a life of such great austerity, could find time to compile twenty-two tomes in folio, works with such variety of subject matter. I myself had the privilege of being his friend for

---

[13] Thomas Wall, 'A distinguished Irish humanist', p. 100.
[14] Burke, p. 482.

some time, while he resided at the convent of St. Francis on the mountain, outside Florence, and I observed not only was he deeply pious, but also most regular in his attendance at choir, and in spite of his advanced age was never absent from Midnight Matins.[15]

The length of his stay is uncertain but, by 1683, after a lifetime of travel and scholarship, he had returned to his beloved St. Isidore's. He resumed his duties as professor of theology but advancing years had taken their toll. In a touching reference to his failing health he said, 'bowed with the weight of years, broken by toil, my eyes are growing dim, my hearing impaired, my teeth gone, my legs refuse to bear me up. It is time to lay down the pen worn by so many volumes'. He died on 18 March 1696 at the great age of eighty-six and was buried in a crypt beneath the church of St. Isidore's.

Baron was a man who was very conscious of his own worth. Before he died he carefully composed his own epitaph, making sure to record all of his distinctions, omitting nothing that might impress the passer by with an awareness of his achievements and importance:

Bonaventure Baron
Several times Emeritus Lecturer
Author of 22 volumes
to wit
An Orator, a Poet,
A Philosopher and Historian,
Theologian of sundry Princes,
Once Guardian of Ireland,
Later Commissary of Croatia,
Having rejected the Prefecture of this Convent
(Not to mention episcopal mitres)
He yielded to Mortality
More than an Octogenarian.

---

[15] Cited in Fr. Benignus Millett, 'Bonaventure Baron, O. F. M.' in *Tercentenary Record* (Clonmel, 1950), p. 44.

His vanity extended to his writings, which include tributes from various admirers testifying in flattering terms to his literary ability. He could be peeved if anyone who quoted from his books refused to acknowledge him. It would also appear that he was not averse to have his portrait painted, and no fewer than four of these survive. The first is an oil painting depicting him when he was about thirty-five years of age. The original hangs in St. Isidore's and there is a copy in the Friary in Clonmel. He is profiled in a scholarly pose, with his left hand resting on a book and the other raised, as if lecturing. A second, which also hangs in St. Isidore's, sees him seated at the end of a library table facing his uncle against a background of bound volumes. The third image is a copperplate engraving which forms the frontis-piece to a number of his publications. It depicts Baron, aged fifty-two in a Franciscan habit, flanked by two columns, holding a book in his left hand and a pen in the other. The final work is preserved in the Franciscan friary in Merchant's Quay, Dublin. Here we see the face of a plump and pleasant-looking old man, unlike the stiff and formal face of the earlier representations.

Like his uncle, Luke Wadding, he sought to cultivate an elegance of style in his writings which caused an admirer to exclaim, with some degree of exaggeration, that he had brought the muses back to Italy.[16] In our age of specialisation the diversity and extent of his writings is impressive. A biographer wrote in awe: 'we cannot but wonder how one man could have written so much, so learnedly, and on such a variety of topics'.[17] While posterity may not have given him the recognition he felt he deserved, his brilliance won for him a reputation among his contemporaries as a historian, philosopher and theologian of the highest calibre.

---

[16] Cited in John J. Silke, 'Irish Scholarship and the Renaissance' in *Studies in the Renaissance*, vol. xx, (America, 1973), p. 184.
[17] Burke, p. 481.

Chapter 7

The Three Martyrs

Protestantism was introduced into Ireland during the course of the Tudor conquest but the new faith made little progress among either the Irish or the old English, as the descendants of the Norman settlers were called. Resistance to these doctrinal changes was met with periodic bouts of persecution, particularly during the reign of Elizabeth I and following the Cromwellian occupation in the 1650s. In the course of a century, many Catholics who refused to abandon their religion were left to rot in prison, banished or hanged. On 27 September 1992, Pope John Paul II selected seventeen of those who had died, for beatification as martyrs. Three had been executed in the market square in Clonmel.

Maurice MacKenraghty (?–1585)

Maurice MacKenraghty was the first of these martyrs to die in Clonmel. He was the son of Thomas MacKenraghty from north Kerry who became a burgess of Kilmallock, a prosperous walled town in the heart of Desmond territory. Thomas is mentioned in the records of the period as being a goldsmith and silversmith by trade. Maurice was born in Kilmallock but the date of his birth is unknown. Neither have we details of his religious training other than that he was a bachelor of theology. His early ministry was spent in Kilmallock where he won a reputation for being an inspiring preacher.

Gerald, 14th earl of Desmond, hearing of the young man's reputation, appointed him as his chaplain and confessor. In 1579 the Earl took up arms in a futile attempt to protect his ancestral lands from a Tudor monarchy determined to extend its control over the whole of Ireland. With the Desmond rebellion drawing to an end, a contemporary described the Earl wandering from mountain to mountain attended only by a priest and a few faithful followers. The priest in question was Maurice MacKenraghty who had accompanied him to war and endured the physical hardships of the campaign. On 17

September 1583 a party of Elizabethan soldiers, under the command of Maurice Roche, Viscount Fermoy, surprised Desmond and his remaining followers in the Sliabh Luachra area near Duhallow on the borders of Cork and Kerry. The Earl escaped, but MacKenraghty, who was riding a slower horse, was taken prisoner.

Roche wrote to the Earl of Ormond telling him that he had captured MacKenraghty. Ormond sent Captain Roberts to bring the prisoner to Clonmel. He also sent his servant, Patrick Grant, to be chained to the priest, so that no one might speak to him until he had the opportunity of questioning him. In a letter to Lord Burghley, Queen Elizabeth's treasurer, Ormond wrote, 'I would this chaplain, and I, were for one hour with you in your chamber, that you might know the secrets of his heart, which by fair, or foul means, he must open unto me'. The phrase 'fair or foul' suggests that Ormond intended to torture him but there is no record of any such interrogation.

MacKenraghty was to spend the next eighteen months in Clonmel jail. Conditions were primitive but he was allowed to receive visitors. On the eve of Easter Sunday 1585, Victor White, one of the town's leading citizens and a pious Catholic, bribed the jailer to release the priest so that White's family and friends could celebrate the Easter ceremonies in his house. MacKenraghty was to return to prison the following day with no one the wiser. On Saturday he made his way to the oratory in White's house. An eye-witness account tells of how the priest spent all night hearing confessions and during the following morning preparations were made for Mass. Those who had been to confession were divided among the different bedrooms, where they devoted themselves to prayer in preparation for communion. Some were in the chapel making the altar ready, while others were still receiving absolution. Victor White greeted new arrivals in the hallway and brought them to the chapel.[1]

Unfortunately, Sir John Norris, President of Munster, accompanied by a troop of soldiers paid an unexpected visit to the town. The jailer, in an effort to save his own skin, informed him that if he wished to catch the principal men of the town hearing Mass he could do so at the house of Victor White. Under his orders soldiers rushed White's house. In the ensuing panic some made their escape through

---

[1] Desmond Forristal, *Seventeen Martyrs*, (Dublin, 1990), pp. 40, 41.

back doors and windows, others fled to the basement, while a married lady fell from a window and broke her arm. MacKenraghty hid in a clump of straw in the yard where his leg was wounded by a probing sword. Despite this he remained silent and escaped.

The soldiers dismantled the altar and seized the sacred vessels. They arrested Victor White and threatened him with death, if he failed to persuade the priest to return. White refused. Hearing of this, MacKenragthy sent word that he was willing to give himself up, if the life of his friend was spared. White tried to dissuade him, saying that he would prefer to die rather than let this happen. But MacKenraghty would not hear of it and surrendered. This time his fate was in the hands of Norris, a man from whom he could expect no mercy.

Seeking a speedy resolution, Norris had MacKenraghty tried under martial law. To proceed against him as a Catholic priest in accordance with the common law would have demanded a long process. There might also have been a public outcry and even the possibility of an acquittal by a local jury. MacKenraghty was offered his freedom if he would renounce the Catholic faith and accept the Queen as head of the church but he resolutely refused to do so. Neither would he supply the name of any person who had attended his Mass or received the sacraments from him. A Protestant minister also tried unsuccessfully to convert the priest by engaging him in debate. It is said that Norris, 'after much invective', condemned him to death. The reasons for MacKenraghty's martyrdom were clear cut. He was sentenced to die for hearing confessions, making preparations to say mass and denying the royal supremacy in matters spiritual.

He met his fate with a serene countenance, gave thanks to God, and advised bystanders to be true to their faith and loyal to the Pope. As he moved to the scaffold, which had been erected in the market square in front of the present Main Guard, he addressed the people so devoutly that many were moved to tears. He was allowed to complete the final stage of his journey to the scaffold on his knees. In this fashion he moved forward, praying all the time, while some of the heretic onlookers mocked him. However, another account said that he was dragged at the tail of a horse to his place of execution. On the scaffold he asked the people to pray for him and gave them his blessing.

MacKenraghty was hanged on 30 April 1585. Those who

witnessed his death were impressed by his composure. He was taken down from the gallows while still alive, beheaded and quartered. The following day the four quarters were set up on the market cross in the centre of the town. The head, which was placed on a loftier eminence so that it could be seen by all, was alleged to have become red and perspired each day at 10 a.m. This marvel was attributed by the townspeople to the fact that he had been accustomed to say Mass at that time every day. It was said that a number of the local Catholics bribed officials to hand over the body and 'rendered the highest burial honours they could'. The memory of MacKenraghty's death remained alive in Clonmel for many generations. The street off Lough Street, the present Market Street, where Victor White lived, became known as Martyr's Lane.

The large number of young men from the town who became priests in the years that followed was attributed to his martyrdom. The Franciscan historian Donagh Mooney, who visited Clonmel about thirty years later, recorded that Mac Kenraghty's remains were laid to rest behind the high altar of the suppressed friary. Canon Burke said that his grave in the Franciscan Church would have become a place of pilgrimage had not the friars, to escape persecution, attempted to conceal it. Consequently, in 1647, his remains were conveyed amid great religious honours to their final resting place in Askeaton Abbey.[2]

John Kearney (1619–1653)

Sixty years later, John Kearney became the second martyr to be executed in Clonmel. He was born in Cashel, the son of John Kearney and Elizabeth Creagh. The Kearneys were one of a group of Catholic families, which included the Salls, Hacketts, Everards and Creaghs, who were prominent merchants in the town. The family could be justifiably proud of its contribution to the church, with many of its members in the ranks of the clergy. They also played an active part in the political life of Cashel and the name Kearney occurs frequently in the lists of aldermen and burgesses. The head of the family, being the hereditary custodian of a relic known as Bachall Phádraig or 'the staff of St. Patrick', enjoyed the title 'Kearney Crux' or 'Kearney Bachall'. When John Kearney was born, this title was held by Donagh Kearney, a

---

[2] William Burke, *History of Clonmel*, p. 40.

relative of his father.

The Kearney's home became a place of refuge for the local clergy, especially the Franciscans, during times of persecution, and it was from them the young John Kearney learned his catechism. He also came under the influence of the Jesuits, who had opened a school under Barnaby Kearney, brother to David Kearney, Archbishop of Cashel. When John decided to become a priest, he seriously considered entering the Jesuits. On the advice of his father, he paid a visit to Joseph Everard, Provincial of the Friars Minor, who was also a friend of the family. Everard sent him to the Franciscan Friary in Kilkenny where his school friend, Joseph Sall, joined him. When they completed their novitiate they were sent to St. Anthony's College in Louvain, the famous seminary founded by the Irish Franciscans in 1607, to study for the priesthood. In the course of the journey there is a story told that the ship on which they sailed ran into a violent storm off Bristol. John Kearney led the prayers for their deliverance. The storm passed and they reached their destination safely.

He spent six years in Louvain studying philosophy and theology before being ordained in St. Catherine's church in Brussels on September 1642, at the age of twenty-three. He was a further two years in Belgium before asking permission to return home. Whether he realised it or not, John Kearney was returning to a far different Ireland from the one which he had left. Catholic Ireland was on the brink of catastrophe. Apart from sporadic outbursts of persecution, the religious freedom enjoyed by the Irish Catholics, under James I and in the first fifteen years of the reign of Charles I, was about to come to an abrupt end. In England the Puritan dominated parliament was in revolt against the king, and the outcome of this conflict was to have disastrous consequences for Ireland.

Parliamentary forces intercepted the ship on which John Kearney sailed for Ireland. He was landed at Bristol and brought to London where he was imprisoned. Under cross examination, he admitted to being a Catholic and a Franciscan friar. In an effort to persuade him to renounce his Catholicism, the judge ordered that he be tortured on the rack. He was then confined in a dungeon until he should come to a change of heart. While there he attracted the attentions of the jailor's daughter and she got her mother to ask him if he would marry her.

Although this would have guaranteed him his freedom, he refused. After three months he was returned for trial and sentenced to death, a sentence he greeted by singing the Te Deum in court until silenced. While awaiting the hangman's rope, he was helped to escape by a wealthy Catholic layman who bribed the guards. He was lowered from the window of his cell in a basket and hidden in his benefactor's house, until he escaped to France.

From Calais he set sail once more for Ireland and landed in Wexford. He spent the next two years teaching philosophy in Cashel friary, while at the same time winning a reputation as a preacher. People found his sermons so spiritually uplifting that there was a great demand for his services in neighbouring areas. In response to numerous requests, the Provincial sent him to Waterford as master of novices. The following year the Catholics of Ireland received a sharp reminder of the treatment they could expect from a victorious parliament. On 13 September 1647 the notorious Lord Inchiquin, commander of the parliamentary forces in Munster, laid siege to Cashel. Clergy and lay people sought refuge in the Cathedral on the rock. Inchiquin or Murrogh the Burner as he was also known, true to his reputation, burned it with much loss of life. Among those who perished was the mother of John Kearney.

In August 1650 when Fr. Kearney attended a Provincial Chapter meeting of the order held at Kilconnell, Co. Galway he was appointed guardian of the Friary in Carrick-on-Suir. However, by this time the town and the surrounding countryside were under Cromwellian control, so for the next three years he kept on the move, preaching, saying Mass and administering the sacraments. He had decided to remain in Ireland and continue his ministry, despite the pleas of friends and clerical colleagues that he should seek safety overseas.

On 6 January 1653 the Cromwellian authorities issued a proclamation ordering all priests to leave the country within twenty days, or face the penalty of death. Two months later, Fr. Kearney was taken prisoner by Captain Wilmer in Cashel. He was transferred to Clonmel where the area's military governor, Colonel Sankey, ordered him thrown in jail. The arrest of this leading Franciscan preacher was a coup for the authorities and they lost no time in dealing with him, for he was tried the very next day. He stood in the dock with the other imprisoned priests accused of having said Mass and administering the sacraments in various parts of Munster, and preventing Catholics from being converted to the true Protestant religion. Witnesses were produced to prove these charges and he made no attempt to deny them. He freely admitted that he was a Catholic and a Franciscan, as he had in London, and said what he did was no more than his duty.

Immediately, he was led back to prison where he put aside his lay clothes, which he wore as a disguise over his religious garb. Dressed in his Franciscan habit, with rosary attached, and with a cross in his hand he was taken to the scaffold. A crowd quickly gathered, made up of Catholics and Puritans, the latter scoffing in amazement at the strangely dressed prisoner. When he reached the place of execution, Kearney knelt down and, with tears in his eyes, prayed briefly. He then ascended the steps and got permission from the commander of the company of soldiers to address the crowd. He explained the details of his arrest and trial and stated that the only reason for his conviction was that he had carried out his duties as a Catholic priest. He then professed his loyalty to Catholicism as the one true church for which he was now willing to die.

Following his hanging, Sankey gave permission to Kearney's friends for the removal of his body. They brought it to Cashel for burial in the chapter hall of the suppressed friary, which stood in the area now occupied by the recently built town hall. His habit was cut up into little pieces and distributed as relics all over Ireland and to Irish colleges abroad. One of these fragments is still preserved in the Franciscan friary in Killiney, near Dublin. A portion of his hair was also preserved, but has since disappeared.

Impressed by the way he lived and equally by his manner of dying, Fr. John Kearney's fellow priests were convinced that he was a martyr, for it was they who played a major role in spreading his reputation at home and abroad. Within a year his Franciscan friend, Joseph Sall, who described him as a man of the utmost integrity, had written an account of his life. A question arises as to why Father John Kearney was singled out for execution, while his fellow clerical prisoners in Clonmel were simply banished. The answer lies in his conduct during the trial. On being charged with having exercised his priesthood he admitted his guilt, showed no regrets, refused to apologise or be intimidated by threats and insisted that the laws, which forbade him to function as a priest, were unjust. These emphatic pronouncements probably angered Sankey, who decided to apply the full penalty of the law. Steadfast in the face of death and confident in the mercy of God, John Kearney faced his executioner.

William Tirry (1608–1654)

The third martyr to die on the scaffold in Clonmel was William Tirry. He was born in Cork in 1608, the son of Robert and Joan Tirry. The Tirrys were prominent in the commercial and civic life of Cork and from 1505 to 1719, twenty-two members of the family had filled the office of mayor. There are no details of William's early life. From his family background we can assume that he had a privileged upbringing and was well educated. We do not know where or when he entered the priesthood or why he should have chosen the Augustinian order. His novitiate may have been spent with the Augustinians in his native city or possibly on the continent. Contemporary documents make it clear that he was ordained at Valladolid in Spain. From there he proceeded to Paris where he continued his theological studies and then went to Brussels, the city which at that time served as a rallying point for those about to embark on the Irish mission.

Fr. Tirry returned to Ireland in 1637 or 1638 and was appointed to the Augustinian community in his native Cork. For a few months he served as secretary to his uncle, Bishop Tirry of Cork, before returning to his community. Shortly afterwards he became chaplain to his second cousin, the 2nd Viscount Kilmallock, while at the same time acting as tutor to his two sons. In 1646 he was sent to Fethard as secretary to the Augustinian Provincial, Father Denis O'Driscoll. He remained there until 1649 when he was appointed prior of Skryne abbey in Co. Meath. Two months later Cromwell landed in Ireland and following the fall of Drogheda and the capture of the surrounding district it is most unlikely that Fr. Tirry was able to take up his appointment.

In the Spring of 1650, Cromwell received the surrender of Fethard, and desecrated the church and friary. He then proceeded to scatter the priests and outlaw the celebration of holy Mass. Although placing himself in mortal danger, Tirry returned to Fethard in 1651 where he enjoyed the protection of Mrs. Amy Everard, who was the widow of a wealthy landowner and his distant relative. She invited him to become tutor to her two small children. The Everards were one of the leading Catholic families in the area and several of them are buried in the grounds of the local Augustinian Abbey.

The old abbey church was then in ruins but tradition says that prior to his capture, Tirry hid in the old priory buildings. He lodged in a small room, adjoining the church which could only be reached by a narrow stone stairway, and is still known as Fr. Tirry's room. Here he celebrated Mass, wrote and prayed and, when circumstances permitted, ventured out to minister to the needs of the townspeople, often adopting the disguise of a soldier to avoid arrest. His whereabouts were betrayed by three of the locals for five pounds, the standard sum offered to those who supplied information leading to the capture of a priest. On the morning of Holy Saturday, 25 March 1654, while vested for Mass, a group of soldiers with swords drawn broke into his quarters and took him to Clonmel jail where four secular priests were already imprisoned.

One of them, Canon Walter Conway, described how Tirry's presence and behaviour transformed their cell 'into a place of prayer'. Another prisoner, Father Matthew Fogarty, a Capuchin friar, left the following account of Tirry's piety:

> Every morning between 3 and 4 of the clock he would get up roundly and put on his apparel with all expedition, and soon after fall on his knees and there continue till 8 o'clock, still either praying, weeping or striking his breast through sensible contrition, to the great edification of all his fellow prisoners.[3]

The four secular priests were tried on 23 April 1654 and were banished. Three days later, the two friars, Fathers Tirry and Fogarty, were brought to trial. They were delivered to the sacristy of old St. Mary's Church in Clonmel accompanied by the jailer and a company of musketeers. He was charged with remaining in the country, contrary to the proclamation of 1653. In reply, Fr. Tirry stated that his superior general had sent him to Ireland and that he could only leave with his permission. The prosecutor, in exasperation, then asked him did he

---

[3] John O'Connor, O.S.A., *A priest on the run*, (Dublin, 1992), pp. 16, 17.

acknowledge any higher power in this kingdom than theirs. Tirry replied that in temporal matters he accepted the authority of the law, but in spiritual matters he had to obey his superiors and the Pope.

The result was a foregone conclusion as can be seen from Fr. Fogarty's description of the proceedings. The trial was presided over by Colonel Solomon Richards, one of the four commissioners appointed to administer Clonmel after the Cromwellian conquest. Referring to Richards' carefully hand picked jury, Fogarty described them as consisting of 'twelve base and poor churls of base condition'. He overheard one of them remarking to the Colonel before they retired, 'Shall we find them all guilty?' To which the Colonel replied, 'Who doubts it? What else is to be done?' A verdict of guilty was duly returned and Tirry and Fogarty were sentenced to hang.

The day after sentence was passed, the jailer, Mr. Richard Rouse, had the prisoners unfettered and transferred to the more comfortable surroundings of his own house while they were awaiting execution. Though they could not celebrate mass, the two condemned priests received visits from their former fellow prisoners, who had been given parole on the undertaking they would go into exile. They brought hosts consecrated at Masses they had furtively celebrated elsewhere. Other friends and well wishers left alms, which Father Tirry promptly gave away. On one occasion he arranged to have forty six loaves of bread distributed to the poor in atonement for the sins he had committed during each year of his life. The treatment Fr. Tirry received at the hands of Rouse was very generous under the circumstances. Whether the jailer was impressed by his pious demeanour, or benefited from the offerings of sympathisers, is not clear.

On hearing the order for his execution, Tirry threw himself upon his knees, saying in Irish, 'God Almighty be thanked who choose me to this happy end!' Fr. Fogarty, whose sentence was commuted to imprisonment, claimed William Tirry was singled out because on the day of his arrest he was vested for mass and that he was also engaged in writing a book refuting the teachings of Protestantism, the manuscript of which had been found on his desk. Bound with iron cuffs, he was led to the scaffold. The other priests were refused permission to accompany him to the market square and Canon Conway gave him last absolution before he was taken away.

Wearing his Augustinian robes, his hair freshly tonsured and fingering his rosary beads, Tirry was escorted by a company of horse and foot soldiers. He was accompanied by a Mr. Peter Power, a Catholic layman, who was to be executed for reasons unknown. The street was crowded with men and women, some weeping and kneeling before him, craving his blessing. At intervals, he knelt and prayed until he came in sight of the gallows. He gave Peter Power absolution and continued kneeling until his companion was hanged.

Then he accepted the halter from Rouse and put it around his own neck. Standing on the scaffold, he exhorted the people to remain true to the church and its teachings. A nearby Protestant minister, fearing that the priest would lead his listeners astray, requested that he be silenced. Rouse ignored the minister and gave Tirry permission to continue. Tirry asked forgiveness for his sins and for the three people who had betrayed him. He requested any priest who might be in the crowd to grant him absolution and then made a sign to Mr. Rouse to do his duty. As soon as he was dead the crowd surged forward, tearing at his clothing, seeking relics.

Various miracles have been attributed to Father Tirry. A blind woman was reported to have had her sight restored when a piece of his habit was applied to her eyes. Canon Conway claimed that on his way to the continent a storm blew up off Dunkirk putting the ship in grave peril but, through recourse to a piece of Fr. Tirry's clothing, the storm abated and the ship reached port in safety. The Catholic sovereign of Fethard got permission from the military governor of Clonmel to take Fr. Tirry's body to Fethard where he had it buried in the ruins of the abbey. when a new floor was being laid in the church during the autumn of 1956, a unsuccessful search was made for his grave.

On 27 May 2004, a memorial to Maurice MacKenraghty, John Kearney and William Tirry, three brave men who faced death rather than abandon their principles, was unveiled in front of SS. Peter & Paul's church in Clonmel.

1. Athassel Abbey

2. Richard de Burgo (c.1193-1243)

3. Otho de Grandison (1138-1328)

4. Thomas Butler, 14th earl of Ormond (1530-1613)

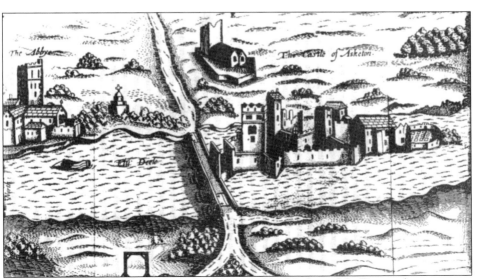

5. Askeaton Castle and Abbey, principal residence and burial place of the Desmonds

6. Thomas White, S.J. (1556-1622)

7. Oliver Cromwell
(1599-1658)

8. James,
   1st duke of Ormonde
   (1610-1688)

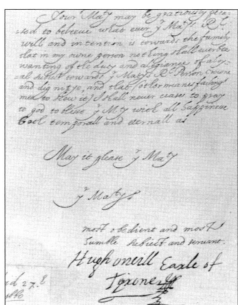

9. Letter from Hugh
   Dubh O'Neill
   (c.1611-1660) to King
   Charles II seeking
   recognition as earl of
   Tyrone.

10. Bonaventure Baron, O.F.M. (1610-1696)

11. Martyrs' Memorial Stone

12. Second earl of Mountcashell (1770-1822)

13. Barne House

14. Laurence Sterne (1713-1786)

15. George Borrow (1803-1881)

16. Anthony Trollope (1815-1882)

17. The grave of Fr. Nicholas Sheehy (1728-1766).

18. David Malcomson (1765-1844)

19. Charles Bianconi (1786-1875)

20. Lady Blessington (1789-1849)

21. Senator John Bagwell (1874-1946)

22. Marlfield House

Chapter 8

Moores of Barne

Under the terms of the Cromwellian settlement the Catholic Anglo-Norman burgers, who had dominated the civic and commercial life of Clonmel for centuries, were uprooted and banished to Connacht. They were replaced by a new breed of settler, mostly craftsmen and traders whose descendants were destined to monopolise the political and economic life of Clonmel until challenged by the rise of the Catholic middle class in the nineteenth century.

There was to be one final act in the drama before the new arrivals could enjoy the security of the possessions they had received. The accession of the Catholic convert, James II, to the throne of England in 1685 posed a threat to 'the beneficiaries of the Cromwellian plantations loosing out to the heirs of dispossessed Catholics'.[1] The situation was resolved when, five years later, James was defeated by William of Orange at the Battle of the Boyne, and the Irish parliament became the preserve of the Protestant ruling class. In 1692 the new assembly set about consolidating its position by devising measures to crush any possible signs of Catholic resurgence.

The so-called Penal Laws aimed at keeping the Catholic population in a state of permanent subjection by attempting to eradicate their religion. Catholics were not allowed to sit in parliament, to hold any government office, to enter the legal profession or have commissions in the army and navy. They could not buy land or secure leases for longer than thirty one years and the estates of deceased Catholics landowners had to be divided equally among the male heirs. Having curtailed the Catholic threat, the way lay open for capable and ambitious Protestant families to make their fortunes and 'there was a steady procession of well-to-do merchants who

---

[1] R. V. Comerford, *Ireland*, (London, 2003), p. 100.

purchased landed property and thus made their way into the ruling class'.[2] One such family, who were ideally positioned to take advantage of such favourable circumstances, were the Moores who became the most prominent and influential family in eighteenth century Clonmel.

The Moore family is reputedly descended from Thomas de More who came from Normandy with William the Conqueror in 1066. This Thomas is said to be listed among the survivors of the battle of Hastings. In the reign of James I, Richard Moore, a glover from Barnstable in Devon, came to Ireland. A supporter of Cromwell, he received a grant of a 'house, garden and 11 acres 24 perches' at an annual rent of £6 in Clonmel and the surrounding burgagery lands under the Settlement of 1654.[3] The degree of success his family achieved caused Burke to exclaim, 'the part which they were to play in Clonmel affairs he (Moore) could not have foreseen in the wildest dreams of ambition'.[4]

Richard Moore soon established himself as a person of some importance. In a proclamation of 1672 he was described as 'formerly being a poor glover, but was by that time an esquire worth £2,000 a year'. It is said that 'he prospered exceedingly' as a land broker and property agent. He established himself as a successful sheep rancher and the ledger of Clonmel merchant, William Vaughan, records that, in 1673, Richard Moore of Kilworth supplied him with 128 bags of wool valued at £1,443.[5] His enhanced status was reflected in the prestigious appointments he received, sheriff of County Waterford in 1666, and sheriff of County Tipperary in 1675. In 1688 he is listed as an alderman of the Clonmel Corporation.

By time he died in 1690 at his home in Lough Street, the present Gladstone Street, he was a man of considerable property. His estates included lands in Kilworth, Chancellorstown, Garrinlea, Hore Abbey and Barne. While Richard Moore's investments helped to propel the family up the social ladder, it was their involvement in politics which provided them with access to the many lucrative appointments and favours in the gift of

---

[2] Aiden Clarke, 'The English' in Patrick Loughrey (ed.), *The People of Ireland,* (Belfast, 1988), pp. 127-28.

[3] William Burke, *History of Clonmel*, p. 246.

[4] *Ibid*, p. 91.

[5] *Ibid*, p. 110.

the crown. In the words of Burke, 'the process by which Clonmel was converted into a pocket borough, the several steps by which the family of a Devonshire glover ascended into a peerage without military services or civic distinction, deserve careful notice'.[6]

Richard Moore was survived by two sons, Stephen, whose descendants were destined to become Earls of Mountcashell, and Thomas, or Thomas of Chancellorstown as he was known, founder of the Barne branch of the family.[7] In 1684, Stephen Moore purchased 40,000 acres in counties Waterford and Cork.[8] He selected about 1,000 acres of it to form his demesne and enclosed it with a wall twelve feet high and seven miles long. This became known as Moore Park, outside Fermoy, where he built a magnificent three storeyed Georgian residence on the hill overlooking the Funcheon river. It was subsequently destroyed by fire in 1908, and today the lands are now the property of government agency, Teagasc.

In 1685, Stephen Moore created an endowment of 300 acres of land for the establishment of a Free School in Clonmel, where the sons of Protestant freemen would receive free education. The site of the original school, which had a long and sometimes troubled history, is now occupied by the Sisters of Charity primary school. By the time the Free School closed its doors in 1921 it had been transferred in 1830 to Irishtown to a building which ironically is now home to Gael Scoil Chluain Meala. Stephen had the honour of being acquainted with King William, and on his arrival in England lent the monarch a sum of £3,000 which was not, however, repaid. In compensation for services rendered, the king appointed him governor of Tipperary and colonel of the Tipperary militia.

The emergence of the Moores as a political force in local politics was facilitated by the decline of the local power brokers, the Ormonds. While the Dukes of Ormond still held considerable property in Clonmel, the Moores and 'other substantial landholding interests had emerged following the Cromwellian confiscations, to challenge the family's predominance in county politics'. The general election of 1692 'brought

---

[6] *Ibid*, p. 113.
[7] see Appendix 1, pp. 333, 334.
[8] Catherine Anne Wilson, *A new lease of life*, (McGill-Queen's University Press, London, 1994), pp. 13, 15.

home to Ormonde the limitations of his influence'[9] when Stephen Moore (1653?-1793) became an MP for county Tipperary and Stephen's son, Richard Moore (1671-1699) was elected MP for Clonmel. All vestiges of Tory Ormond influence had vanished in Clonmel when, in 1713, the borough returned a pair of Whigs.[10] One of them was Colonel Stephen Moore, who was to initiate the contest for control of Clonmel borough.

Colonel Mooree was the grandson of Richard Moore of Barnstable and the younger son of Thomas of Chancellorstown. The Colonel was one of the most colourful and controversial members of the Moore family. Soldier, landlord and politician, he was a noted duelist, an unscrupulous and ambitious politician and yet, an enlightened and progressive landowner. In 1712 he married Judith Dowdeswell of Poole Court, Worcestershire and took up residence at Barne, outside Clonmel.

When he was elected mayor of Clonmel in 1724 he lost no time in taking steps to manipulate the borough to the advantage of his family. The electorate at the time was largely comprised of a small number of resident freemen. Since freeman status could be obtained by grace of the mayor, the Colonel created ninety-two additional freemen to act in the Moore interest. Despite this, the Moore backed candidate, James Going, was defeated in the 1725 mayoral election by Robert Hamerton. Moore ignored the wishes of the electorate and proceeded to certify Going, leaving the town with two mayors. The case was placed before the privy council in Dublin who gave judgment in favour of Hamerton. Moore retaliated by refusing to swear in Hamerton as his successor and by retaining the mayoral regalia and the corporation minute books.[11] When the case was later referred to the King's bench a judgment was obtained on a technicality against Hamerton.

The Moore family continued to virtually dominate the corporation until 1747. In that year the opposition group succeeded in having their own mayor, Jeremiah Morgan, elected. He proceeded to enact a set of by-laws designed to break the Moore influence, but in 1754, with the support of the

---

[9] D. W. Hayton, 'Dependence, clientage and affinity: the political following of the second Duke of Ormonde' in T. Barnard & J. Fenlon (eds.) *The Dukes of Ormonde, 1610-1745*, p. 223.
[10] *Ibid*, p. 227.
[11] Burke, p. 116.

then mayor, William Kellett, the by-laws were repealed. From then until the end of the century Moore control over Clonmel Corporation remained undisputed.

Colonel Stephen Moore also set about influencing the selection of the two parliamentary representatives for the borough of Clonmel.[12] He had been elected MP for Clonmel in 1713, and was returned again in 1715, serving until parliament was dissolved in 1727 upon the death of the king. Moore felt that the forthcoming election presented him with the ideal opportunity to secure the second parliamentary seat for his brother, Guy Moore.

After a campaign that was accompanied with much riot and bloodshed, the Moores achieved a majority. As soon as parliament met, Robert Hamerton and Robert Marshall, the defeated candidates, lodged a petition on the grounds that victory was achieved through the number of freemen Colonel Moore had created during his occupancy of the mayoral chair. Their objections were upheld on the grounds that these freemen, not being residents of the borough, were not properly qualified and the Moores were unseated. This setback was compounded by the failure of Guy Moore to achieve a by-election success on the death of Hamerton in 1733, despite polling 140 votes to 81 for Sir Thomas Prendergast. The latter successfully petitioned parliament on grounds of bribery and intimidation by the Moores.

In 1754, a further by-election took place when the sitting MP, Robert Marshall, became a member of the judiciary. On this occasion Guy Coote Moore, son of Guy Moore, was selected as a candidate. He was opposed by local landlord, William Bagwell. The subsequent election was described as the most notable in the history of the borough. Although Moore secured a majority, the result was, once again, reversed following a petition from Bagwell. Bagwell's triumph however, was short-lived, as he died the following year, leaving Guy Coote to fill the vacancy.

Thereafter, until the end of the century, two members of the Moore family or their nominees were returned at every election, turning Clonmel into a pocket borough. Similarly, 'the corporation of Clonmel as a free

---

[12] Up to the Act of Union (1800), Clonmel returned two members to the Irish House of Commons in Dublin.

Chapter 9

Sterne, Borrow and Trollope

Laurence Sterne, George Borrow and Anthony Trollope, who are among the leading figures in English literature, all had associations with Clonmel. One was born in Clonmel, another attended school in the town, while the third worked there for a time.

Laurence Sterne (1713-1786)

Laurence Sterne was a great-grandson of Richard Sterne, Archbishop of York, and a relative of John Sterne, founder of the Irish College of Surgeons in Dublin. His father, Roger, however, never rose beyond the rank of ensign in the army and, in Laurence's words, was 'a little smart man, active to the last degree in all exercises – most patient of fatigue and disappointments, of which it pleased God to give him full measure'.

The circumstances in which his parents met were as bizarre as some of the incidents Sterne later described in his novels. Roger Sterne was campaigning in Flanders when he found himself in debt to an army provisioner, named Nuttle or Tuthill, who had Clonmel connections. Nuttle had a step-daughter called Agnes Hebert, who was the widow of an army captain. To settle the debt, Roger agreed to marry Agnes. Their first child, Mary, was born in Lille, but Agnes was anxious that their next would be born amongst her own people. She arrived in Clonmel from Dunkirk on 21 November 1713, just three days before Laurence was born. Opinion is divided as to the precise location of his birth. Mary Street, Suir Island and the Military Barracks have been suggested as possible locations, while a plaque over Allen's shop in O'Connell Street also lays claim to the honour.

Roger Sterne's regiment left the town shortly after the birth of his son and Laurence spent his first two years with his wealthy paternal grandmother at Elvington in Yorkshire, and the following eight trailing after his family from barracks to barracks throughout England and Ireland. It is hardly surprising that army-life was to provide him with much background material for his most famous work, *Tristram Shandy*. When he was ten years old, he went to live in Yorkshire where he would spend almost his entire adult life.

Laurence attended school near Halifax for the next eight years. When his father died in Jamaica in 1731 he was briefly re-united with his mother. The Sterne family were unwilling to aid her so she returned to Ireland where she opened an embroidery school, probably in Clonmel. For the next eleven years Sterne heard little of her nor is there any indication that he ever came to visit her.

He left school shortly after his father's death and spent the next two years in idleness at Elvington, supported by a cousin of his called Richard. With Richard's assistance he entered Jesus College, Cambridge in 1733 where he took his B.A. in 1736 and an M.A. in 1740. While he was at university he became friends with the wit, John Hall-Stevenson, whose main delight was in coarse jesting and the perusal of obscene literature. Laurence became a frequent visitor to John's home, Skelton Castle, where he took great pleasure in exploring his friend's library.

His Uncle Jacques, who was a clergyman and a whig supporter, suggested that his nephew should enter the Church. Although Laurence had no vocation whatsoever, on his uncle's advice he took orders and, through his influence, secured the living at Sutton in Yorkshire. In return for Jacques' patronage, he contributed political tracts to *The York Journal*, supporting the whig interest, but soon afterwards he informed his uncle that he would write no more. 'Though my uncle was a party man', Sterne declared, 'I was not, and detested such dirty work, thinking it beneath me. From that period he became my bitterest enemy'. However, local gossip attributed the cause of the quarrel to the fact that Sterne had alienated the affections of his uncle's mistress.

In 1741, Sterne married Elizabeth Lumley, daughter of a clergyman, and she bore him several stillborn children and one living daughter, Lydia. From the beginning his marriage was unhappy due to the fact that Sterne, amoral and self-indulgent, was a born philanderer who took his matrimonial obligations lightly. His 'small, quiet attentions' to various ladies were described as disturbing his conjugal life. He did not neglect his responsibilities however, and in later years following their formal separation, he always provided financial support for Elizabeth and his daughter, Lydia, to whom he was devoted.

His relations with his mother were also strained and Byron said he 'wept over a dead ass but let his mother starve'. She eventually died in a debtor's prison, but whether or not Sterne knew of her predicament is uncertain. We do know that his mother was mercenary and demanding and, when news reached her in Clonmel that he had married a woman of means, she departed for England with his younger sister, Catherine, and pursued him relentlessly for money.

For over twenty years the Sternes lived in Sutton where he enjoyed a comfortable living of two hundred pounds a year. But parochial duties were irksome to him. His parishioners found it difficult to understand his light-hearted indifference to his sacred functions. He was a good shot, and the story is told that on one Sunday when he was on his way to conduct service his pointer dog sprang a covey of partridges. At once he went back for his gun, leaving his congregation to wait in vain. Sterne was not popular with his flock because he was actively engaged in securing the enclosure of the common lands of the farmers. This might explain the 'unreadiness' of his parishioners to rescue him when he fell through ice during a skating accident.

To relieve the monotony of rural existence, Laurence consoled himself with visits to nearby Skelton Castle where his former college friend Hall-Stephenson kept an open house 'to a rather questionable and roistering crew, of whom his clerical friend made cheerfully one'.[1] He also devoted his attention to 'books, fiddling and painting', and to beginning his career as a writer. An incessant reader, he was rarely seen riding around the parish without a book in his hand.

In 1747, he first appeared in print under his own name and over the succeeding years he published a number of sermons. These were followed by *The History of a Good Warm Watchcoat,* a satire on a quarrel among a number of cathedral officials in York, which was not published until after his death. Around the time it was written, his wife, having found her husband in a compromising position with a member of the domestic staff,

---

[1] Stanley J. Kunitz and Howard Heycraft, *British authors before 1800*, (New York, 1952), p. 494.

became insane and had to be committed to psychiatric care. For a while he was full of remorse, but his desire for female company led to a flirtation with Catherine Fourmantelle, a young French singer living at York.

In 1760, the opening two volumes of his masterpiece *The Life and Times of Tristram Shandy, Gentleman* appeared, and the succeeding seven volumes came out at intervals up to 1767. It was an innovative work which revolutionised English fiction. Tristram Shandy is a novel of character, not of narrative. In this respect, Sterne, acknowledged his debt to John Locke whose *Essay on Human Understanding* seemed to him 'a history book .... of what passes in the mind of a man'. He concentrates on the unspoken thoughts of his characters, often without logical sequence or context, anticipating the stream-of-consciousness technique perfected two centuries later by James Joyce. The whole work consists of prefatory remarks to a narrative that never actually begins, in the course of which the reader is introduced to an eccentric cast of characters.

Sterne employed every device to break the thread of the story. There are many digressions which have no discernible connection with the plot of *Tristram Shandy* or anything else. He had a love of anecdote, often coarse, which he inserted as the humour took him. Sterne delighted, too, in puzzling his readers by interpolating text with blank pages, asterisks, black chapters, and graphic doodles marking the chronology of events and lapses in the narrative.

The immediate popularity of the novel made Sterne a wealthy man and an overnight celebrity. It was said that a wager laid in London claimed that a letter addressed to Tristram Shandy anywhere in Europe would reach him in Sutton where he had built a house called *Shandy Hall*. As the poet John Gray said, 'Sterne proved as great an object of admiration as the book'. He received the congratulations of such luminaries as Lord Chesterfield and the famous actor, Richard Garrick, while Lord Ossory commissioned Joshua Reynolds to paint his portrait. Others, however, including Goldsmith and Samuel Richardson, denounced the novel's obscenity, while Dr. Johnson dismissed it with the famous remark, 'Nothing odd will do long'.

Sterne, as Garrick remarked, 'degenerated in London like an ill-transplanted shrub; the incense of the great spoiled his head as their ragouts had done his stomach'. He was increasingly troubled by tuberculosis, which he had contracted as a student. Doctors recommended the benign French climate and several trips to the continent followed. In 1767, during a visit to London, the most celebrated of his romances took place. He fell in love with Mrs. Elizabeth Draper. She was married to an East India Company official, who was twenty years her senior. When she left for India to rejoin her husband Sterne was inconsolable. The story of his affair was recorded in *The Journal of Eliza* which was described as being self-indulgent and sentimental.

Sterne died of pleurisy in London in 1786, intestate and in debt. English literature had lost its most original and eccentric novelist at the age of fifty-four. After his burial, his body was disinterred by grave robbers. An old acquaintance witnessing a body being decapitated during an anatomy lesson recognised the head of his friend. His remains were brought to St. Michael's in Coxwold where they were re-buried.

Goethe regarded him as a great liberating influence showing that there were untried possibilities in the novel. Acknowledged as an original genius, he is a difficult and complex author, who influenced many writers such as Byron, Dickens, Stevenson and Joyce.

George Borrow (1803-1881)

George Borrow was the second son of Thomas Borrow, captain in the Norfolk Regiment of Militia. He accompanied his father to Ireland in the latter part of 1815. They were to spend nine months in the country, mainly in Clonmel. There is a mystery surrounding the origins of his mother's family. Some accounts claim that she was an actress in a touring company, or that she was possibly of gypsy origin. George, however, described her as belonging to a Norfolk family which had resisted the 'tyranny of Rome'.

From his writings, it is apparent that Clonmel had made a lasting impression on the young George Borrow. He recalled that the best salmon were caught in the Suir 'a river which flows past the beautiful town of Clonmel in Ireland'. With his father's regiment stationed in the local barracks, George was duly enrolled as a pupil in the Free School which was then situated in Mary Street. He later gave a vivid description of the schoolroom and the schoolmaster, the Reverend Richard Carey:

> The schoolroom with its long, high, stone-floored hall was dirty and dilapidated. The boys used to crowd on stools and benches round a roaring fire, and the only master at the time, an old man who taught the most elegant Latin, sat at a desk of black, Irish oak. Occasionally he would raise his head, mumble out a few instructions about Latin or Greek tastes, and then bend again to his own reading. Nobody paid any attention to him. The boys had their books on their knees, and talked in low voices among themselves. They were not construing Latin or Greek. They were telling each other wild stories of adventures or playing cards.

During his time in Clonmel, Borrow developed an interest in horses and languages, both of which became abiding passions. One day he was standing at the door of the army barracks when he was asked by one of the grooms to 'give the cob a breathing this fine morning' and quickly found that he had that strange affinity which can exist between horse and man. His first introduction to the Irish language was, as he said, 'on a wild road in Ireland I heard Irish spoken for the first time; and I was seized with a desire to learn Irish, the acquisition in my case, became the stepping stone to other languages'. In his lifetime he was to master an astonishing range of tongues. Apart from Irish, these included Welsh, Old Norse, Romany, Russian, Persian, Portuguese, Manchu and Modern Greek, among others.

It was in Clonmel's Free School that George received his first lessons in Irish. His tutor was a fellow student to whom he gave a pack of playing cards in payment. The boy was a Papist called Murtagh and was described by Borrow as 'sixteen years old and standing over six foot'. He lived in a place called the Wilderness, a district now occupied by a modern housing estate in north Clonmel. Murtagh was later to feature in a number of Borrow's novels. For Borrow, who had a life-long obsessive hatred of Roman Catholicism this friendship seems unusual. Perhaps, that's what his father meant when he said that his son 'kept very strange company when he was in Ireland'.

Early in the new year, Captain Borrow took up duty for a short time in Templemore, before returning to Norwich in May 1816. George won a scholarship to the local grammar school but thirteen years of wandering was poor preparation for the confinement of the classroom. The delights of the countryside held more attractions for him and he spent endless hours hunting and fishing. He became unhappy and rebellious which resulted in his leading a truant party, an incident for which he was publicly horsewhipped before the whole school. He was belligerent by nature and loved a fight. He was fortunate in having a powerful physique, standing six foot three inches and described as having long powerful hands. He was totally fearless and ready to fight at all times. He learned the art of boxing from Thomas Thurtell, a well known bruiser and war veteran, later hanged for murder, who features prominently in the pages of *Lavengro*.

After he left school, his father had him articled to a solicitor in Norwich for five years. It is said that at the end of his time he knew more about shoeing a horse than he did of jurisprudence. He devoted his energies to learning Welsh from an ostler, and German and Hebrew from 'a fraudulent, wandering Jew'. He also made the acquaintance of William Taylor, another disreputable character, who introduced the young Borrow to Danish poetry. In 1824, he set off for London to seek his literary fortune but his early efforts met with little success. Instead, he became acquainted with the Bohemian element of London's back streets and spent his time brawling in the local alehouses. On one occasion when Borrow got involved in a disturbance outside his lodgings he dived into the Thames to avoid the police, swam to the south bank and made his escape. Such an incident might have chastened another, but Borrow was thrilled with the notoriety of it all.

In 1832, he returned to Norwich where he met Mary Clarke, the wealthy widow of a naval officer. The future Mrs. Borrow had a fifteen year old daughter and was a member of a pious evangelical family. She introduced him to the Rev. Francis Cunningham, a strong supporter of The Bible Society, an organisation which specialised in translating the scriptures into innumerable heathen and exotic languages. The Society was looking for agents at the time and, as somebody who could read the Bible in thirteen languages, Borrow seemed highly suited for such a position.

However, he was also a man who had no religion whatsoever, so all who knew him greeted his appointment with great glee. In 1833, the Bible Society sent him on an extensive tour of Russia and in November 1835 he went on the first of three missions to Spain. In a country plagued by civil strife his travels were marked by bizarre adventures, disasters, and sufferings during which time he found himself imprisoned, contracted malaria and encountered a host of strange and colourful characters. Eventually, his wayward behaviour and his unwillingness to obey instructions left his employers with no alternative but to terminate his contract.

In 1840 he left Spain after four and a half tempestuous years and that April he finally married Mary Clarke and went to live in Norfolk, where his new wife, a comfortable middle aged woman had extensive property. Mary was remarkably understanding and prepared to tolerate his frequent tantrums and depressions. But for all his waywardness he was totally dependent on her. Two years later his book, *The Bible in Spain,* was published. Based on his travels there, it was an immediate success and he found himself the focus of attention in London's literary world. But Borrow could not cope with the demands of celebrity status anymore than he could endure the confines of Norfolk. As his biographer put it, 'he belonged to two mutually exclusive worlds and could not bring himself to give up one in favour of the other'.[2]

He became restless and melancholic and overcome with the desire to be on the move again. He took off on an extensive tour of Europe, reaching Russia and Turkey. This was to be the first many such excursions he made 'in search of the roving, raffish and unconventional life that always attracted him'.[3] In his meanderings he walked the length of the Thames, reached as far north as the Orkneys, tramped through Wales and made a return visit to Ireland. He was a man blessed with extraordinary physical energy. A contemporary describes Borrow, then aged seventy, bathing in the Pen Ponds in Richmond Park 'with a north-east wind cutting across the icy water like a razor, run about the grass afterwards, like a boy

---

[2] David Williams, *A World of His Own. The Double Life of George Borrow*, (Oxford University Press, 1982) p. 147.
[3] *Ibid*, p. 164.

to shake off the water drops, stride about the park for hours, and then, after fasting for twelve hours sit down to dinner'.

Between his bouts of rambling he managed to publish his two great books upon which he had been working intermittently. *Lavengro*, which was issued in 1851, was described as a semi-autobiographical novel of gypsy life. It was viewed as a 'Bohemian pilgrimage around Britain' and scorned as an 'epic of ale'. This was followed six years later by *Romany Rye*, which could be regarded as a sequel to the earlier work. Although they are now recognised as Borrow's literary monuments they were, at the time, condemned by the critics, a reaction which Borrow deeply resented.

The death of his wife in 1869 left him bereft and distracted:

> The link attaching him, however loosely, to the real world had gone, and his habits of dreaming, wandering and fighting, and generally standing up for himself did not suit his sixty six years. He had outlived himself. He was a man born to live the life of a Lavengro, a hard aggressive life, a life quite oblivious of all routine, all convention. Temperamentally he was not a man born to be old, yet the limitless toughness of his constitution forced old age on him.[4]

He outlived his wife by twelve years, but for the most part they were dismal and empty ones. He hated being old and became morose and resentful of his declining, physical powers. In 1880 he made his will and ordered a new suit to be buried in. He must, he said, be 'ready for the resurrection'. On 22 July 1881 he died and was laid to rest beside his wife in Brompton Cemetery.

Anthony Trollope (1815–1882)

In the Autumn of 1844, the newly married Anthony Trollope and his wife arrived in Clonmel and took up lodgings in a first floor apartment of a house off Main Street, the present O'Connell Street, close to where O'Gorman's drapery shop stands to-day. He had been appointed postal

---

[4] *Ibid*, p. 168.

surveyer to the district but little did anyone think that this shy, awkward, young man would one day become a celebrated novelist.

Indeed, up to this point in his life there was little to suggest that Anthony Trollope was destined for greatness. In his *Autobiography* he declared that from the day he was born until his arrival in Ireland his life had been one of abject misery and failure. The Trollopes were impoverished gentlefolk and the young Anthony was brought up in the utmost squalor and cruelty. His father, a one-time lawyer and failed gentleman farmer, gradually became melancholic and demented. In 1827, his mother, the novelist Frances Trollope, took off on her own for America to redeem the family fortune. Anthony was twelve at the time and did not see her again for four years.

As a charity boy at Harrow, and briefly at Winchester, he was brutally abused by staff and pupils. Neglected at home and bullied at school, where it was said that he was 'not only slovenly in dress' but that 'his work was equally dirty'. Rejected and despised, he came close to suicide, and only survived 'because he learnt to escape into daydreams of handsome men and beautiful women – a habit that, by his own account, generated his novels'. For seven years, he served as a post office clerk in London at a salary that left him constantly in debt, and under supervisors who frequently upbraided him for his idleness and incompetence.

He finally extricated himself by applying for a position of post-office surveyor in Ireland, a country which was often regarded as the graveyard of ambitions for many an aspiring English gentleman. For Trollope, it was to be his salvation. At Banagher in County Offaly and in Clonmel, he successfully reorganised the postal system. He was received as a gentleman and was entertained by lawyers, doctors, prosperous merchants, garrison officer and their families, being invited to dinners, balls and hunts. For recreation he took up hunting which became a lifelong obsession. No wonder he could write that 'it was altogether a very jolly life that I led in Ireland'.

In 1844 he married an English woman, Rose Heseltine, whom he met while staying in Kingstown (now Dun Laoghaire). The newlyweds having set up house in Clonmel, Trollope began his literary career. He wrote his first novel, *The MacDermots of Ballycloran*, after a visit to a ruin in Drumsna, Co. Leitrim. During his stay in Clonmel, he became firm friends with Charles Bianconi who, since 1815, had been carrying the mails on his successful coach system. Anthony was a welcome visitor to Bianconi's home in Silver Spring where he mixed business with pleasure. It was there that he wrote part of his *Irish Sketch Book*, and Eliza Bianconi said that 'Silverbridge' in *The last chronicle of Barset* was so called 'in memory of his happy visits to Silver Spring, where he would always wake up early to write for an hour or so before going out hunting'.[5]

In his report to the Post Office in 1857, he mentions Mr. Bianconi with admiration and respect. Few others contributed more to Trollope's understanding of Ireland than Charles Bianconi who, as a result of operating his coach service, had gained extraordinary insights into the complex social and economic relationships that characterised Ireland in the middle of the nineteenth century.

Trollope's years in Clonmel were to prove fruitful for him both as husband and aspiring author. His two sons were born here, Henry Merivale on the 13 March 1846 and Frederick James Anthony, a year later. Both were baptised in Old St. Mary's. Interestingly, the baptismal register shows Trollope did not declare his occupation as 'postal surveyer' but instead he is listed as 'gentleman'. Travelling alone on horseback on post office business, Trollope' imagination was stimulated by the countryside and by the people he met, and in a literary career that encompassed almost sixty novels, Trollope's fascination with Ireland is obvious.

Many of his writings reflect his years spent in and around Clonmel. His friendship with Bianconi contributed to the creation of Melmotte, the foreign tycoon in *The Way We Live Now*. A handsome, aristocratic rake called de Burgo Fitzgerald makes his appearance in *The Small House at Allingham*, a name which recalls the connection the de Burgo family and the Fitzgeralds of Desmond had with the manor of Clonmel. The title of one of his most famous works *The Pallisers* also has resonaces of Clonmel. A family of that name lived over the Old Bridge in the seventeen hundreds, and the rector of Old St. Mary's during Trollope's stay in Clonmel was the Reverend Bury Palliser.

---

[5] M. O'Connell Bianconi & S. J. Watson, *Bianconi: King of the Irish Roads*, (Dublin, 1962), p. 119.

In the spring of 1848, Anthony Trollope and his family left Clonmel for Killarney. By the time of his return to England in 1859 he had achieved much. He had become an authority on the postal system, was responsible for introducing the post-box to the United Kingdom and, in addition, was recognised as one of the leading literary figures of his day. He is best remembered for a series of novels known as the Barchester Chronicles, so-called because they were set in the imaginary town of Barchester.

Many social historians regard his novels as key documents in tracing the contours of nineteenth century Britain and Ireland, and it is said that no one had a clearer vision of the social structures of Victorian England. His final years were spent in the seclusion of a small Sussex village, where he worked on in the face of gradually diminishing popularity, failing health and increasing melancholy. He died in London, having been stricken with paralysis.

The connection of all three famous writers with Clonmel was short-lived. The fact that the fathers of Sterne and Borrow served in the British army, while Trollope himself was a postal official meant that none of these literary figures spent any great length of time in the town. Obviously Sterne's writings were not influenced by his birthplace since he only lived in Clonmel for a few months as an infant. Borrow and Trollope, however, remained long enough in Clonmel to be inspired by the people, the town and the surrounding countryside.

Chapter 10

A Cloud over Clonmel

The execution of Fr. Nicholas Sheehy in 1766 on a trumped-up charge of murder is still remembered in Clonmel today. Tragic deaths often create their own mythology and his made a lasting impression on the minds of the people. Charles Kickham in *Knocknagow* tells of a dark cloud that hung over Clonmel since that fatal event, and in the town it was widely believed that it always rained on the fair day.

We know little of the early life of Fr. Nicholas Sheehy. He was the son of Francis Sheehy, a well-to-do Catholic, who came from Drumcollogher in County Limerick. Francis Sheehy married a woman whose surname was Power from Bawnfaune, a townland situated in the parish of Kilronan in the barony of Glenaheiry in Co. Waterford. Some claim that this is where Nicholas Sheehy was born in 1728, but others suggest that Barretstown, near Fethard was his birthplace.[1] He enrolled in the Irish College in Salamanca on 17 March 1749 to train for the priesthood. It would appear that he was quite clever as the results of his first year theology examination, taken the following August, were regarded as being 'superior'.[2] In May 1751, for reasons unknown, he left Salamanca without completing his theological course.[3] It is not certain where he was ordained but around 1752 he was appointed to the parish of Newcastle.

At the time there was growing unrest among the tenant farmers of rural Ireland who, all too often, had been the victims of callous landlords and an oppressive legal system. Throughout the eighteenth century their position had steadily worsened. With a growth in

---

[1] P. Lonergan, 'The life and death of Father Sheehy' in *Irish Ecclesiastical Record*, xvii (July, 1896), p.602; Thomas A. Murphy, 'Father Nicholas Sheehy, P. P., Clogheen' in William Darmody (ed.) *Tercentenary Record* (1950), p. 47.
[2] Anon. 'Students in the Irish College, Salamanca' in *Archivium Hibernicum*, iv, (1915), p. 34.
[3] Patrick Corish (ed.), 'Correspondence of the superior of the Jesuit mission in Ireland with John O'Brien, S.J., Rector of Salamanca' in *Archivium Hibernicum*, xxvii, (1964), p. 91.

population, competition for farms increased accordingly. Holdings were subdivided into uneconomic units to accommodate the demand, and rents, which were already high, were pushed up even further. To add to their woes the unfortunate peasantry had to pay tithes, consisting of one tenth of their income, for the upkeep of the Protestant clergy.

Fr. Sheehy felt a deep sense of outrage at this injustice and advised his parishioners in Newcastle to withhold the payment of tithes on the grounds that there were no Protestants in the parish. In 1756, when he was appointed parish priest of Shanrahan, Templetenny and Ballysheehan, later to be known as the parishes of Clogheen and Ballyporeen, he continued his protest against what he considered to be this most unfair form of taxation. In 1762, two Protestant clergymen, Foulkes and Sutton, rented their tithes to a Ballyporeen inn-keeper called Dobbyn. This unscrupulous tithe proctor instituted a new claim by demanding five shillings for every marriage performed by the parish priest. Fr. Sheehy responded by denouncing these levies and encouraged his parishioners to resist payment.

In 1759, the laws prohibiting the importation of Irish cattle into England were relaxed, creating a greater demand for pasture. Local landlords responded by enclosing the commonages. This was resisted by a quasi-military group known first as Levellers, and later as Whiteboys, so-called because they disguised themselves by wearing their shirts over their clothing. The first outbreak of violence occurred in 1761, when the fences around the commons in Drumlemmon were levelled. These were on the estates of John Ross, a tenant of the Catholic landlord, Lord Cahir.

This incident sparked off a decade of lawlessness and violence. Soon the Whiteboys turned their attention to other injustices and to the tithe question in particular. Cattle were maimed and property was destroyed. The Protestant population became thoroughly alarmed. Their clergy resented the attacks on tithe proctors and the landlords feared for their lands and property. The authorities in Dublin Castle were not slow to act. Lord Drogheda and his dragoons were dispatched to Clogheen. The soldiery scoured the countryside brutalising and terrorising the people. Father Sheehy was a witness to these raids and, according to tradition, he visited and consoled the families who were victimised.[4]

The prime persecutor at local level was the Rev. John Hewetson, who held estates at Suirville, Co. Kilkenny, as well as the tithes of several parishes in Tipperary. He was described as 'a lowly curate in the Established Church' who 'was keen for advancement by a firm display of loyal activity against the Whiteboys and Catholic gentry'.[5] In Hewetson's opinion, Sheehy was 'a very capital ringleader of those insurgents and the very life and soul of those deluded people'. Being the parish priest at the centre of the disturbances, together with his outspoken opposition to the tithes and to the enclosure of the commonages, made Sheehy a marked man. It was only a question of time before his formidable enemies made a determined effort to get him.

This vindictive campaign began in June 1762 when Fr. Sheehy was presented to the grand jury as an unregistered priest – a charge that scarcely needed proof. However, since no conviction followed, this appeared to be no more than a warning.[6] Fr. Sheehy was again in the dock at the Clonmel Assizes the following year when he was charged in connection with the levelling of the fences at Drumlemmon, two years earlier. It is difficult to assess Fr. Sheehy's involvement in this incident because Ross, the landowner in question, refused to testify against him. At the Spring Assizes in Clonmel in 1764, more serious charges were brought against him when he was accused of acting as a leader in a treasonable conspiracy by exercising men under arms and swearing them to allegiance to the French king.

On the advice of his friends, Fr. Sheehy went into hiding. An offer of £300 was made for his capture but he found shelter in the houses of his loyal parishioners and, for a period, he hid in the O'Callaghan family vault in Shanrahan cemetery. At night, he was protected by a Protestant gentleman called Griffith, whose home adjoined Shanrahan. Subsequently, on the night before his execution, Fr. Sheehy left Griffith his watch, as a token of appreciation to his former benefactor.

---

[4] Philip O'Connell, 'The plot against Father Sheehy' in *The Irish Ecclesiatical Record*, series v (December, 1967), P. 374.

[5] Cited in T. P. Power, *Land, politics and society in eighteenth century Tipperary*, (Oxford, 1993), p. 260.

[6] Corish, p. 123.

After some months, to prevent further harassment of his parishioners by a frustrated soldiery and realising that he could not remain on the run indefinitely, Fr. Sheehy decided to give himself up. He feared that if he fled the country it would be seen as an admission of guilt. Realising that he could expect no mercy from a local jury, he wrote to the chief secretary Waite requesting that he be tried in Dublin and not in Clonmel 'where he feared the power and malice of his enemies were too prevalent for justice'.[7]

It was on this understanding that he surrendered to a local magistrate, Cornelius O'Callaghan, who later became 1st Baron Lismore. O'Callaghan was a humane man who rightly feared that Sheehy would not get a fair trial. He offered Sheehy a hundred guineas and advised him to flee the country but the headstrong priest, confident that he would be proved innocent, declined. On 16 March 1765 Sheehy was brought to Dublin and lodged in the Lower Castle Yard. Following four months imprisonment, a preliminary hearing indicated that the authorities were convinced of his innocence. He was released on bail of £4,000 and was free to go anywhere within the city limits.

On 10 February 1766, Sheehy was brought to trial in Dublin. The witnesses, who had been procured and tutored by Hewetson and his cohorts, were discredited and Fr. Sheehy was acquitted on all counts. Although, the Tipperary justices were once again frustrated they remained determined to obtain Sheehy's conviction at any cost.[8] On leaving the court, Fr. Sheehy was immediately re-arrested and accused of being an accessory to the murder of a man called John Bridge, who had been allegedly killed by Francis Meehan, because it was said that he refused to take the Whiteboy oath.

Shortly after Sheehy had been arrested and brought to Dublin, the grand jury had offered a reward of £50 for the conviction of those involved in the alleged murder of Bridge. Bridge was a foundling, so-called because he was abandoned on a bridge. He was described 'as a drivelling, begging idiot' and Fr. Sheehy had been previously accused of assaulting him in connection with the theft of a chalice from the chapel of Carrigvisteal which went missing a few years earlier. It transpired that Bridge had nothing to do with the robbery but the altercation between

---

[7] Burke, p. 372.
[8] T. P. Power, *Land, politics etc.,* p. 263.

the priest and Bridge presented Fr. Sheehy's enemies with an ideal opportunity. In October 1764, Bridge went missing. Hewitson and his fellow conspirators circulated the rumour that he had been murdered and that Sheehy was implicated in the crime.

Sheehy was brought to Clonmel from Dublin on horseback with his hands pinioned behind his back and his legs firmly bound together. He was lodged in the town jail which then stood in Lough Street, the present Gladstone Street, where 'he was double bolted and treated in every respect with rigour'.[9] This unnecessary brutality resulted in the wounds on his hands and legs becoming ulcerated. Now that his enemies had him in their grasp, they were not going to let their prey escape. The trial of Nicholas Sheehy and Francis Meehan began on 12 March at the back of the Tholstel, now known as the Main Guard.

His accusers left nothing to chance. It was said that 'a great military force' roamed the town intimidating sympathisers of the accused on the pretence that the 'prisoners Sheehy and Meehan intended an escape', and it was rumoured 'that it was discovered that they had disengaged themselves from their irons'.[10] Another account stated that:

> On the day of the trial a party of horse surrounded the court, admitting and excluding whom they thought proper; while others of them with a certain Baronet (Sir Thomas Maude) at their head, scampered the streets in a formidable manner; forcing into inns and private lodgings in the town; challenging and questioning all comers; menacing his (Sheehy's) friends and encouraging his enemies.[11]

This harassment was so effective that no local attorney could be found to defend the prisoners. Eventually Mr. Sparrow, an obscure Dublin lawyer, had the unenviable task of representing them. Such were the intimidatory tactics, that even after the death sentence had been passed, he found it necessary to steal out of town at night for his own safety.

A carefully selected jury, united in its determination to deliver a

---

[9] Burke, 375.
[10] *Ibid*, p. 376.
[11] *Ibid.*

verdict of guilty, was sworn in by Sir Thomas Maude of Dundrum, a rabid anti-Catholic. They were a motley collection, consisting of some landlords and grasiers, a soldier and an attorney. Two were Clonmel men, John Dumville, a tallow chandler who had a premises in the Main Street, and Osborne Tuthill, who lived on Suir Island. The same witnesses who had been discredited at the Dublin trial were produced once more. They included John Toohy, a convicted horse thief, John Lonergan, a young man who was described as a 'villain' and one of 'low intellect', and the notorious Moll Dunlea 'a lady of easy virtue well known to the common soldiers' whose immoral activities had already been denounced from the altar by Fr. Sheehy. During the course of the trial she was referred to as Mrs. Mary Brady, adopting the surname of the soldier with whom she co-habited.

They were all 'genteely dressed' for the occasion. Toohy was said to have been decked out 'in an elegant suit of fine new clothes, a superfine blue cloth coat, the waistcoat and breeches of black silk'. They were housed in The Spread Eagle Inn, one of the town's leading hostelries situated between Sarsfield Street and Quay Street. They performed to the satisfaction of their masters and afterwards were financially rewarded for their services. The Tipperary Grand Jury later gave a sum of £600 to be divided equally between Toohy and Lonergan, since Moll Dunlea did not live to claim her share.

During the course of the trial, Toohy swore he was present with a party of Whiteboys when Sheehy asked Bridge to swear an oath that he would not divulge any information about them to the authorities. When Bridge refused, Toohy claimed he saw him being killed by a blow of a billhook delivered by Meehan. He also said that Sheehy swore all present to silence. Lonergan testified that he encountered a crowd on the way to bury Bridge's body and that Sheehy paid him three half crowns not to inform on them.

Moll Dunlea gave evidence that she lived with her mother at Clogheen, and that a man called Kearney was at the house that night. She said that Sheehy called for him, and that she followed them to Shanbally where she saw the priest, Kearney and others carrying Bridge's body, which they buried at a place called Baron, later removing it to Ballysheehan. Her mother however testified that she slept with Moll on the night in question and that she could not have left the house without her knowledge. This was corroborated by Eleanor Dunlea, Moll's sister. Moll's mother also stated that Kearney was not in their house that night.

Sheehy's defence was a simple one. He proposed to account for his whereabouts during the period when the murder was alleged to have taken place and stated that he could produce witnesses of the utmost integrity. The first of these was Robert Keating, a member of a highly respected Catholic family from Cahir, who testified that Sheehy had spent the night of the murder in his house. In an effort to discredit Keating, Hewitson accused him of being involved in the murder of two soldiers at Newmarket in Co. Kilkenny. As a result, Keating's evidence was struck from the record and later he found himself in Kilkenny gaol awaiting trial. Fortunately, he was acquitted.

Another of Fr. Sheehy's witnesses received similar treatment. James Herbert, a Protestant farmer from County Limerick, was also arrested and charged as being an accomplice in the murder. Fearing for the safety of his friends, Fr. Sheehy decided not to call his remaining witnesses with the exception of William Egan, parish priest of Clonmel, who was to become the future bishop of Waterford and Lismore.

Father Egan refused to come forward. He was reluctant to become involved in a matter of public controversy. At a time when there was a relaxation of the penal laws he had no desire to see these new-found freedoms jeopardised. Indeed, Fr. Sheehy's activities had been viewed with increasing alarm by the Church. Even the ageing Dr. Creagh, bishop of the diocese, felt it his duty to supply the authorities with information concerning the Whiteboys. These were seen as an embarrassment to the Catholic establishment at a time when cautious moves for civil recognition were being made.

Father Egan's failure to act was not forgotten. When the corpse of Fr. Sheehy was subsequently being carried past the parochial house in Irishtown, which stood until the mid-1980s, the dead priest's sister smeared the front door posts with her brother's blood. A contemporary Irish lament contains the following line, 'Bagwell and Maud pierced you in the heart' and adds bitterly 'Egan and Creagh sold you'.

Sheehy and Meehan were found guilty on the evidence of a convicted horse-thief, a vagrant of ill-repute and a prostitute. Before sentence was passed Fr. Sheehy, on behalf of Edward Meehan and himself, spoke with dignity of the shameful injustice, the gross perjury, and the deadly malice of which they were victims. He added that he left it to God to distinguish between the innocent and the guilty. One clergyman who stood staunchly by the condemned was Sheehy's friend and colleague, Fr. Doyle, parish priest of Ardfinnan, who comforted him in his last hours.

On 16 March 1766, Sheehy and Meehan were hanged on a scaffold erected outside the town gaol across the street from the entrance to the present SS. Peter and Paul's Church. Facing the assembled multitude, Sheehy prayed that God might spare those who had sworn his life away. He then shook hands with Father Doyle, begged to be remembered in his prayers and indicated his readiness to the hangman. His body was cut down, quartered and drawn through the streets of the town. The head was severed and spiked on a pole in front of the prison where it remained for the next twenty years. When a new gaol opened in Emmet Street in 1786, the skull was given to his sister, Mrs. Catherine Burke, who had it buried with his other remains in Shanrahan churchyard, outside Clogheen.

To say that the trial was a gross miscarriage of justice is an understatement. It was never proved that the crime for which the two men were hanged actually took place. Every effort to find the whereabouts of John Bridge's body failed. It was a known fact that Lord Drogheda had Bridge arrested on suspicion of being a Whiteboy and had him savagely tortured and flogged. It was said that he was given his freedom on condition that he would turn informer, but rather than do so he left the country. Some say he had emigrated to Newfoundland and that he had previously indicated his intentions to many of his acquaintances. Peter Crowley, a native of Clogheen, was reputed to have met him many years later in a tavern in Newfoundland and to have reported that Bridge was horrified when he heard of the executions.

Another account records that Bridge was murdered by two men in County Cork on the grounds that he might testify against the Whiteboys and possibly implicate Father Sheehy. This story derived from the confession of a condemned man, Damian Dwyer, who was executed on 25 April 1768. The alleged incident was corroborated by Fr. Sheehy himself who, on the day before he was executed, wrote to Joseph Sirr in Dublin stating that Bridge was strangled by two men on the night of 24 October 1764 but that he could not make use of this information since he received it in the confessional.

The perpetrators of Sheehy's murder had every reason to feel satisfied. Hewitson was only too pleased to have had the opportunity to exercise his 'poor abilities' in the services of his king and country. He received two hundred and twenty seven pounds ten shillings for his trouble. It gave Maude the 'greatest pleasure and satisfaction to find that' his 'endeavours to assist the many worthy and loyal persons in the County of Tipperary, who on every occasion have appeared in defence and support of the Constitution, have been honoured'.[12] No doubt it gave him even greater pleasure to hear that he had been raised to the peerage as Baron de Montalt for services rendered.

It was obvious from the reactions of the authorities, that they neither cared about nor understood what prompted the unrest in the first place. This was no more than a response by the poor to a worsening economic situation, and the protests were in no way sectarian nor even in any sense political.[13] Indeed, the actions of those who pursued Fr. Sheehy were vehemently condemned by the Protestant peer, Lord Charlemont, who declared that 'the furious and bigoted zeal with which some Protestants were activated was shocking to humanity and a disgrace to our mild religion'.[14] The sweet taste of victory was soon to turn sour for many of Sheehy's enemies. As Dr. Madden wrote, 'the extraordinary judgements which fell on the persons who were involved in the death of Father Sheehy, are still fresh in the memories of the inhabitants of Clonmel and Clogheen'.[15]

Though obscured by legend, many of those involved in the trial did in fact die in strange and violent circumstances. The most dramatic were the deaths of Sir Thomas Maud, who contracted a fatal repulsive disease with his eyes dropping out of their sockets, while John Bagwell of Kilmore died tormented by a vision of the headless body of Father Sheehy. Several members of the jury died in equally gruesome and bizarre

---

[12] *Ibid*, p. 391.
[13] P. J. Corish, *The Catholic community in the seventeenth and eighteenth centuries*, (Dublin, 1981), p. 122.
[14] Cited in Power, p. 267.
[15] Cited in Brian O' Higgins, 'Cloud over Clonmel' in James Maher's *Romantic Slievenamon,* (Tralee, 1954), p. 100.

circumstances. One cut his throat, another choked at dinner, while a third was killed by a horse. The witnesses fared no better. Soon after the trial, Moll Dunlea fell down a stairs and broke her neck, Toohy contracted leprosy, while Lonergan was afflicted from head to toe by ulcers.

Two more scenes were yet to be played out in this sad drama. Four years later, Darby Brohan, the hangman who carried out the sentence on Father Sheehy, was engaged in a similar task in Daingean, Co. Offaly when he was stoned to death by a hostile crowd. It was said that it was in retaliation for his involvement in the Clonmel execution. The second occurred when the people of Clogheen decided to erect a memorial cross over Fr. Sheehy's grave in Shanrahan churchyard, outside the village. Lord Lismore objected vehemently and threatened to draft in the military. What makes this so extraordinary is that it occurred over a hundred years after Sheehy's death. Today that cross still stands in front of Clogheen parish church.

In reviewing Sheehy's trial and the surrounding legal proceedings the general consensus is that his execution was judicial murder, engineered by his enemies to get rid of a known troublemaker. To-day, Fr. Sheehy would be regarded as a man with a social conscience, moved to compassion by the injustice and poverty he saw around him. His outspoken involvement made him a thorn in the side of the authorities. In his efforts to help his people he fell foul of those who found in him a convenient scapegoat. In the face of growing agrarian outrages he became the victim of a witch hunt. Unfortunately for him, Sheehy was a man who was in the wrong place at the wrong time. His execution was designed to subdue all protest and unrest and cower the peasantry into submission and compliance, but instead it created a popular martyr, who is still remembered to this day.

Chapter 11

The Quaker Industrialist

Mid-eighteenth century Clonmel was described by Burke as being 'as somnolent as a backwood settlement'. Trade was mainly of a local nature, and apart from a few scattered houses in the suburbs, the town had scarcely extended beyond its medieval dimensions. By 1799, however, the population had doubled, reaching a figure of 9,212[1] and the urban landscape had been dramatically altered. The ancient town walls on the quays were demolished to accommodate the town's growing fabric and its expanding river trade. The catalyst for this transformation was the corn trade which had been revolutionised by a series of acts passed by the Dublin parliament. In 1759, subsidies were paid on the inland carriage of flour to Dublin. This was followed by the passage of Foster's Corn Laws in 1784 which offered bounties on the export of grain to England to feed an increasing urban population, while at the same time imposing restrictions on the importation of foreign grain. Clonmel was ideally placed to take advantage of this legislation. Its rich agricultural hinterland and its links with the port of Waterford helped to make it the largest milling centre in Ireland.

Clonmel's milling industry was monopolised by the Quakers. This small, enterprising group, whose numbers scarcely exceeded three hundred, was noted for its business acumen and entrepreneurial skill. The successful involvement of such families as Dudley, Grubb, Hughes and Sparrow, initially in the woollen industry, generated the necessary capital which enabled them to exploit the possibilities presented by the developing corn trade. While their multi-storeyed mills dotted the skyline, related industries such as bacon, brewing, tanning and butter-making were also largely in Quaker hands. They were prominent in the provision of such essentials as groceries, drapery and hardware, as well. Although they were a dominant force in the economic life of Clonmel almost up to the middle of the nineteenth century, none created a commercial dynasty to match that of the

---

[1] Grubb collection, Ms box 44, SGA 33 (F.H.L.D.).

Malcomsons.

The Malcomsons were Scottish Presbyterian emigrants who settled at Lurgan in County Armagh in the seventeenth century. The first Malcomson to come to Ireland was Andrew, a skilled linen weaver, who married a local girl, Jane Tough or Tugh. In 1748, one of Andrew's sons, Joseph, married Rachel Greer, a Quakeress. Although Joseph never became a Quaker, his eleven children were all brought up as members of the Religious Society of Friends, as the Quakers were also known. When Joseph died in 1774 his son David, future founder of the family's commercial empire, was only nine years old. We cannot say what circumstances brought David to Clonmel but, since the Quakers saw it as their duty to look after the welfare of widows and their children, it is likely that David was entrusted to the care of the Clonmel Meeting. It would appear that he did not receive much formal education for he subsequently regretted not having the opportunity of learning 'the history and occurrences of past ages'. Since it was customary for young Quakers to pass directly from school to apprenticeship, it seems certain that he had served his time in business before arriving in Clonmel where his older brother John had settled a few years earlier.

In 1784 David took up employment with his cousin Sarah Grubb of Anner mills, who had advertised for 'competent clerks to aid her in the administration of her late husband's estates'. He soon came into conflict with his employer whose strong personality had earned her the name 'Queen of the South'. Two years later, John Barclay Clibborn, her future son-in-law, came to Anner mills as a replacement for David, who had been reputedly sacked for poor time-keeping. It would appear that the incident did not damage his relationship with Sarah Grubb, for she subsequently acted as intermediary when he wished to propose to his future wife. There is a story told that on the day David Malcomson left Anner mills he had only a sovereign in his pocket, and meeting a beggar woman on the road he gave it to her, whereupon she is said to have prophesied that he would have luck in whatever he did.

After this he became involved in whiskey distilling and in 1790, became agent to John Bagwell, owner of Marlfield corn mill, the largest in Clonmel. When Bagwell was made colonel of the Tipperary militia, David Malcomson took on a most un-Quakerly role, acting as paymaster for the regiment. The Bagwell connection was to produce additional benefits when, in 1800, the colonel purchased the town of Clonmel from the trustees of the Ormond estate. Through Bagwell's influence Malcomson was made a freeman of the borough, in the process acquiring the attendant commercial and political privileges bestowed by that honour. One irate citizen, referring to the preferential treatment that Malcomson and some others had received, said that although they had corn stores near his 'they had no tolls to pay' and that he 'was mulcted every way out of 150 guineas'.[2]

In 1801, David Malcomson went into business for himself when he purchased the first of three corn stores on the quay. He had been fortunate enough to receive a legacy of £300 on the death of his mother in 1791. Four years later, his marriage to Mary Fennell of Cahir Abbey, daughter of a wealthy Quaker farmer, brought him a share in an estate in Crohane, near Killenaule, and a dowry of £1,500 which was to be invested in lands for David. He also enjoyed the support of his elder brother, John, who was well established in the commercial life of Clonmel as a draper and distiller and who, in 1808, bought the Corporation mill on Suir Island for the sum of £3,000, on David's behalf.

Becoming a mill-owner was to prove the defining moment in David Malcomson's career. An inventory of David's property shows his rapid rise to wealth and fortune, his assets increasing from £33,888 in 1809 to £67,434 in 1816.[3] His new-found prosperity was reflected in a change of residence. Following his marriage he lived in Mary Street and later moved to Flag Lane where he had already purchased a corn store. In 1813, he decided to build an imposing mansion, known as Melview House, in the north suburbs at a cost of £3,500. Its outward appearance led to it being affectionately known as 'the tea caddy'. Consisting of three storeys it provided adequate accommodation for David's large family of seven boys and four girls. It was solidly built and planned with care which led Richard Lalor Shiel to exclaim that it seemed to reflect David's character. He went on to say that 'notwithstanding all its elaborate plainness, I everywhere observed the lurking indications of luxury, which was only thinly veiled by

[2] Rev. Wm. Burke, *History of Clonmel*, p. 145.
[3] Notes on the Malcomson family (National Library, MS. 8146).

ostentatious simplicity'.[4]

Until 1818, David Malcomson traded under his own name but, in that year, he took his sons, Joseph, Joshua and John into partnership with him and the firm became known as David Malcomson & Sons. Two years later, he set about enlarging his mill on Suir Island by leasing a site from the Earl of Glengall which lay between his own mill and that of Thomas Hughes. Malcomson's new mill was later known as Baron's mill, to distinguish it from his other mill which continued to be known as Corporation mill. In 1828, Shiel who paid a visit to the Malcomson mills in Clonmel, described them as 'the finest in Ireland where half the harvest of the adjoining counties as well as of Tipperary is powdered under the huge mill stones that I saw wheeling with incalculable rapidity, and it is thence poured into the London markets'.

Four years previously, David Malcomson had extended the base of his operations when he acquired a lease of Pouldrew corn mills, situated on the river Clodiagh about two miles from Kilmeadon, in County Waterford. Increased business necessitated the purchase of an additional corn store in Carrick-on-Suir. The success of his milling ventures can be illustrated by the exports of flour from the Malcomson owned mills which rose from 34,398 cwt for the period 1815 to 1819, to 357,618 cwt for the years 1825-29. From 1820-29 he supplied an average of 21% of the flour exports from the port of Waterford.

Despite his success, David Malcomson was well aware that the well being of the Irish corn industry depended on the maintenance of the corn laws and any moves to abolish them was a cause of concern. 'We fear', he wrote that 'we are on the eve of such a change in the Corn Laws as will be very serious to this country'. He realised that Ireland could no longer compete with other countries, who were opening their corn market to Britain at very cheap rates. 'It is clear that for every barrel of foreign corn imported from other countries into England, she wants so much less from Ireland'.

These concerns prompted him to seek an alternative source of investment. At sixty years of age David Malcomson embarked on the most ambitious project of his career. He purchased sixteen acres of land at

---

[4] Richard Lalor Shiel, 'A glimpse of Industrial Clonmel in 1829' in *Catholic Record*, (September, 1918), p. 117.

Mayfield in Portlaw in what he described as having 'a most eligible situation with full command of the river Clodiagh' where he decided to build a cotton mill. Although his decision to engage in the cotton trade was guided by practical business he was 'conscious of the fact that they were strangers to the cotton business'. He sounded a note of warning when he wrote, 'if we fail we must admit to a serious loss but which we expect to be able to bear up against'. He was also influenced by philanthropic motives, adding 'if we are able to succeed we will we expect lay the foundation for employing many thousands of people of this country'.

The Portlaw site contained a small flour mill which had formerly produced iron. This was demolished and David re-structured the weir on the river Clodiagh to ensure the availability of the necessary water supply and also built a canal to link the Clodiagh to the Suir. This meant that barges could convey raw materials up to sixty tons from the port of Waterford and into the factory where they were unloaded. Building commenced in 1825 and the completed structure measured 268 feet long, 47 feet wide and 72 feet high, comprising six storeys and was reputed to be the largest single span building in the world. Its flat roof contained a reservoir for water, 260 feet in length and 40 feet in breath. Alongside the spinning mill was a single storey glass roofed structure covering an acre and given over to weaving operations. When the complex was completed it was bigger than the two largest mills in Belfast combined. The original building cost £15,000 but by the time various additions had been added upwards of £60,000 had been spent. By the mid eighteen thirties it had become the largest cotton factory in Ireland. It initially provided employment for 260 workers, rising rapidly to almost 2,000 in David's lifetime.

David's extraordinary commercial success provided him with the means of transforming Portlaw into a model industrial village inspired by Quaker principles. Various measures for the moral welfare and social improvement of the workforce were introduced. Houses were built which were let at a low rent. David Malcomson set up a school where 'no sectarian animosities, no quarrels about the bible are allowed to prevail'. He also provided a dispensary and, in 1837, appointed a resident doctor. In the following year, a temperance society and savings club were formed. One of the rules of the latter stipulated that if a member had 'brought illness or accident on himself by drunkenness, debauchery, rioting, quarrelling or playing at unlawful games on the Sabbath, they shall direct his allowance money to be suspended'.

This reflected David's aversion to alcohol which he felt contributed to the misery and destitution of the Irish peasantry. Shiel observed that no employee was allowed smoke in the presence of their employer and the strictest morality prevailed, it being a rule to dismiss any girl who was guilty of the slightest impropriety. Another contemporary source pointed out that 'the health, education and morals of this newly created colony have been strictly adhered to by its' patrons'.[5] The Malcomsons also made provision for the recreation of the workers by providing a billiards room, handball court, concert hall and the formation of a brass band.

Fresh water, lighting and shopping facilities were introduced to the village. Since the nearest shop was eight miles away David decided to open a company store which supplied such essentials as clothing and groceries at reasonable prices. With limited banking facilities and the danger and inconvenience of transporting large sums of money to meet the weekly wage bill of almost £1,000, the Malcomsons introduced a system of cardboard tokens, usually referred to as 'leather money'. These tokens which first appeared in 1834 had values of 4d. 1/-, 2/- and 2/6d. They were used to pay the workers and could be exchanged to procure goods in the company shop. It was only by choice that the workers received these tokens, instead of cash. Their use became so widespread that they were even accepted by merchants in Waterford and Clonmel and by farmers and the gentry in the locality. This led to a bitter attack in 1844 by the proprietors of the *Warder* and *Statesman*, two Dublin newspapers, who attacked the Malcomsons for employing 'slaves' who received no money but small tokens to procure goods in the shops of the 'tyrants'. The Malcomsons took an action for libel and received an apology and £500 damages, proving in the process that their goods were cheaper than elsewhere.

In 1826, David Malcomson had built another cotton factory on the Quay in Clonmel, located in the car park between the present Clonmel Arms Hotel and the river. One hundred girls were employed in the

---

[5] Samuel Lewis, *Topographical dictionary of Ireland*, vol. ii (London, 1837), p. 466.

manufacture of calico by hand looms. They worked from 7 a.m. to 8 p.m. in winter and from 6 a.m. to 7 p.m. in summer. They were paid 1/6d. to 6/- per week (average 2/9d.), while superintendents were paid 15 shillings. Two years later, when Shiel visited the mill, he was impressed by the perfect cleanliness (in fact each girl was obliged to wash and comb their hair each morning), the freshness of the air, the whiteness of the walls and the air of cheerfulness that was diffused over the whole assembly. He says of David Malcomson that 'he evidently felt that best of all luxuries, the consciousness of being the creator of felicity'.

David Malcomson was acutely aware that the provision of an efficient network of communications was vital to the expansion of his commercial interests and critical to this end was the maintenance and improved navigation of the Suir. In 1816, when the Waterford Harbour Commissioners Board was established to improve access to the port of Waterford, David Malcomson was one of six nominees of the traders of Clonmel. In 1835, he was the principal speaker at a meeting held in Carrick-on-Suir promoting the River Suir Navigation Company. This organisation aimed at making the river Suir navigable for vessels of 300 tons burden, twice the existing tonnage, trading between Waterford and Carrick. From there the cargo was transported in horse drawn barges to Clonmel. In the course of his address he pointed out that 'the cheaper the freight, the more we can give for the produce'.[6] The company obtained parliamentary powers and a grant of £8,000 and he was elected joint treasurer.

Another priority for the Malcomson firm was to gain control of cross-channel freight charges. Their Portlaw interest was dependent on the importation of large quantities of American raw cotton out of the port of Liverpool and supplies of Welsh coal for the factory's steam engines. David Malcomson joined forces with other Waterford merchants to break the shipping monopoly of Pope Brothers, proprietors of the Waterford Line, who were charging exorbitant rates on freight carried on the Waterford-Liverpool-Bristol routes. He was also acutely aware that the days of the traditional sailing vessel were numbered and that the steamer offered a far more efficient and consistent service. The Malcomsons began by chartering steamers, but later became owners themselves in 1836 when they took a

---

[6] Burke, p. 196.

twenty per cent interest in the newly-formed Waterford Steamship Company and eventually acquired all the share capital.

Central to the Quaker ethos was concern for the injustices and poverty in the wider world around them and they set about applying their resources, time and expertise to alleviating distress and destitution of those in need. David Malcomson showed a lifelong commitment to assisting the poor and the marginalized. In 1800, he was presented with a silver cup by the inhabitants of Lurgan in recognition of his efforts to help the needy people of his native town. In his cotton factories in Clonmel and Portlaw he provided employment for a number of young girls from the Clonmel workhouse and the slums. He said that 'in order to save these little girls from the wretched fate to which their poverty had doomed them, I have snatched them out of garrets and of cellars, and placed them here'. A contemporary wrote of how Mr. Malcomson's extensive concerns gave 'employment to many hundreds who but for him should pine in want'.[7]

He was also active in various organised efforts and institutions which were designed to assist the less fortunate. Following the opening of Clonmel District Asylum in 1835 David Malcomson was appointed as a member of the first board of governors and directors. The following year he was elected chairman of a relief fund set up in Clonmel to provide fuel and straw for the poor. At the inaugural meeting of the Clonmel Mechanics' Institute set up for the education and improvement of the working classes in 1843, David Malcomson became one of its patrons.

He started life in 'slender circumstances, but by reason of his shrewdness and foresight, he was able to take advantage of the opportunities of his time'. His first employer, Sarah Grubb, was astute enough to recognise young Malcomson's ambition and ability. She may have dismissed him but 'she felt he would have left anyway unless his situation became more lucrative, and she acknowledged that she was 'much indebted to his ingenuity'.[8] After his departure from Anner Mills he showed a willingness to apply himself to any form of commercial activity that might be useful and profitable. He was fortunate that his arrival in Clonmel coincided with the milling boom. Here he enjoyed the support of a well-established Quaker community and their highly developed network.

---

[7] *Clonmel Advertiser*, 5 May 1826.
[8] Grubb Collection, Ms Box 44, SGB, 12 (Friends' Historical Library, Dublin).

Business acumen was combined with the Quaker virtues of hard work, thrift, honesty and scrupulous reliability in his trade dealings. He had the vision to appreciate the fragile state of the corn industry and the entrepreneurial spirit to seek an alternative venture. His success at Portlaw was combined with his philanthropic concern for the welfare of the workers.

By the time David retired from business on 1 November 1837 he had amassed a considerable fortune and laid the foundations for an industrial dynasty. Although many Quaker entrepreneurs became extremely wealthy, none of them could remotely match the achievements of the Malcomson family, whose economic activities transcended both county and national boundaries and who, in the course of time, 'built up a multinational, multifaceted empire'.[9] At its peak it included shipbuilding, corn milling, cotton manufacture, salmon fisheries and railway interests, in addition to the ownership of a coalmine in the Ruhr and a tea plantation in Ceylon.

David Malcomson died at his home in Melview on 6 June 1844. He was then in his seventy ninth year. Shortly before his death he received a visit from one of his grand-daughters, Mrs. A. R. Barcroft, who spoke of him as 'an elderly man, very stately in manner, and somewhat of a martinet'. Another impression was of a gentleman-like individual in sober dress. Lalor Shiel, who was a great admirer of his achievements, approved of the practical training he gave to his children. When Shiel saw 'a young man shovelling the flour with his own hands into a large tube, and covered with its particles' in his Suir Island mill, David introduced him as his son with the comment that 'he will teach others, by having first practised his business himself'.

His obituary in *The Tipperary Free Press* was surprisingly brief. It simply stated that:

In the demise of this much respected gentleman the commercial world has lost one of its most enterprising and useful members, and the poor have lost a liberal benefactor, who was never known to turn a listless ear to the application of the distressed.

---

[9] Cormac Ó Gráda, *Ireland. A new economic history 1780-1939* (Oxford, 1994), pp. 278.279.

Chapter 12

An Empire on Wheels

'I shall never forget the ludicrous figure I cut in going into the street saying "buy, buy" to every person I met and, when questioned as to the price, I was unable to reply except by counting on my fingers the number of the pence I wanted'. This was how the sixteen year old print seller, Charles Bianconi, introduced himself to the people of Dublin. Little did anyone realise that one day this bedraggled urchin would revolutionise Irish transport, become the friend of some of the most important people in the land and die a millionaire.

Charles Bianconi, the second of five children, was born on 24 September 1786 in Tregolo in Northern Italy, not far from Lake Como. His father, Pietro, was a farmer, owner of a small silk mill and an agent for an important local family. His grandmother had hoped Charles would become a priest but he was, in his own words, a very wild boy and not given to study. When he left school at fourteen his father had him apprenticed to Andrea Faroni, an itinerant dealer in prints, barometers and spy-glasses. There are various opinions as to what prompted this course of action. Some say that it was to enable him escape conscription. Others maintain it was because Charles had fallen in love with a young woman who was promised to another, so family honour demanded that the relationship be ended.

In July 1802, Bianconi was one of four boys, between the ages of fifteen and eighteen, who set off for England under the care of Signor Faroni. Travelling on foot, they crossed the St. Bernard Pass into Switzerland. There was obviously a change of plan, for several months later the little group found themselves in Dublin. Faroni set them to work making small leaden frames for his stock of cheap prints which contained scriptural pictures, portraits of the British royal family, and of Napoleon and his generals. As Bianconi learned a little English, he was sent out from Dublin every Monday morning with fourpence in his pocket and with strict instructions to be back in the city by the following Saturday night. For the next eighteen months this young, friendless foreigner, with his few words of English, humped his heavy pack of prints through the countryside.

He was soon to discover that the roads of Ireland could be fraught with danger. Following the 1798 rebellion and with England embroiled with the armies of Napoleon, Ireland was in a state of political turmoil. At Passage, outside Waterford, he was arrested by the order of a magistrate for selling Bonaparte's effigy. He later recalled that he was kept perishing all night in a guardroom without fire or bedclothes, but the next morning was let go. On another occasion, when he was plying his wares, Fr. Matthew, the Apostle of Temperance, rescued him from the hands of local bullies in the streets of Thurles. As a result, the two men became firm friends.

The young Bianconi could not have found a better testing ground to develop his entrepreneurial skills than the little villages and towns of Ireland. He became a familiar caller at the homes of the landed gentry throughout the country where the handsome 'curly-headed Italian boy', with his charm and cheerful manner, helped to loosen the purse strings. After eighteen months, his apprenticeship had been completed and Faroni offered to take him back to his father, but Bianconi felt it was too soon, for he had not yet made his fortune. 'My pride was so mortified that I declined his offer. Faroni gave me back my purse with its entire contents, about one hundred louis d'or which seemed to me then to be a very great sum'.

He invested some of his money in prints and went into business for himself. The hardships of hawking made him realise 'the great difference between the pedlar doomed to tramp on foot' and 'his more fortunate fellow, who could post or ride on horseback'. He soon decided to abandon his career as a pedlar and, in 1806 he set up shop in Carrick-on-Suir as a carver and gilder. Shortly afterwards, he moved his business to Waterford, where he got to know Edmund Rice, a man who was to have a profound influence on his life. Under his guidance Bianconi was encouraged to resume his studies. The young man who once said of himself that learning took as little effect on him as pouring water on a duck's back now became a keen student. Bianconi was not one to forget a kindness and later, when the Christian Brothers were struggling to establish their schools, he proved himself a generous benefactor to their founder, Edmund Rice.

Bianconi arrived in Clonmel in 1808. His first small shop was in

Dublin Street but he soon switched to a larger premises at 1 Johnson Street, opposite the Main Guard, where the exotic-looking Italian with the funny sounding name became known to the locals as 'Brian Cooney'. With his flair for self-promotion, he lost no time in making his premises a focus of local interest. He ordered a large mirror from London which he placed in the front window. Besides startling the passing horses, it caused an old lady to faint. Seeing herself for the first time in a mirror was obviously too much for her. He took on four skilled employees and set about making picture frames and looking glasses which he sold throughout the countryside from his eye-catching, yellow gig.

His experiences tramping the roads of Ireland had convinced him of the need for an efficient transport system. In later years he said that 'his cars grew out of his shoulders'. The end of the Napoleonic Wars provided him with an ideal opportunity when the market was flooded with a supply of cheap army horses. He invested £10 in a horse and jaunting car and on the 6 July 1815 the first Bianconi car ran from Clonmel to Cahir and back. It registered an average speed of seven and a half miles per hour and carried six passengers at a fare of 2d. per mile. In later life he was asked why he selected this route for his first venture. His answer was that with one horse and cart at his disposal Cahir was the ideal distance for a horse to make a return journey in one day.

People were reluctant to use the service at first, preferring to walk, but Bianconi devised a clever scheme to catch the public's attention. He secretly bought 'a yellow horse', as he called him, and a second car which he set up in competition with the first one, a contest which he realised would arouse the sporting instincts of the public. Soon cheering crowds lined the roadside and wagers were placed on the outcome.

One evening his own driver rushed into his office and exclaimed in a state of great pride and excitement, 'You know the great big yallah horse under the opposition car. Well, sir, he'll never run another yard. I'm after breaking his heart this night. I raced him in from beyond Moores of Barne, and he'll never travel again'.[1] Bianconi was obliged to express his delight at the loss of the beast. The opposition car had

---

[1] M. O'Connell and S. J. Watson, *Bianconi. King of the Irish Roads,* (Dublin, 1962), p. 58.

served its purpose and by now the people had become aware of the advantages of Bianconi's service. Success was assured and, by the end of the year, further routes had been opened, and it was not long before he closed his shop in Clonmel to concentrate on his coach business.

The cars, which became affectionately known as 'bians', were very distinctive and attractive in appearance. They were painted in crimson and yellow with the names of the towns en route shown on the back in gold letters. The horses, which were uniform in size to facilitate a fast change, had a silver plated harness engraved with the initial 'B'. Just as he prided himself on buying the best horses, he used nothing but the finest of materials in the construction of his coaches. He eventually opened three car factories, one at his chief depot in Clonmel, another in Sligo and a third in Galway. His workshops in Clonmel employed over a hundred people, including carpenters, harness makers, painters, wheelwrights and many other skilled craftsmen.

The first car was a modest affair, but as his business grew so did the size of the cars. To accommodate the increase in passengers Bianconi introduced his famous four wheeled vehicles which became known as 'The Long Car'. Officially called the Finn Mac Cool, this colossus could accommodate twenty passengers. Their departure was a cause of considerable excitement to onlookers. The scene was one of hustle and bustle with porters carrying trunks and baggage, horses being harnessed and placed in position, the driver arriving with an assortment of rugs and capes, accompanied by a boy carrying the whips. With everything in readiness, the reins were handed to the driver by the groom. Finally, with the horses rearing in anticipation, following a blast on the horn the coach departed to the applause of the onlookers.

Bianconi kept a close eye on things, and it was said that he knew every man and horse who worked for him, and that no matter where he was, or who he was with, he would always keep an ear open for the toot of a distant horn and then pull out his watch to make sure his coaches were running on time. It was the regularity of his services that won for him the contracts for carrying mails. In 1833 when the Post Office decided to deal directly with coach owners, he paid a visit to London to secure an official contract from the British Post Office for carrying mails in Ireland. His command of English was inadequate to explain the design of his cars, so he wrote home to a son of an artist friend, Michael

Angelo Hayes, who supplied drawings of each vehicle. Some years ago, An Post featured two of these illustrations on their Bianconi Commemorative stamps.

His employees were well paid in relation to the standard of living of the time. Daniel Hearn, his chief agent, received a salary of £120 a year. As an employer Bianconi was strict but fair. He demanded that his workers be punctual, truthful and sober. If they were found to be dishonest or caught drunk on duty, they were instantly dismissed. He supplied each of his drivers with a watch to ensure punctuality. They were not allowed to carry any letters apart from the official mail, for as Bianconi said:

> I do so because if I do not respect other institutions like the post office, my men would soon learn not to respect my own. Then, for carrying letters during the extent of their trip, the men probably would not get money but drink, and hence, become dissipated and unworthy of confidence.[2]

The wives of his grooms were forbidden to keep hens, in case they were tempted to feed them with the oats provided for the horses. Each agent was responsible for the daily food ration for each horse. If this was exceeded, the agent in question had to pay for it, but it also ensured that each horse got his proper rations.

Agents were entrusted with the task of preparing a way bill at the start of each trip. This showed the names of drivers, names of passengers and fares paid, the towns passed through and the hours of arrival and departure. Bianconi would personally check each return. His diligence was such that he often remarked that he had no time to read anything but waybills, a comment which provoked Cardinal Newman's barb when he heard that Bianconi had been promoted a trustee of the Catholic University: 'a gentleman well read in waybills I presume'.

Despite travelling over rough roads and exposure to the elements, every effort was made to improve the comfort of the passengers. In wet weather, oil cloths were provided which could be pulled up to the chin, wooden slats were placed under the cushions to help drain off the water, while it was company policy to ensure that no

---

[2] Ibid, p. 63.

138

militia and yeomen. A drive for recruits was launched in the Clonmel area by Lord Donoughmore. In Edmond Power he found a willing tool, a victim of vanity goaded by greed. Power was appointed a magistrate and given command of a company of dragoons which he employed to terrorise the countryside.

Power's behaviour at home was no less obnoxious, where as a drunken host he presided over scenes of continuous revelry. One of the local army officers to enjoy this hospitality was Maurice St. Leger Farmer, a wealthy landowner from Kildare. Farmer began to take an interest in Margaret, who by this time had blossomed into a most attractive young woman. Power, whose lifestyle, not surprisingly, found him in straitened circumstances, realised all too well the financial and social benefits such an alliance might bring. Neither Margaret nor her browbeaten mother was in a position to object. So, with callous indifference, he sold his fifteen year old daughter into marriage and, on 7 March 1804 in St. Mary's Protestant Church, Clonmel, Margaret Power became Mrs. Margaret Farmer.

Margaret's marriage was doomed from the beginning. Farmer was subject to violent fits of insanity and for three months he brutally mistreated her. What sufferings she endured at the hands of her sadistic husband can scarcely be imagined. In the words of her biographer, from that time, although she grew in loveliness, she never provoked real passion nor sought to encourage it, because her sexual sensibility was dead. She was not yet sixteen.[1]

When her husband was transferred to the Curragh she refused to accompany him and returned home to Suir Island, where she became the chief victim of her father's drunken rages, who irrationally blamed her for his many difficulties. In 1800, Edmund Power had taken over a local newspaper called *The Clonmel Gazette* which he converted into an organ of propaganda for his patron, Lord Donoughmore. An article was published attacking Donoughmore's political rival, John Bagwell. A libel action followed at the Clonmel Assizes on 11 August 1804 and Power was left to pay damages which further impoverished him. Three years later, on one his rebel raids, Power shot and killed an innocent boy. Although acquitted of murder, he was relieved of his office of magistrate. When he was deserted by his lordship, who now found him

---

[1] Michael Sadleir, *Blessington D'Orsay: a masquerade (London, 1933)*, p.10.

145

an embarrassment, his ruination was complete. In his own warped way he felt that all his troubles had started with the departure of the wealthy Farmer for which he held Margaret responsible.

Accompanied by her sister Ellen, she sought refuge with various relations in Cahir and Fethard. It was during this time that she made the acquaintance of another army officer, an Englishman, by the name of Captain Thomas Jenkins. Captivated by her beauty and feeling sorry for her because of her unhappy home life, he invited her to come away with him. It is thought that Margaret spent the next two years in Dublin with the amiable Jenkins before settling down with him on his estates in Hampshire. While there she enjoyed the hospitality of his house and the stimulation of his library. Five years later she emerged a well read and very cultured young lady.

During this time she renewed her acquaintance with the Hon. Charles Gardiner, Viscount Mountjoy, who paid a visit to Jenkins' house. When the Viscount had been based in Clonmel as Lieut. Col. of the Tyrone Militia, he had been an occasional caller to her home on Suir Island. He was a man of considerable wealth, having an annual income of £30,000 and enormous estates in Omagh, covering an area of fifty square miles. In addition to this, he was the owner of a palatial residence in London and considerable properties in Mountjoy Square and Gardiner Street in Dublin.

Enchanted by Margaret's beauty, the Viscount became a frequent caller to Jenkins' house. On 12 January 1816, he was created Earl of Blessington and shortly afterwards made Jenkins an unusual proposition. In return for £10,000 he would take Margaret under his protection. Jenkins willingly obliged and the Earl promptly installed her in his London mansion. Any misgivings on her part were softened by the prospect of a life of unrivalled luxury with the indulgent Earl. For the second time in her life she had been sold for money. On the first occasion, she was little more than an innocent child but she was now an accomplished lady, and a fitting social companion for her new benefactor.

As the Viscount set about initiating divorce proceedings to secure Margaret's release from Farmer, a lucky accident helped facilitate matters. Soon after she left him, Farmer had drawn his sword on a superior officer and was forced to resign his commission. He had gone for India, but by now had returned to England where he wound up in the King's Bench Prison for debt. Security was lax enough to allow him to get drunk and fall through a window to his death on the streets below. With this marital obstacle removed, the daughter of Edmund Power of Clonmel became the first and last Countess of Blessington at Bryanston Square Church, London on 16 February 1818. For the next eleven years she was to live a life of unrestrained extravagance with the volatile, erratic and eccentric earl whose means allowed him to live a life of gross self-indulgence.

The Viscount kept the wedding as quiet as possible and then left for Dublin with his bride. With his flair for the theatrical, he planned a spectacular introduction for her in the capital. He brought Marguerite, as she was now known, to his mansion in Henrietta Street. Having had the house decorated from top to bottom, he sent out invitations to what his unsuspecting guests thought was to be a dinner party. When they were all gathered, to their utter amazement, the groom entered with his wife in full bridal attire. The pair spent subsequently their honeymoon in a residence known as 'The Cottage' on the Mountjoy estate in County Tyrone. Quickly tiring of their Tyrone retreat, the newly weds returned to their London residence in St. James's Square.

Marguerite's efforts to establish herself in society were met by rejection from those who were disgusted by her lack of pedigree and outraged by her sexual behaviour. The fact that an Irish commoner:

> by means unknown but certainly sinister, had snatched a titled and wealthy husband from under the very noses of match-making mammas, should now presume to act the smart London hostess, was an outrage to morals and to society'.[2]

In other respects, Lady Blessington was detested by her competitors for being more beautiful, more intelligent and far more congenial company.

It was not long however, before her lavish entertainments at St. James's Square gave Blessington parties a special reputation of their own and invitations were eagerly sought. Among the celebrities who attended over the years were the Irish poet, Thomas Moore, the novelists Dickens and Thackeray, and the artist Sir Thomas Laurence, who

---

[2] *Ibid*, p. 26.

painted Marguerite's portrait. These soirees also attracted the noted American poet, Longfellow, and the famous Hans Christen Anderson. The world of politics was represented by such notables as Wellington, Disraeli and Prince Louis Napoleon.

The proceedings were presided over by 'the most gorgeous Lady Blessington', a compliment conferred on her by the famous classical scholar, Doctor Parr. Her husband was content to glory in watching her captivate the famous and win the admiration of the clever. She had all the qualities of the successful hostess. She was gifted with a good speaking voice with which she enthralled her listeners. In the opinion of Mrs. Newton Crossland, she told a good story capitally, and was the best raconteuse she had ever met. Being well read, she was able to hold her own with the distinguished company that sat at her table and possessed the ability to evaluate the merit of any literary work presented to her. Always careful not to dominate, she encouraged her most timid guests to contribute towards the proceedings. With a tact unsurpassed:

> she contrived to draw out even the most modest tyro from his shell of reserve, and, by appearing to take an interest in his opinion, gave him the courage to express it. All her visitors seem, by some hidden influence, to find their level, yet they leave her house satisfied with themselves.[3]

Her beauty was beyond question:

> Her dazzling clear complexion, dark hair, and rich dark eyebrows and lashes, delicate features ever radiant with the warm light of her mirthful nature, small mouth and thin pink lips curling with playful irony, small white hands, tiny feet, and incomparable shape, were the theme of universal admiration.[4]

Possessing a superb dress sense, she was at all times conscious of the devastating effect she had on the opposite sex. A contemporary, William Archer Shee, wrote:

---

[3] *Ibid*, p. 382.
[4] *Ibid*, p. 385.

Lady Blessington is conspicious for her dress, which is always in excellent taste, and, though it may be sometimes more elaborate than is necessary in a circle generally composed of men, it is always adapted to set off the attractions, and soften the exuberance, of a figure where the only defect is the embonpoint, the effect of which, however, she knows how to mitigate with much skill.[5]

Around this time a French nobleman, Count Albert d'Orsay, who was destined to become a life-long friend of Lady Blessington, arrived on the scene. He was the son of General Count d'Orsay and Anne, daughter of the Duke of Wurtenburg. A man of independent means, his distinguished appearance and easy manners allowed him to assume the role of society dandy. His relationship with Lady Blessington provoked much comment. It has been said that the pair fell in love and that her husband assumed the role of complacent dupe, but the general feeling is that they were never more than friends.

In August 1822 the Blessingtons, accompanied by Ann Power, Marguerite's sister and Count d'Orsay set out on a continental tour which was to last for six years. They sojourned in all the fashionable resorts of France and Italy. Paris, Nice, Naples, Florence, Pisa and many other enticing spots formed part of their itinerary. Their progress through the continent resembled an army on the march with its cavalcade of carriages filled with mattresses, pillows, writing desks and countless accessories. This was constantly being augmented en route by the purchase of books, paintings, statues and anything else that caught their fancy.

The pièce de résistance was her ladyship's double springed sleeping carriage, with its soft cushions and eiderdown pillows. It included a bookcase, a canteen of plate and glass and innumerable other comforts. In addition to this, a formidable retinue of servants pandered to them. The magnitude and extravagance of it all caused one wag to dub it 'The Blessington Circus'. It must be said that Lady Blessington was not adverse to such ostentation, but she did have a discerning eye when it

---

[5] *Ibid*, p. 381.

came to quality. 'Her taste in everything was towards the gay, the superb, the luxurious; but, on the whole, excellently good'.[6]

Her every whim was gratified. On one occasion Lord Blessington heard his wife admire the coach of Lady Burghersh as it drove through the streets of Florence. He promptly sent instructions to England and ordered a replica shipped to Genoa. They later took over a mansion outside Paris called the Hotel Ney, named after one of Napoleon's generals. The cost of its refurbishment was such that all previous extravagance paled into insignificance. Some idea of the opulence and luxury with which they surrounded themselves can be gleaned from a description of her ladyship's bed:

> which is silvered, instead of gilt, rests on the back of two large silver swans, so exquisitely sculptured that every feather is in alto-relievo, and looks nearly as fleecy as those of the living bird. The recess in which it is placed is lined with white fluted silk, bordered with blue embossed lace; and from the columns that support the frieze of the recess, pale blue silk curtains, lined with white, are hung, which, when drawn, conceal the recess altogether.[7]

The ladies passed the time sightseeing, reading, writing, and drawing. For exercise the men went horse riding, walked, swam and fenced. In the evening, they held dances or organised literary gatherings. Perhaps, one of the most memorable events of these years occurred in Genoa, where Lady Blessington made the acquaintance of the notorious Lord Byron. She had been intrigued by his brilliance and debauchery but her first impression was one of disappointment. Pale and slight in stature she felt he 'did not match the Promethean figure of her imagination'. However, she would have been favourably disposed to any person who had suffered rejection, as she herself had, at the hands of English society. She was later to record her recollections of the bard in one of her most successful books entitled *Conversations of Lord Byron with the Countess of Blessington*.

In Byron's letters there are several references to her intellectual abilities and he was sufficiently impressed by her beauty to dedicate a

---

[6] *Ibid*, p. 383.
[7] *Ibid*, p. 127.

poem to her:

I pray thee, lady turn these leaves
And gaze upon the face
Whose lineaments no artist's skill,
Methinks, could truly trace.
The outline knows art's fine control
There are no colours for the soul.

If I can read that face aright,
'Tis something more than fair:
Ah! not alone the lovely face,
The lovely heart is there.
The smile that seems to light and win,
Speaks of the deeper world within.

Hatred, and toil, and bitterness,
And envyings, and wrath,
Masked, each in some fair disguise,
Are round the human path.
May every evil thou hast shown
Be safely guarded from thine own.

In spite of his self-indulgence the Earl of Blessington was not a man totally without principle. In April 1829, he was requested to attend the House of Lords to support The Duke of Wellington's Catholic Emancipation Bill. Although in ill health, he refused to send a proxy. He duly presented himself, recorded his vote and returned to Paris. The following month, riding his horse up the Champs Elysees, he was struck with an attack of apoplexy and died two days later on 25 May 1829.

After his burial in the family tomb in St. Thomas's Church, Dublin, the most glamorous chapter in Lady Blessington's life was over. She no longer had the earl's unlimited resources at her disposal. From now on she would have to live within a fixed income. Her life of luxury had drawn to a close. Under the terms of her late husband's will she was to receive £2,000 a year, in addition to the unexpired portion of the lease of the house in St. James's Square. Though more than ample to maintain her comfortably it was totally inadequate to keep her in the style to which she had become accustomed. Why he had been so niggardly in his bequest to her must remain a mystery, and Lady Blessington herself was not forthcoming on the matter.

Worse was to follow. The Earl's family held nothing but contempt for the upstart Lady Blessington and when the opportunity presented itself to harm her they seized it with relish. Charles, the late Earl's illegitimate son, decided to contest his father's will and they gave him their full support. Although the final outcome favoured neither party, it involved Lady Blessington in long and costly litigation.

Lady Blessington sold her interest in the house in St. James's and took a lease of another property in Seymore Place where she went to live, together with her two nieces, d'Orsay and his wife. Her presence in the capital added spice to the gossip columns of the London periodicals which hinted at an illicit relationship between herself and d'Orsay. In spite of this and regardless of her straitened circumstances, she mounted a brave and brilliant challenge to regain the social leadership of London. Her dinners were glittering occasions with exquisite food served by her green and gold liveried staff, and the atmosphere was enlivened by the stimulating conversation of the various notables, including Charles Bianconi who, when in London, always paid her a visit. The expense of entertaining on such a lavish scale made it increasingly necessary for her to raise money from other sources.

To help solve her financial problems she turned, or rather returned, to writing. In 1822 she had published a collection of four essays entitled *The Magic Lantern or Sketches of Scenes in the Metropolis*. They described in a simple and unaffected way a public auction, a visit to an Egyptian tomb, a walk in Hyde Park and an evening at the Italian Opera. The demands imposed by her literary career her left her with less time to devote to other pursuits. Her appearances in public were now reserved for outings to the theatre and the opera and her famous green carriage was rarely to be seen in Hyde Park.

Her first literary efforts, as has been stated, were contributions to various magazines. In 1832 her *Conversations with Byron* began to appear in serialised form in the *New Monthly*. Biographers of the poet have expressed their indebtedness to this work. The following year, *The*

152

Repealers, the first of a dozen novels she was to write, was published. Her books 'distinguished by delicacy of sentiment' gave them a certain current popularity, but they lacked the quality to endure. Lady Wilde found that 'there was such a total want of elevation of feeling or depth of thought in her works that it was impossible to read them with profit or remember them with interest'.[8]

Constant financial pressure forced Lady Blessington to write at speed and to pander to public taste. Six hundred of the nine hundred and eighty pages of *The Repealers* were completed in four weeks. She admitted herself that 'they are written on the everyday business of life without once entering the region of imagination. I wrote because I wanted money, and was obliged to select subjects that would command it'. Her books were based on her own experiences and were firmly rooted in the world she knew so well. They depict the jealousies and affectations of English society and her characters are no more than thinly veiled portraits of people who inhabited it.

She also left behind her an extensive correspondence which shows 'the implicit trust that was put in her judgement and integrity by the most eminent men of her time in politics, literature and art'. They seemed 'to have had entire confidence in her honour, discretion, and common sense and kindness of heart' and consequently 'they communicated with her with the utmost freedom, and evidently with a firm conviction that their confidence would never be abused'.[9]

In 1835, when her lease of Seymore Place had expired, she moved to Gore House, Kensington. Its secluded, rural setting enabled her to concentrate on her writing. *Victims of Society* which appeared in 1837, traces the story of an innocent young girl who is driven to death by the malicious slander of fashionable society. Crabb Robinson maintained that the book expressed Lady Blessington's anger at the women who rejected her. In 1839 *The Governess* appeared, which many consider to be her best work. It tells the story of an orphan girl who is sacrificed to feed the vanity of an ageing society queen. She departs from her usual theme of charting the vanities of society and focuses attention on the plight of the underprivileged. A further five novels

---

[8] *Ibid*, p. 386.
[9] R. R. Madden, *The literary life and correspondence of the Countess of Blessington*, ii (London, 1855), p. 1.

were to follow, none of which made any impact.

She also became the editor of *The Book of Beauty* and *The Keepsake*, two of the many annuals which very popular at the time. These productions, which had a certain snobbish appeal, were lavishly presented in watered silk, velvet or Moroccan leather. They were filled with contributions by well-known literary figures and contained engravings by established artists. Although her publications were considered of a higher standard than those of her competitors, the pressure of meeting deadlines and getting suitable contributions imposed an intolerable strain on her health. Ironically, it was to this style of writing that her talents were ideally suited. She had a gift for the trivia and titbits of gossip which the public find fascinating, qualities which would have made her an invaluable asset to today's tabloids and celebrity magazines.

The last of her works to win popular appeal were two travel books based on her journals. In *The Idler in Italy* and *The Idler in France* she drew on her continental experiences. Although she continued to write 'she had exhausted her meagre vein of fictional originality' and all that remained was the 'listless re-handling of material already used'.[10] *The Cambridge Guide to English Literature* dismissively states that 'her novels are not likely to be read again'.

In spite of all her difficulties she was exceptionally generous to others, constantly making use of her connections to gain favours for friends who were down on their luck. Mrs. S. C. Hall said, 'she never lost an opportunity of doing a gracious act or saying a gracious word'. As a result of her troubles with her late husband's family, her brother, Robert Power, lost his position as agent for the Tyrone estates. Not alone did she send him financial assistance, but she took in his two daughters and her sister, Mary Ann. One of her maids, writing after her death, spoke of her 'great many charities'. These included helping impoverished, literary people, musicians, and old servants. One young writer to benefit from her generosity was the struggling Charles Dickens. Apart from being quick to spot his talent, it was she who helped him to become established.

Her finances were delicately balanced and as long as nothing untoward occurred she could survive. However, a series of calamities

---

[10] Sadleir, p. 278.

ended in her ruination. As the forties progressed the earning power of her writings diminished, and even the annuals lost their popularity. *The Book of Beauty* went into liquidation leaving £700 owing to her. Her income from the Blessington Estates in Ireland was seriously curtailed by the Famine. Debts mounted and creditors grew impatient. Bailiffs stalked the grounds of Gore House awaiting their opportunity to gain entry. One debt to a silk merchant for shawls and jewellery reached the enormous sum of £4,000. She was forced to sell her jewellery, but it was not enough.

Finally, she offered Gore House and its entire contents for sale and, in the middle of April 1849, left for Paris where she rented a moderately sized residence. On June 4 that year she died, aged sixty, with her two nieces and d'Orsay at her side. She was buried in the cemetery of Cambourcy on the outskirts of Paris overlooking the Seine. Her tomb consists of a granite pyramid, faced with a little porched doorway. Three years later Count Alfred d'Orsay, the man known as 'The Last of the Dandies', was laid to rest by her side.

Lady Blessington's life was as remarkable as it was controversial. She was sometimes condemned her because of the scandal and notoriety that surrounded her, yet she won the admiration of some of the most famous men of her day. Considered by Charles Grenville to be 'ignorant, vulgar and commonplace', Lady Longford, however, regarded her as being 'the most cultured, intelligent and most famous literary hostess of the period'. There can be little doubt that her great beauty and charming personality enabled Sally Power, the daughter of a lowly Clonmel merchant, to rise from her obscure beginnings and become one of the queens of London society. That was the extraordinary achievement of this very remarkable woman.

Chapter 14

The Bagwells of Marlfield

Canon Burke in his *History of Clonmel* stated that the origin of the Bagwell family previous to the 1730s is, like the source of the Amazon, obscure. However research carried out on behalf of the family suggests that John Bagwell[1], a captain in Cromwell's army, was the first member of the family to come to Ireland. His son, William, settled at Ballylaffin, north of Ardfinnan[2]. His grandson, another John, married the daughter of a Presbyterian clergyman from Dublin named Shaw and became a successful banker in Clonmel.

John's success led to his appointment as an agent for the banking houses of La Touche and Keane of Dublin, and for Harper and Armstead of Cork. His extensive land purchases in the County of Tipperary marked the entry of the Bagwells into the ranks of the landed class. In 1726, he bought the burgagery lands of Clonmel for £12,000. Three years later he secured 900 acres of the ancestral lands of the bankrupt Lord Dunboyne at Ballydoyle, Ballyduff and Lough Kent Upper and Lower for £5,592. In 1733, he expended a further £13,500 on 1,500 acres of lands at Kilmore, Cahirclogh, Redmondstown and Lisronagh, the estate of John Slattery, a Catholic lawyer and agent of Lord Cahir.

Bagwell was a committed Presbyterian. He was one of the trustees of the Clonmel Presbyterian community and, in 1747, made a contribution of £140 to building a residence for the local minister in the present Mitchel Street.[3] In 1733 The Incorporated Society for the Promotion of Protestant Schools in Ireland was set up to provide a network of schools where the children of poor Roman Catholics would be brought up in the Protestant faith. Bagwell collected subscriptions for the Society, and the opening of

---

[1] see Appendix 2, p. 335.

[2] Documents in the hands of the author.

[3] David Butler, 'Presbyterianism in Clonmel, 1650-1977' in *Tipperary Historical Journal*, xvi, (2003), p. 86.

the Charter School in Clonmel in 1748 was mainly due to his efforts.[4] The deserted school building at Silver Springs, which later became home to Charles Bianconi, is one of the town's most striking landmarks.

When John Bagwell died in 1754, he left a substantial estate of 2,730 acres reputed to yield £20,000 a year. He conducted his banking business in what was described as a slate house on the Quay, purchased in 1720 from Robert Marshall. The business passed to his son-in-law William Riall, and continued to be operated by two further generations of the Riall family, until it went bankrupt in 1820. In the same year it was sold to The Provincial Bank and in recent times the building formed part of the Clonmel Arms Hotel.

John Bagwell had two sons, John and William. He set John up as a country gentleman at Kilmore whose son, also called John, gained notoriety through his involvement in the trial of Father Sheehy. His other son, William (1728-1756), married Anne, daughter of John Harper of Cork, partner in the banking firm of Harper and Armstead. He received the burgagery lands his father purchased, as well as inheriting the Harper estate at Cobh, county Cork. He stood as an independent member for the borough of Clonmel in 1755 but was narrowly defeated by Guy Moore. He contested the result and, following a petition, secured the seat, but he did not live long to enjoy the fruits of his success, dying the following year.

William had one son, John (1751-1816), later known as Colonel John Bagwell, who was brought up by the Harpers in Cork. He entered Oxford University at the age of sixteen, graduating in 1771 with an M.A. degree. Three years later he married Margaret Hare, sister of the first Earl of Listowel, by whom he had three sons and four daughters. Although he gave an annual contribution of £16 for the maintenance of the local Presbyterian minister[5], he later found the Presbyterianism of his ancestors 'an obstacle to his social progress', so he changed his allegiance to the Church of Ireland. In 1775, he contested the parliamentary election for Cork city but was unsuccessful. Shortly afterwards he returned to Tipperary, and in 1781 purchased the lands of the bankrupt Stephen Moore

---

[4] Michael Ahern, 'Clonmel Charter School' in *Tipperary Historical Journal*, v, (1992), pp. 148-152.
[5] *Clonmel Chronicle*, 22 September 1877.

of Marlfield. This included an estate of some four hundred acres on which he built a mansion at a cost of £13,000. He also took over Moore's corn and rape business and made considerable money during the Napoleonic War, producing bread and biscuits.

It was said that Colonel Bagwell 'from his prepossessing appearance and urbanity of manner commanded great respect'. He also enjoyed a considerable reputation for personal valour. Described as a man who 'stood fire', he fought at least three duels.[6] When war with France appeared imminent, the formation of the Tipperary militia on 25 April 1793 gave him an outlet for his bellicose tendencies. He was appointed colonel and commanding officer through the influence of the then Lord Lieutenant, Lord Cumberland, who had been an old friend and school fellow of Colonel Bagwell.

When Toulon was attacked by British forces during the Napoleonic war, it was generally believed by the common people that Bagwell was to be tried for treason. Great quantities of flour bags marked 'John Bagwell, Marlfield Mills' were reputedly found in the town and he was accused of supplying the enemy. The combination of Bagwell's militia and milling activities led to the local wags dubbing him 'Marshal Sacks' and his son 'the Flour of Tipperary'. During the Rebellion of 1798, Bagwell fully approved of the harsh methods being employed to crush the rebels. He wrote to the notorious Judkin Fitzgerald, Sheriff of Tipperary, telling him 'that if any good be found to come from floggings he might go on with it but let it not reach my ears', a remark which reflects little credit on him.

He contested three elections for the county of Tipperary and was each time returned to parliament where he adopted an independent position. In the course of the Union debates he changed sides twice before finally voting for its acceptance. It appears that his decision was one of expediency rather than conviction, as in parliament 'Bagwell seemed always to have been motivated by personal gain and political advantage'. This assessment is borne out by the patronage he later demanded for his support of Pitt, the British prime-minister. This enabled him to ensure that his son, William, succeeded him as colonel of the Tipperary Militia, while he obtained the

---

[6] James Kelly, *That Damn'd Thing Called Honour. Duelling in Ireland, 1570-1860,* (Cork, 1995), pp. 143, 146.

Deanery of Clogher for another son, Richard, MP for Cashel. In 1801, he applied unsuccessfully to Dublin Castle seeking further preferment for Richard, who was to remain at Clogher until his death twenty years later. It would appear that Bagwell did not endear himself to the powers that be, for it was said that he was not thought 'proper' for an Irish peerage.

In 1800, Colonel John Bagwell purchased the town of Clonmel from the trustees of the Earl of Ormond. It gave the Bagwell family absolute control over the political affairs of the borough and up to the passage of the Municipal Reform Act of 1832 they returned a member of parliament unopposed for Clonmel. Their dominance was highlighted by the report of the commission set up by the government to enquire into the existing state of municipal corporations in Ireland which was published in 1835. It described the Bagwell family as 'patrons of the borough' which meant 'that their recommendations and wishes were always attended to in the appointment of mayor, burgesses and other officers' and 'in the return of Members of Parliament for the borough'.

Like their predecessors, the Moores, they had sufficient influence to procure the admission of any number of freemen they pleased. As the new owner of Clonmel, John Bagwell lost no time in consolidating his position and immediately set about unseating the Moore representation on the Clonmel Corporation and replacing them by freemen of his own choosing. In 1801, John Bagwell was elected both as M. P. and Mayor of Clonmel and was to serve in the latter position on three further occasions. In 1812, he was described by Wakefield as 'proprietor of the whole town of Clonmel, together with an immense estate in the neighbourhood'[7] from which he received an annual income of £18,000.

When Colonel John Bagwell died, his eldest son, William Bagwell (1775-1826), succeeded to his personal fortune and estates. He was educated at Westminster and in Germany. Like his father, he opposed the union but in February he had joined him in deserting to the government camp in time to benefit from the rewards of his change of mind.[8] In 1805

---

[7] Edward Wakefield, *An Account of Ireland, Statistical and Political,* i, (London, 1912), p.276.
[8] Edith Mary Johnson Liik, *History of the Irish Parliament 1692-1800,* v, (Belfast, 2002), p. 129.

he took over command of the Tipperary Militia when his father relinquished the post. In addition he became a Privy Councillor and Joint Muster Master General of his majesty's forces in Ireland for which he received an annual salary of £4,007. He also served as governor of County Tipperary and mayor of Clonmel and sat in parliament for 29 years. From 1798 to 1800 he was a member of parliament for Rathcormack in Co. Cork, and represented Clonmel in a similar capacity from 1801 to 1819. In that year, a by-election led to William being returned unopposed as a member of parliament for the county. He continued to serve until the dissolution of parliament in May 1826, ill health preventing him from contesting the next election.

William was regarded as a good landlord, a gentleman of honour and integrity whose word was his bond. He disposed of the family's milling interests during the economic slump that followed the Napoleonic war. In 1817, John Stein and Company converted the Marlfield corn mill into a distillery. Later, in the 1850s, it was sold to the Jamesons but closed a few years later.

His architectural legacy can still be seen in Marlfield. In 1819, William built St. Patrick's Chapel on the site of the former Cistercian Abbey, overlooking the river Suir. Subsequently, his daughter-in-law, Fanny Bagwell, laid out the church avenue and had the sexton's lodge built. Later still, Richard and Harriette Bagwell made further improvements to this picturesque building. She recorded how:

> An open roof was put into the church, and stone mullions replaced the old wooden ones in the windows. I collected money for the American organ, and to re-pew and wainscot the church. This was done with orham, an Australian wood. We made other minor improvements.[9]

The most attractive feature was the incorporation of a stone door-case from the thirteenth Cistercian abbey of Inishlounaght which occupied the same site.

---

[9] Memoir of Harriette Bagwell in possession of the author. Unpaginated and undated.

William was also responsible for building Inislounaght House which he erected as a residence for his heir in waiting. He is perhaps best remembered for the construction of the dry, stone Martello tower to celebrate the defeat of Napoleon on Mount O'Neill, the highest point in Kilnamac Wood. Unfortunately, the difficulty of quarrying sufficient building materials led to his abandoning the project. As a result, it was dubbed 'Bagwell's Folly'. The incomplete tower was ten metres in diameter and one metre in height and bore the following inscription:

> Erected by the Right Hon. William Bagwell
> In the year of our Lord 1814
> And of the return of peace to Europe
> By the overthrow of the Tyrant
> Napoleon Bonaparte.[10]

John Bagwell (1811-1883) was the son of the Dean of Clogher. In 1826 he inherited the family estates from his unmarried uncle, William Bagwell. They covered an area of some 5,157 acres with lands in counties Tipperary (3,519), Cork (509), Waterford (778) and Galway (351).[11] In addition, he was by far the biggest property owner in the borough of Clonmel.[12] In 1832 he married the Hon. Frances Eliza Prittie, daughter of the 3rd Baron Dunalley. Coming from a family that for three generations had been involved in politics, John Bagwell sought a seat in the House of Commons as a member of parliament for Clonmel.

His ambitions were thwarted by the reform act of 1832 which radically altered the politics of the borough. The act extended the franchise to all householders whose dwellings were worth at least £10 freehold and increased the Clonmel electorate almost fivefold to 531. These changes were detrimental to the Bagwell interest and he was defeated in 1832 and 1835, in what were the first contested elections in Clonmel since the passage of the Act of Union. John Bagwell's opponent on both occasions

---

[10] *Clonmel Advertiser*, 8 October 1814.
[11] U. H. Hussey de Burgh, *Land Owners of Ireland*, (Dublin, 1878), p. 16.
[12] Sean O'Donnell, *Clonmel 1840-1900: Anatomy of an Irish Town*, (Dublin, 1999), p. 105.

was Dominick Ronayne, a supporter of Daniel O'Connell's repeal movement whose politics contrasted sharply with Bagwell's unionism. Bagwell once stated publicly that he was not a repealer and rather than compromise his principles he would not accept parliamentary office even if were offered to him.

Bagwell may have derived some consolation from his appointment as High Sheriff of Tipperary in 1834. His subsequent political rehabilitation began with his election to the Clonmel Corporation in 1849, a seat he held until 1874. His success could be attributed to several factors. His practical assistance for the victims of famine had boosted his popularity and the repeal question, at the time, was no longer a major political issue. He publicly proclaimed himself to be committed to civil and religious liberty and an advocate of the rights of the poor. This declaration has been described 'as the first public breach with his conservative roots. Henceforth he was always politically liberal'.[13] Membership of the corporation was to prove a significant step on his way to becoming the parliamentary representative for the borough.

After the resignation of the sitting MP, John O'Connell, son of The Liberator in 1858, the resultant by-election witnessed one of the crowning achievements of Bagwell's political career. His victory over Patrick Joseph Murray after a hotly contested campaign 'represented the remarkable resurrection after a quarter of a century of the political power of the Bagwells. They had left as hardline tories; they returned in the person of John Bagwell as liberals'.[14] He was returned unopposed until 1874 when, as a convinced unionist, he fell victim to the growing enthusiasm for home rule. He was replaced by Count Arthur John Moore of Mooresfort, who held the seat until 1885, in which year Clonmel ceased to be a parliamentary borough.

His integrity was such that in the House of Commons he was generally known as 'honest John Bagwell'. He favoured religious and civil freedom, church disestablishment and land reform. He voted for the retention of the Maynooth College grant and the abolition of minister's

---

[13] *Ibid*, p. 157.
[14] R. V. Comerford, 'Representation at Westminster 1801-1918' in William Nolan & Thomas G. McGrath, *Tipperary: History and Society*, (Dublin, 1985), p. 330.

money. In 1859 he accepted a post from Lord Palmerstown as a junior lord of the treasury but resigned two years later on a matter of principle. This gave him more time to devote to local affairs. He became very active in parliament on urban matters of particular interest to Clonmel such as the policing of towns at night, the regulation of fairs and markets and the billeting of troops, and on all these matters he was in frequent communication with Clonmel Corporation. It was said that 'he represented the borough of Clonmel and the interests of the country at large in the Imperial Parliament with unswerving integrity and with an unselfishness of purpose that redounded to his honour and deserves more than a passing recognition'.[15]

On one occasion, during a debate on the renewal of the Insurrection Act, a northern member declared that the life of any man of property, or even of any man with a good coat, was not safe in Ireland. Bagwell replied that he lived in Ireland, had considerable property there, and would go at any time through the most disturbed district, fortified with no other weapon than his umbrella, a remark which earned him the name, 'Umbrella Bagwell'.[16]

For many years he also served as chairman of the Board of Guardians in Clonmel, and as a trustee of the Clonmel Mechanics' Institute. He was regarded as being a good landlord with a kind and humane disposition who, during the famine of 1846-47, took an active part in the alleviation of distress. No tenant was ever turned out of his holding or forced to emigrate. He always said that he had then learned the lesson that starving people can be relieved only by food and not by the sham of useless public works.[17] Writing of him his daughter-in-law said that he:

> saw a great deal of his constituents, and was on the most friendly terms with them and there were constant dinner parties for them at Marlfield. The parish priests were often there, but after the Home Rule question became for a time merged in the land agitation this

---

[15] *Clonmel Chronicle*, 3 March 1883.
[16] Burke, *History of Clonmel*, p. 323.
[17] *Clonmel Chronicle*, 7 March 1888.

intercourse came to an end.[18]

Despite his extensive estates, he had little interest in farming, but became a keen gardener with a wide knowledge of shrubs and flowers. In later years, he lived a life of easy and cultured retirement, accumulating a rare collection of objects d'art. On a personal level, he was a talented athlete, impressive on the racquet court, and a rower and yachtsman of note. He was blessed with extraordinary stamina. When building his house in Eastgrove, near Cobh, he used to ride and drive there from Marlfield and return on the same day – a distance of one hundred and sixty kilometers. On another occasion, while hunting at Fethard, twenty kilometers distant, he bought a large number of young cattle, which he drove home with his whip.

With the death of John Bagwell in 1883 his estates devolved on his eldest son, Richard (1840-1918). He was educated at Harrow and Oxford and while still young was called to the English bar. In 1873 he married Harriette, daughter of P. J. Newton of Dunleckney, and had one son and three daughters. Recalling these years Harriette wrote in her memoir:

> This was in some ways the happiest time of our lives, before the clouds began to gather over Ireland which caused so much anxiety increasing with each year that came. Richard was intended and fitted for political life. His family had been members for Clonmel for generations. He was a good speaker, and a leader of men, but when the Home Rule question came to the fore in 1874, the year his father lost his seat, which he had held for eighteen years, he saw that this career was barred to him. From the first, he said it would be a government of factions, and would divide Ireland in two, and he never changed his mind.

He decided instead to take an interest in local politics but his involvement was to be short-lived. He was the last of the Bagwells to become a member of the corporation, serving from 1884 to 1886. He had previously served as a Justice of the Peace for County Waterford and High

---

[18] Memoir of Harriette Bagwell.

Sheriff for Tipperary in 1859. From 1896 to 1903, he acted as Special Local Government Commissioner and was a Commissioner for National Education in the period 1905-18. A committed unionist he felt that home rule would plunge the country into civil war. The Bagwells did not feel any less Irish for insisting that Ireland should remain part of the union. Membership of the greatest empire the world had ever seen guaranteed their status and security. It is understandable that they looked on with growing concern 'at what they considered the vain and illogical aspirations of their fellow-countrymen for independence from such a powerful entity'.[19] It could be said that 'their unionism came from the head rather than the heart ..... their allegiance was not so much to Britain as to the crown'.[20]

His unionist politics were criticized by an article published in the *Nationalist* of 1889 under the heading 'Who is Dick Bagwell near Clonmel?':

This was the question of a correspondent in the *Star* the other day. Dick's local admirers fancy that he is a familiar notability from China to Peru, not to mind all Great Britain and Ireland. It would appear that he delivered some supremely ridiculous discourse recently at Seven Oaks, which was announced to be 'non-political' but which turned out to be rabidly Unionist. That is Dick all out. For the information of all concerned we desire to say that he is a flippant story-teller, a rampant bigot, an arrogant egotist, a worthless humbug, and an absurdly pretentious bashaw who spews out a lot of driveling bunkum which nobody now-a-days notices seriously.

Richard continued to take an interest in local affairs, acting as a magistrate at petty sessions and for many years he was chairman of the Grand Jury until the passage of the Local Government Act of 1898 which introduced the county councils. He was involved in many benevolent agencies, becoming the first president of the Clonmel Borstal Institution, a member of the I.S.P.C.C., a subscriber to the St. Vincent de Paul Society

---

[19] Anne Chambers, *At Arm's Length*, (Dublin, 2004), p. 114.
[20] Mark Bence Jones, *Twilight of the Ascendancy*, (London, 1987), p. 15.

and a supporter of the Cottage Hospital, which was set up by his wife, Harriette Philippa in 1894 'to supply a need to suit people of moderate means'. The hospital was largely maintained by charitable contributions until 1971, when rising running costs forced it to close.[21] It now operates as a private nursing home.

When Richard succeeded his father, Marlfield village was far from being the picturesque and prosperous-looking place it is to-day. The remnants of the long closed distillery work-force were existing on casual labour and living in hovels. A few years before John Bagwell's death the lease of the distillery came to an end and that portion of the village reverted back to the control of the Bagwell family, bringing with it its poverty-stricken tenants. As Harriette recorded, 'when we inherited the property, for the first time it became possible to do anything'. Many of the houses were little more than mud cabins but, as time went on and people died out, these were by degrees pulled down; the better ones renovated and the village assumed a more respectable appearance.

This was one of many initiatives taken by the Richard and his wife to improve the quality of life of their tenants. They also took responsibility for the management and upkeep of the village school. Harriette Bagwell set up a cookery school, a servant's registry office to enable local girls find employment and she started a penny club to encourage savings. Their most ambitious and successful venture was the establishment of Clonmel Cottage Industries in 1886. This was part of a wider movement when, in various parts of Ireland, an increasing number of ladies were working to encourage handicrafts and home industries as a means of improving the conditions of the country people.

Harriette Bagwell trained young women in the craft of embroidery which they applied to coverlets and quilts, tea clothes, cushion covers, children's frocks and even doll's frocks. The high degree of skill they achieved was acknowledged by Helen Blackburn in her book *Handy book of reference for Irishwomen* which stated that 'Marlfield designs were original and graceful, and the effects excellent'.[22] Mrs. Bagwell had their

---

[21] Anon. *All about Clonmel. A presentation of Irish Life* (n.d.), p. 39.
[22] Nellie Beary Ó Cléirigh, 'Marlfield, a tale worth telling' in Brendan Long (ed.), *The Nationalist centenary supplement 1890-1990*, (Clonmel, 1990), p. 67.

products exhibited at the Cork Exhibition of 1883 and ten years later, their work went on to achieve international recognition, being sold at the World's Fair in Chicago in 1893. When a committee was set up in 1884 to improve the quality and design of Irish lace, Richard Bagwell was one of its members and subscribed five pounds.

Richard Bagwell is best remembered as an outstanding scholar, who wrote two widely acclaimed historical works. In 1890 he produced *Ireland under the Tudors* in three volumes. His wife provided some interesting insights into the nature and extent of her husband's researches when she wrote:

> Much of the material for this period had not been printed, and was only to be found among the state papers in London. He read old Latin and other manuscripts, so dry that he could hardly keep awake over them, but so thorough was his work that nothing was omitted that could throw light on those obscure times. His object became more and more to give the original authorities, and tell future historians the truth in a form which could be read by all. He thought Irish History had been written to prove some political case, and was often untrue.[23]

This was followed by a companion work *Ireland under the Stuarts* published in 1909. In 1917 his contribution was recognised by the award of an honorary D. Litt. from Oxford University. Just as 'George Meredith is the novelists' novelist, so Dr. Bagwell is the historians' historian', said the *Irish Times*. When he died in 1918 his remains were borne on a farm cart driven by the estate's oldest employee to the family plot in Marlfield graveyard.

John Philip Bagwell (1874-1946), Richard's only son, was heir to his father's estates. His childhood was spent at Inislounaght. In 1883, he was sent with his governess to a school in Switzerland, an experience that gave him his first love of mountaineering. He was at a preparatory school at Bournemouth before going to Harrow and his father insisted that he spend four years at Oxford. In 1901, he married Louise, daughter of Major-

---

[23] Memoir of Hariette Bagwell.

General George Shaw. He devoted thirty years of his life to the railway world. He started in 1905 as assistant superintendent on the Midland Railway of England and retired as General Manager of the Great Northern Railway of Ireland. He was appointed Deputy lieutenant for Tipperary and later took a courageous step by becoming one of the first members of the Irish senate where he served from 1922-36. He was no believer in Home Rule but, as his mother said, 'as it had become our only government, he felt it was his duty to do what he could for his country'. It was a decision that cost him dearly.

In December 1922, Liam Lynch, Chief of Staff of the Republican forces, ordered that the houses of all senators should be burnt. In January 1923 Marlfield House, which had been completed by Col. John Bagwell in 1792, went up in flames, destroying one of the finest private libraries in the country. Bagwell moved with his family into the servants' quarters until the main house was re-built. Three weeks later, he was kidnapped at Howth but his prowess as an athlete at Oxford University and as a member of the Alpine Club helped him make good his escape from an upstairs window.[24]

This was not the only indication of his athleticism. He was a keen horseman and a member of the Tipperary Hounds and, on one occasion, at the age of fifty seven, he walked from Clonmel to Cobh. Like his father, he took a keen interest in the life of Clonmel. He was prominently associated with the activities of the Clonmel Horse Show and Agricultural Society of which he was a highly efficient chairman for a number of years. After his death in 1946, he was succeeded by William (1905-1979), who had served as a Lieutenant-Commander in the Royal Navy during the Second World War.

The Bagwells, like the vast majority of the Irish Protestant landed classes were as Sean O'Faolain wrote, 'a separate enclave'.[25] They differed from the majority Catholic population in religion, social status and in cultural orientation. They socialised and married within their own confined circle. Their children attended English public schools, before taking up a career in the British armed forces or in the public service. The Bagwells

---

[24] Donal O'Sullivan, *The Irish Free State and its Senate*, (Dublin, 1940), p. 104-105.

[25] Sean O'Faolain, *The Irish*, (Middlesex, 1947), p. 88.

were also highly regarded landlords who attempted to promote the interests of the community in which they lived by involving themselves in local organizations and serving on public bodies. In 1979, the family's long association with the town of Clonmel was brought to an end with the death of William Bagwell.

Chapter 15

John Hackett and Sons

An imposing Celtic cross which stands in the forecourt of SS. Peter and Paul's church, Clonmel marks the grave of the Hackett family. Among those buried there are John Hackett and his three sons, all of whom played a distinguished and prominent part in the civic history of the town in the nineteenth century. They lived through an era which witnessed some of the defining moments in Irish history including Catholic emancipation, the ongoing agitation for repeal of the union, the horrors of the great famine, the defeat of the Young Irelanders and Fenians and the successful campaign for land reform. As the power of the Protestant ascendancy was gradually undermined the Catholic masses emerged from several centuries of subjugation and legal discrimination. Among those who contributed significantly to the national struggle for liberation were members of the Hackett family of Clonmel.

John Hackett (1796-1872)

John Hackett, who became one of the best-known nineteenth century Clonmel personalities, was the first member of the family to become involved in the affairs of the town. He was born on Suir Island and was the only child of John Hackett and Catherine Riordan. Through his father he was descended from the Hacketts of Ballysheehan and of Ballytrasna, Baile Tarsna an Haicéadaigh in Irish, both north of Cashel. Their lands had been confiscated in the Cromwellian plantation, and were those of his mother's family, who was descended from the Mocklers of Mocklerstown, a townsland between Fethard and Cashel. He received a private classical education in Clonmel and served his apprenticeship with Thomas Gorman who was then the sole bookseller and stationer in the town.[1]

---

[1] Sean O'Donnell, *Clonmel 1840-1900: Anatomy of an Irish Town*, (Dublin, 1999), p. 264.

He set up business at 101 Main Street as a bookseller. In addition to which, he established a public library and held agencies for the British Commercial, Fire and Life Insurance Company and for various medicinal remedies. Having married Frances Burke from Carrick-on-Suir, they had a family of three boys and seven girls.

In 1826 John Hackett became the owner and editor of a newspaper called the *Tipperary Free Press.* In the prospectus for the new paper he denounced 'the generality of Provincial Journalists' who, according to Hackett 'exist upon official patronage and are as void of public principle, as they are of information' and stated that 'he did not intend to take them for his model'. He claimed that his newspaper would be the 'voice of the common people' and pledged that 'the exactions which are practised upon the peasantry through taxes, dues, tolls and tithes, and all the complicated machinery by which the people are ground down' would be fully and fearlessly exposed to the public eye.

Hackett's paper became an influential and popular voice in supporting current liberal causes. By the late 1830s the weekly circulation figures of the *Tipperary Free Press* had reached 17,500, the highest of any local newspaper. It was launched at a time when his Catholic countrymen were treated as second class citizens by a succession of unsympathetic governments. Angered by injustice and inequality his public utterances and editorials were frequently marked by intemperate language and trenchant prose which, on more than one occasion, involved him in costly litigation and left him on the verge of financial ruin.

Hackett gave extensive coverage to the Catholic Emancipation movement and, in August 1828, was elected as a committee member of the provincial meeting of the Catholics of Munster. Their objective was to refuse support to any parliamentary candidate unwilling to promote emancipation. In the struggle for religious liberty he became a staunch supporter and personal friend of Daniel O'Connell and in deference to the Liberator, he named his second son, Henry O'Connell Hackett.

Following the granting of Catholic Emancipation in 1829, Hackett involved himself in the anti-tithe campaign. Being a gifted public speaker his services were much in demand. At a meeting held in Clonmel's Ormond Hotel, he called for an abolition of tithes, stating that there was never 'a grosser species of tyranny and injustice imposed upon a conquered country than the Irish Tithe System'[2], a reference to the fact that the Catholic majority were legally bound to contribute to the upkeep of the established Protestant church. Hackett helped organise further anti-tithe meetings and published a series of articles in the pages of the *Tipperary Free Press* denouncing the inequities of the system. He invoked the ire of his enemies to such an extent that the authorities decided to make an example of him.

He was charged on a criminal indictment of conspiring to defeat the attempt to collect tithes. To ensure a conviction, this charge was split into sixteen counts – each, if proved, punishable by transportation. Bail was set at the unusually high figure of £2,000. During the next six months, Hackett was arrested three times and brought to Dublin. On each occasion he was forced to enter into securities for the sum of £500. Following many frustrating delays and having paid heavy sums for his defence, charges were eventually dropped and Hackett was released. If the authorities had hoped that the experience would have rendered him more cautious they were sadly mistaken. Hackett responded by promoting the Tipperary Tithe Sufferers' Fund and by continuing 'to denounce the oppressors' in his newspaper.

Despite the inflammatory nature of Hackett's rhetoric he believed that constitutional means were the only acceptable way to achieve the abolition of tithes. At a meeting held in Cashel in 1834 he appealed to the crowd to 'abstain from all illegal and private associations … as it was only through open, constitutional unity of purpose and opinion that they could ever hope to remove the evils under which they at present laboured'.[3] The Tithe Act of 1838 resulted in a reduction of tithes, and removed it as an issue from the political scene.

He detested the act of union which had left Ireland subject to the parliament at Westminster. An ardent repealer, Hackett wrote that 'every day's experience proves that it alone is the true panacea for Ireland … the question may slumber but it cannot die'.[4] His antipathy for those who

[2] *Tipperary Free Press*, 8 February 1837.
[3] *Freeman's Journal,* 30 January 1834.
[4] *Tipperary Free Press*, 15 August 1856.

advocated its retention involved him in one of the most controversial and shameful incidents of his career and culminated in a costly libel action. Following the defeat of the unionist candidate, John Bagwell, who failed to win the seat for Clonmel borough in the parliamentary election of 1835, Hackett launched a series of articles under the pseudonym 'Nemo' attacking Bagwell and his supporters. In the course of one of them Hackett represented himself as having entered Bagwell's election room and proceeded to describe one of its occupants in a most unflattering and derogatory manner:

> Pre-eminently officious was a tall, thin faced young man (about thirty-eight), with light bushy whiskers, long nose, a figure drooped at the shoulders, but not from age. What first fixed my attention on him was the unearthly excitement in his eye – it was terrible, such as no election feeling could conjure up. It was frenzied, and riveted me like a basilisk's. I asked my guide who the young man was, and his answer solved the enigma.

It was obvious to readers of the *Tipperary Free Press* that the person in question was William Strangman, a member of Bagwell's election team. The article continued with the following insinuation:

> Many years have rolled away, and the Suir has often emptied itself into the sea, but time cannot blot out nor the years efface the memory of a fearful deed which put a sudden ending to the lives and loves of two unhappy people. I could not bear to look longer on that miserable and haggard countenance and was glad to turn away.[5]

The phrase 'fearful deed' referred to the tragic drowning of Lieutenant Frederick Close and Anne Grubb in the river Suir which had occurred nine years previously. While the article illustrates Hackett's undisputed skill as a writer, it was also an unwarranted attack on an innocent man's reputation. Not surprisingly, Strangman took an action for damages on the grounds that although the article did not mention him by

---

[5] *Tipperary Free Press*, 25 February 1835.

name, it clearly referred to him, and suggested that he was in some way responsible for the 'Suir Tragedy'. After a half hour's deliberation the judge found for the plaintiff and awarded £750 damages.

Undeterred, Hackett continued at every opportunity to use his editorial privilege to attack his political enemies. In April 1838, a letter on behalf of the county's magistrates was sent to Dublin Castle deploring the lawless state of the county. The reply from Under-Secretary, Thomas Drummond, a man renowned for his liberal views and reforming policies, pointed out that some of the outrages resulted from poor landlord-tenant relationships and included the immortal line, 'Property has its duties as well as its rights'. Although Lord Donoughmore, Lord Lieutenant of County Tipperary, was unwilling to make the letter public Hackett got his hands on it and printed it for widespread distribution as a broadsheet. He announced in the *Tipperary Free Press* with calculated malice that he did so 'in order to gratify the calumniated jurors of this county who desire to have this splendid document in gilt frames to grace their mantelpieces, we have directed that some copies be beautifully printed (but not in letters of gold) on superfine hot-pressed paper'. As a result of a subsequent legal action Hackett was forced to pay another £800.

Prior to this, Hackett's friends and supporters who had become alarmed by the level of damages levied against him decided, on his behalf, to organise an appeal for funds. This resulted in two public meetings being held in Clonmel in March and October 1836 for the 'Protection of the *Tipperary Free Press*'. Hackett was praised for his 'love of country', a man who had a 'respect of law and a passion for justice' and through his paper had denounced 'every species of corruption and tyranny'.[6] A letter of support sent to the October meeting from Daniel O'Connell stressed the unnecessary vindictiveness used against Hackett. Subsequently, the generous response from Clonmel and the surrounding districts ensured the survival of the paper.

His career as a public representative was no less controversial. Although corporations were nominally open to Roman Catholics since 1793, the vast majority, including that of Clonmel, were in Protestant hands. The Reform Act of 1840 ended absolute Protestant control of

---

[6] *Tipperary Free Press*, 30 November 1836.

municipal government in Ireland and increased Catholic influence in local politics. In 1843 John Hackett became the first Catholic mayor since the reign of James II in the latter half of the seventeenth century. In addition to this honour, Hackett was appointed chairman of the town commissioners, a body to which had been first elected in 1834.[7]

Assessing his achievement in becoming mayor, Canon Burke wrote:

> from being a journeyman printer, had, by ability, courage and public spirit, won for himself, the foremost place among his fellow citizens. At a time when the whole machinery of the law was in operation against the rights of the common people, he smote amain (sic), week by week, in the 'Free Press', tithe proctors, partisan magistrates and exterminating landlords. Damages amounting to hundreds of pounds were obtained against him in the law courts, but he survived all and having been the stoutest opponent of the old corporation, he became the first mayor of the new.[8]

John Hackett, the newly elected mayor and editor of a popular newspaper, who enjoyed the friendship of the great O'Connell, was the subject of much petty jealousy and envy. He was accused of giving all the corporation printing contracts to his firm and also of overcharging for them. He had metal plaques bearing his name erected around the town, many of which can still be seen today. While these marked the wards and borough boundaries, his enemies claimed they were a matter of vanity. He was compared to 'a jackal on the prowl for pickings' and of being 'impertinent and overbearing and a dictator'. Whatever about the validity of such personal claims there was no doubt that the new corporation was guilty of jobbery and nepotism.

During his mayoralty, he convened an extraordinary number of meetings, seventy eight in total. By comparison Charles Bianconi, who

---

[7] Under the Lighting of Towns Act 1828, Clonmel had acquired town commissioners, who were given responsibility for the watching, lighting, cleansing and paving of the town.

[8] Burke, *History of Clonmel*, pp. 180,81.

twice filled the office, held no more than a mere fifty for the two years in question. In the thirty years Hackett spent as a member of the corporation he had the best attendance record of any councillor and, despite declining health, he was even present at five meetings in the year that he died.[9] He resisted many efforts to take mayoral office on further occasions, but had the satisfaction of seeing two of his sons succeed to that honour.

Hackett was twice elected chief magistrate of the town, a position also occupied by his three sons. In the twenty years that he held office it was said that he discharged his duties with the strictest honour and integrity and displayed Christianity and humanity to those who came before him. He was also a poor law guardian for the Clonmel Workhouse and during the famine he was elected secretary of the Clonmel Relief Committee, earning the praise of his contemporaries for 'ministering, as best he could, to the wants of the distressed and afflicted'.

John Hackett helped promote the social and intellectual welfare of his fellow townsmen by taking a special interest in various literary, educational and charitable organisations. At a meeting held in Clonmel on 3rd January 1841, he proposed setting up the Clonmel Mechanics' Institute for the educational improvement of the working classes[10], and was later elected vice-president of that institute which occupied the building now known as Mulcahy House in Anglesea Street.

On the 15th May of that year he chaired a meeting which led to the setting up of the Clonmel Literary Institute which provided a library and reading room for the working classes. He also offered financial support to the project and donated a number of books. Hackett became secretary of the steering committee that helped set up the Clonmel branch of the National Bank established as the 'poor man's bank' by O'Connell, and subsequently became a shareholder.

He was elected president of the St. Vincent de Paul Society in 1857, a position he held until the year of his death in 1872. Rev. John

---

[9] Seán O'Donnell, 'Clonmel Corporation 1842-98: A Municipal Study', Ph. D. thesis (St. Patrick's College, Maynooth, 1996), Appendix iv, v, vi, vii, p. 309 et seq.,

[10] *Tipperary Free Press,* 7 January 1841.

Power, then parish priest of SS. Peter and Paul's, in the course of a tribute to his dedicated service stated:

> that no consideration of his own private concerns, however urgent, or no inclemency of season – however severe – could prevent him taking his accustomed place at the weekly meeting of this conference. Even in declining health, and when yielding under those infirmities of age which the most robust must expect, he would not allow himself that ease and repose that nature would require, the interests of the poor being uppermost in his mind.[11]

Hackett, as chief spokesman of the Clonmel liberals, was ably supported by Fr. Michael Burke, parish priest of SS. Peter and Paul's. A native of Kilsheelan he was educated at Maynooth and served as a professor in St. John's College in Waterford before taking up his appointment in Clonmel in 1836. This formidable and influential pastor was responsible for inviting both the Sisters of Charity and the Christian Brothers to Clonmel. A dominant and forceful individual, he was to have a considerable impact on the political affairs of Clonmel. It didn't take him long to make his presence felt and shortly after his arrival, he chaired the meeting called for the 'Protection of the *Tipperary Free Press*', referred to above, at which he pledged his services and support to the beleaguered Hackett.

For the next twenty years Hackett and Burke became leaders of the liberal cause, with Charles Bianconi playing a subsidiary role. However, relations between Hackett and Burke became strained when the latter supported John Bagwell's election to the corporation in 1849. Burke had been impressed by Bagwell's efforts to provide relief during the famine and by his pledge to work for civil and religious liberty, but Hackett remained vehemently anti-Bagwell and condemned his uncompromising attitude to repeal. The rift between the two became complete when they found themselves on opposite sides during the parliamentary election of 1857 which saw John Bagwell become MP for the borough of Clonmel. The

---

[11] Michael Kelly, *Society of St. Vincent de Paul. Conference of S.S. Peter & Paul, Clonmel,* (Clonmel, 1993), p. 23.

result had made it clear that Hackett's influence in the borough was not strong enough to dislodge Bagwell as long as he enjoyed the support of Fr. Burke.

Following this, Hackett took no further part in election campaigning[12]. Instead, he devoted his energies to his continued fight against injustice and inequality through the columns of his paper and to promoting the cause for land reform and repeal. In 1861, he handed over the editorship of the *Tipperary Free Press* to his eldest son, William Louis Hackett. On the 3rd August 1872, John Hackett died after a lengthy illness. He was surrounded by all his family with the exception of his eldest daughter, Sister Bernard, then superioress of the Ursuline convent in Waterford.

For nearly half a century, few men had played a more important role on the public stage throughout the south of Ireland and numerous tributes were paid to him in the national and provincial newspapers. The *Freeman* wrote of him as being 'highly esteemed as a staunch, honest patriot – one who espoused the popular cause and, as a journalist, rendered it valuable service at a time when to do so was surrounded by much difficulty and considerable personal sacrifice'.[13]

The *Clonmel Chronicle*, official organ of the conservative party, stated that while 'he may not always have taken that course which might have commended itself to others; but we fail to recall to mind any occasion where he ever swerved from the path he conscientiously believed to be right'.[14] Edmond Power, political rival and fellow member of the corporation, described Hackett as 'a man whose voice and pen were untiring in the cause of his country and his faith and who in public and private life trod the path that the sons of any man might be proud to follow'.[15]

John Hackett's lifelong contribution is best summed up in the *Cork Examiner* who said that the country is greatly indebted to such men for the

---

[12] O'Donnell, *Clonmel 1840-1900 etc.,* p. 200.
[13] *Tipperary Free Press*, 13 August 1872
[14] *Clonmel Chronicle*, 3 August 1872.
[15] *Tipperary Free Press*, 3 August 1872.

maintenance of its public spirit and for the support they provided for O'Connell's leadership of the Catholic cause. It continued by stating that:

men were needed to stir the popular mind and accustom it to the handling of great questions, such as these touching religious and national freedom. O'Connell did much by his own personal exertions, but it needed men throughout the different districts men of consideration, animated by his own zeal and patriotism, to enforce his teachings, and to sustain the spirit which he had breathed into the people. Alderman Hackett was one of the most able and useful of these men, steadfast and consistent, sincere and earnest, he inspired confidence amongst all those who came in contact with him.

This assessment is reflected in the inscription on his tombstone:

He praised his creed. He served his country,
And he loved his kind.

William Louis Hackett (1829-1876)

William Louis Hackett was the eldest son of John Hackett. He received an MA from Trinity College, Dublin and, in 1849, was admitted as a barrister to the King's Inn, London. In 1854, he succeeded his father as publisher of the *Tipperary Free Press* and he was elected as a member of the Clonmel Corporation in 1858. Though he was the youngest serving member, he became mayor the following year. He was a highly regarded Chief Magistrate of the town, was admired for his considerable ability and respected for his sound judgements.

He was re-elected mayor in 1862 but resigned his corporation seat five years later when he left Clonmel to enter the legal profession. He settled in Dublin and became an advocate on the Leinster Circuit and in the Four Courts. In 1861, he had taken over editorship of the *Tipperary Free Press* from his father but four years later his brother, Henry O'Connell, set up the short-lived *Tipperary People* in opposition. This would suggest that his departure may have been prompted by family tensions.

When a general election was called in 1874 William Louis returned to Clonmel to contest it. Local activists saw an opportunity to unseat John Bagwell because of his opposition to home rule and denominational education. Two candidates, William Louis Hackett and Arthur Moore, were selected to contest the liberal nomination. The odds were decidedly against Moore, who was in holiday in Palestine and would not be back in Clonmel in time for the election, in addition to which some of his principal supporters had never met him.

However, Hackett found himself opposed by the clergy, as had happened his father in 1857 when he had contested Bagwell's candidature for the corporation. Although Fr. Burke had died in 1866, leadership on this occasion was provided by John Power, former parish priest of SS. Peter and Paul's, and now Bishop of Waterford and Lismore. Power felt that denominational education was of far greater importance than home rule and on that score he felt that Moore was a far more suitable candidate.[16]

Local corporation members opposed to Hackett did their utmost to undermine him and went as far as citing his connection with that bastion of Protestant education, Trinity College. Leaving nothing to chance, Bishop Power arrived in Clonmel to address the vital nomination meeting in Hearns' Hotel, which resulted in the selection of Moore by a narrow majority of ninety two votes to eighty eight. Hackett accepted defeat graciously and acted as Moore's agent in the general election, a contest which Moore won easily. Moore proved himself an undistinguished parliamentarian but was created a papal count in 1879 for his stance on Catholic issues. He is perhaps best remembered for being the last MP for the borough of Clonmel and for assisting the Rosminians in building St. Joseph's School at Ferryhouse, outside the town.

Two years after his unsuccessful attempt to win a parliamentary seat William Louis died at his residence in Main Street on the 9 January 1876. For the last two years of his life he had served as President of St. Vincent de Paul Society. He projected a similarly Catholic and nationalist outlook as his father had done, both on his paper and as a member of the corporation. He was regarded as an inspiring public speaker, a man of

---

[16] James O'Shea, *Priests, Politics and Society in Post-famine Ireland. A study of County Tipperary 1850-1891* (Dublin, 1983), p. 210, 211.

culture and high intellectual endowments. As a journalist, he was an accomplished writer who employed his gifted pen in the service of the town's literary, benevolent and social institutions.[17]

Henry O'Connell Hackett (1835-1880)

Henry O'Connell Hackett was the second eldest son of John Hackett. He carried on the family tradition of public service in their newspaper and on the corporation, and through his involvement in many voluntary bodies. He was a member of the corporation from 1868-1880, and was elected mayor in 1872, 1879 and 1880. He was a highly regarded chief magistrate for the town. He was firm, impartial and when opportunity offered, merciful, his decisions being marked with humanity and fairness. Although he was no trained lawyer it was said that he possessed attributes that would have been creditable to any judge.

He was also an advocate of home rule and in the course of his inauguration speech in 1872 he declared that it was 'essential to Irish prosperity ... with it we rise to national dignity and wanting it we remain in provincial degradation'.[18] Although he opposed armed revolt, he supported the call for the release of the Fenian prisoners on humanitarian grounds. While he didn't agree with Charles Kickham's militant policies, he contributed to his testimonial fund which was launched by the *Freeman's Journal* in 1878 to relieve the writer's financial difficulties.

While his elder brother might be regarded as the intellectual in the family, Henry O'Connell could be said to be the innovator. As mayor he proposed that the corporation should have a town hall of its own instead of meeting, on sufferance, in the judge's chamber at the county courthouse. This led, in 1881, to the present town hall being built in Parnell Street at a cost of £6,000. He was also responsible for providing the civic chain which adorns the mayors of Clonmel to the present day. He set an example by donating the first golden link himself, and encouraged various ex-mayors or their representatives to do likewise.

---

[17] *Tipperary Free Press*, 11 January 1876; *Clonmel Chronicle*, 12 January 1876.
[18] *Tipperary Free Press*, 2 January 1872.

He took a keen interest in the children of the workhouse schools and became president of the town amateur band. Like his father he was elected vice-president of the Clonmel Mechanics' Institute, a member of the Literary Institute and his efforts as president of the Society of St. Vincent de Paul, earned him this tribute following his death:

> He generally visited in person the homes of the poor – not always situated in the most savoury localities – and often found his way to the cellar and the garret, to solace and relieve the afflicted and distressed. He loved the poor, and was never so happy as in relieving their wants. He hated ostentation, and delighted in dispensing charity in secret. He was blessed with a humane, a charitable, and noble heart, and by his death the poor have lost a true friend, a warm advocate, and a generous benefactor.

As has been mentioned, he set up the *Tipperary People* in opposition to the *Tipperary Free Press*, then in the hands of his brother, William Louis. It was first published on 15th July 1865. It aimed at advocating the legitimate claims of the tenant farmer, the disestablishment of the state church and the promotion of an Independent Irish Party in the House of Commons through which Ireland's best interests could be 'advanced and promoted'.[19]

The *Tipperary People* lasted no more than five months. Traders did not support it, preferring to place their advertisements with papers that had a greater circulation. His interest in agricultural matters was reflected in such articles as 'Hints for Farmers' and 'Diseases in Horses' which appeared in the pages of his short-lived newspaper. Following the death of William Louis in 1876, Henry took over the family newspaper the *Tipperary Free Press* where he continued to promote his interest in agriculture. He succeeded in establishing the Clonmel District Agricultural Society, becoming one of its secretaries. Perhaps, his greatest achievement was in persuading the Royal Agricultural Society to hold their national show in Clonmel, an event which proved to be an outstanding success.

---

[19] *Tipperary People*, 15 July 1865.

ever. He enlarged and remodelled Rockwell House, which is now the main entrance to Rockwell College, for William Roe. The result was 'a Gothic residence of the late perpendicular style'. The ornate hallway, with its carved wood filagree work, is almost identical to that seen on the porch of Ashbourne House. Roe was sufficiently impressed with Tinsley's craftsmanship to introduce him to John Maher for whom he added crenellated walls and towers crowned with battlements to Tullamain Castle. This, in turn, led to a further contract when Maher's brother, Valentine, engaged him in 1837 to restructure Turtulla House, a building which now serves as the club house of Thurles Golf club.

In the same year he built Adelaide House in Irishtown, next to the Grammar School, to house his growing family. Built in the Gothic style, it had a parlour, dining room and study on the ground floor, four bedrooms upstairs, while the kitchen, scullery, storeroom and the maid's room were in the basement. Various additions were made as further young Tinsleys came along. Unfortunately, this lovely building was demolished in the nineteen sixties to make way for the new St. Mary's Christian Brothers National School.

By now Tinsley had amassed sufficient capital to invest in real estate, building four houses near his workshops in Peter Street and six cottages in what was then known as Cahir Street, later renamed Albert Street to commemorate the marriage of Queen Victoria. During this time his young daughter, Mary, died tragically when a number of planks fell on her in his lumber yard in Peter Street. She is buried in the grounds of old St. Mary's where other members of the Tinsley family are also interred.

By the 1840s he had given up the building side of the business and practised solely as an architect. In 1841 his career entered a new phase when he was introduced by John Bury Palliser, the rector of Clonmel, to Robert Daly, the new bishop of Waterford. Sometime previously, Tinsley had renovated the residence of the rector's brother, Colonel Wray Palliser of Comeragh House, outside Kilmacthomas in county Waterford. As a result of his meeting with the bishop, he was appointed diocesan architect, in succession to James Pain, Jr. The two architects were close friends and Tinsley had his fourth son christened, James Pain Tinsley. William's duties consisted of designing and erecting a number of churches in the diocese, including those at Clonbeg in the

Glen of Aherlow, Kilbehenny near Mitchelstown and Kilvemnon, halfway between Fethard and Cloneen. His work on Clogheen Protestant church almost resulted in his death when he fell from the roof. He also inspected existing ecclesiastical buildings throughout the diocese, for which he received a fee of £2 a day, in addition to travelling expenses.

The most important commission Tinsley received during the Irish phase of his career began in the early 1840s. In his memoirs he wrote that he was employed by the Earl of Glengall to remodel the town of Cahir. Part of his contract was to erect town and country houses for the earl's tenants. He was also engaged to build a residence for Glengall's agent, John Chaytor. Today this house which is situated in Castle Street is occupied by the Allied Irish Bank. He was also required to renovate part of the batter of Cahir Castle. The Cahir project which was his most ambitious undertaking to date occupied Tinsley for most of the decade and transformed the centre of the town.

The decorative surrounds to doors and windows which he introduced to Cahir have resonances of Renaissance Italy, while the renovations to the castle won the approval of contemporary observers who felt that the repairs had been effected so judiciously 'that its picturesque effect is in no degree injured'.[3] Set into the street front of one of the houses are the initials 'W.T.', later to be found in the buildings he erected in America. Glengall expressed his pleasure in a letter to Tinsley, 'I have had dealings with you for many years & you have built for me & my tenants a very handsome town – the handsomest in Ireland – where your talents & taste as an architect are evident to the admiration of all'.[4] Unfortunately, before the work was completed the earl went bankrupt, and it was many years before Tinsley received payment.

In 1843, while the Cahir project was in progress, Tinsley embarked on what many would regard as one of the architectural gems of Clonmel, the Methodist church in Gordon Street, now known as The White Memorial Hall. He took the plans of the proposed church to Cork to show them to Edward Robinson, an old school friend and now a wealthy businessman. The cost of construction was to be £600 and Robinson instructed Tinsley to return to Clonmel and secure funds by

---

[3] Mr. & Mrs. S. C. Hall, *Ireland, its scenery, character,..* p. 89. (London, 1842).
[4] Forbes, p. 37, 38.

public subscription and that he would make up the deficit. The small Methodist community raised half the sum, Tinsley himself contributed £100, and Robinson duly obliged with the remainder. This building, designed in the Greek Revival manner, was described by a clergyman, named Jobson, as 'the most beautiful chapel in Methodism'.

Tinsley adopted this 'modified Greek Temple' with its classic portico as a favourite style. The façade of ionic columns was first used by him some years previously when he re-modelled the entrance to William Barton's house at Grove, near Fethard. The Gordon Street church was a labour of love for Tinsley since he had recently become a convert to Methodism. So imbued was he by this new doctrine, that at one stage he considered learning Gaelic to convert the peasantry, but the complexities of the language defeated him. Yet, for all his enthusiasm for this new religion, he was far from pleased when, many years later, one of his sons gave up a promising future as an architect to enter the Methodist ministry in Indiana.

The church in Gordon Street also exhibits an integral feature of Tinsley's style, the floral-like pattern of sculpted palmettes which makes much of his work readily identifiable. These can be seen on the ceiling of the church, the tops of the railings, on the corners of the pediment. They appear on a number of other Tinsley buildings in Clonmel. These include the former County Museum in Parnell Street, the Presbyterian church in Anglesea Street which bears the date 1838, and on the porch of Knocklofty House in Marlfield. This motif also featured on the façade of the former Clonmel post-office in O'Connell Street, which was removed to Glenconnor House, sometime after 1901, when the new post office was opened in Gladstone Street, and on the gate piers leading to Melview House in Clonmel.

Towards the end of the eighteen forties Tinsley took on further assignments in County Waterford when he built a range of new stables and a church for Lord Waterford at Curraghmore. This was followed by a contract from one of his lordship's neighbours, Joseph Malcomson, for whom he re-modelled the facade of his house at Mayfield. During the Young Ireland disturbances in 1848, Lord Waterford summoned him once more to fortify Curraghmore. Writing of his experience Tinsley said, 'I constantly drove through a very disaffected part of the country' and 'met and conversed with men known to be rebels and tried to reason with them on the folly of the attempt'.[5] After the rising, he got a further contract from his lordship to build a police barracks at Portlaw.

In 1851, prompted by a combination of circumstances, he decided to emigrate to America. He said that the recent political upheaval caused by the attempted rebellion of 1848 and the unfavourable economic climate following the recent famine had led to a downturn in business. In his journal, he also mentions certain grievances he suffered at the hands of former patrons. The failure of John Bagwell to honour his agreement to give him the contract to build a bridge over the Suir was a source of acute disappointment, and he was 'further distressed' when his Quaker friends offered the design of their new girls' boarding school at Prior Park to one whom he described as 'a pretender from Dublin'.

A will he made on 21 June 1849 indicates that his finances were in a healthy state. It shows that he had a steady income from rented properties, while he admitted that his position as diocesan architect and other professional engagements provided him with enough to meet all 'reasonable wants in a modest way'. Nevertheless he felt he could not face the prospect of his sons not being able to secure a satisfactory livelihood. Before his departure for the United States, he put his affairs in order. He sold some of his property, rented part and entrusted the care of the remainder to the Rev. Charles Foy, the family's sometime lodger, who had married his daughter, Ellen. William handed his brother, Thomas, the responsibility of collecting and remitting his rents.

On 21 September 1851 William Tinsley, accompanied by his wife Lucy and his nine unmarried children, set sail from Waterford to Liverpool, where they boarded the *Queen of the West* bound for America. The crossing proved to be a stormy one and the ship 'was imperilled by savage gales to such an extent that every able bodied man on board was called upon to man the pumps'. Some of the cargo had to be jettisoned and William led prayer meetings invoking divine assistance for a safe delivery. Weary and shaken by their ordeal, they landed in New York where they stayed for eight or nine days. William presented letters of introduction to Fletcher Harper, one of the founders of the famous magazine *Harper's Bazaar*. Harper introduced him to John Price Durbin, a leading figure in the Methodist Church who, in turn,

---

[5] *Ibid*, p. 51.

recommended him to prominent members of the Methodist clergy in Cincinnati.

His arrival in that city did not meet with immediate success and for a time he contemplated a career in farming and even considered speculating in coal-mining properties. The impracticalities of such schemes soon became apparent and he decided to open an architect's office, assisted by his eldest son, Thomas. Business was slow and the few contracts that came his way didn't even pay the rent. A local builder, Harvey Decamp, suggested to him that his style of architecture was too far advanced for the people of Cincinnati. He was also not helped by his proud and uncompromising attitude and the scorn he poured on the work of his contemporaries.

Following a series of disappointments, fortune finally smiled on him when he answered a newspaper advertisement placed by the Board of Directors of the North Western University (now Butler University) in Indianapolis. He received a fee of one hundred dollars to design an extension to the campus and he was also employed to superintend its construction. This was to be the first of seven such college buildings which Tinsley designed in America. The most notable was the Center Hall at Wabash which is regarded as one of the best preserved Tinsley buildings in America. He also designed several churches, and various state buildings including gaols and courthouses.

His public success was somewhat spoiled by domestic difficulties. When his wife died in 1857 his young teenage daughter, Jenny, had to assume the responsibilities of keeping house and caring for her three year old sister, Sarah, a situation that was far from satisfactory. As a solution to his difficulties, he decided to seek a wife to look after his family, hardly a recipe for domestic bliss. On 30 January 1859, Tinsley married Mary Eliza Nixon, his third wife. The marriage was not a success. It was punctuated by violent outbursts of temper from his unhappy partner, who left him several times and, on one occasion, threatened to throw herself into the Ohio River. In spite of their obvious incompatibility, she bore him three children making him the father of seventeen in all.

His marital unhappiness was compounded by the death of his son, William, on the day after his twenty first birthday in July 1859. Two other sons became involved in the American Civil War, Harvey enlisted in the army, while James served in the navy. Both had their health impaired by the rigours of service. The black sheep of the family, Alfie, who had a taste for low company, caused him further grief with his laziness and aversion to work and his habit of running into debt. All this stress proved too much for William. His health failed and he was advised to take a vacation.

He went to Canada where he spent several months recuperating. Feeling much better he decided to visit Ireland. After a pleasant Atlantic crossing, he landed at Derry where he was 'moved to thanksgiving' remembering how the supporters of William of Orange helped to deliver the city from the forces of Popery. Back in Clonmel, after an absence of fourteen years, his former acquaintances found him reserved and aloof. Following a short stay he went on to visit London and Paris.

On his return to America, he embarked on what he regarded as the climax of his architectural career when he received a contract to design a new building for the Ohio Institution for the Education of the Blind at Columbus. With a budget of $318,000, it was the largest and most ambitious contract that he had undertaken. Unfortunately, the project was dogged by controversy from the beginning. A committee charged with inspecting the building criticised its design, claimed that defective materials had been used, that the workmanship was shoddy, and that it was only a matter of time before it collapsed.

The Ohio legislature appointed a five-man commission of enquiry. Their report upheld the charge of faulty design. They also claimed that the contractors were pressurised to hire Tinsley's sons in supervisory positions on the project, and that further nepotism was involved in giving another son the contract to supply ventilation ducts. Tinsley dismissed these accusations by saying it was a trumped-up affair, inspired by corrupt contractors deprived of opportunities for graft. A subsequent report of the Institution's trustees cleared him of all charges and praised his skill and integrity.

On completion of the contract, William Tinsley decided to retire and his son, Thomas R. Tinsley, took over the business. In July 1873, William wrote in his memoir that he was 'in feeble health'. Family pressure and the attack on his integrity in connection with the Ohio Institute were said to have been largely responsible for this decline. Little is known of Tinsley's remaining years. He died at his home on

Bigelow Street, Cincinnati, on 14 June 1885, in his eighty-second year. He was buried beside his second wife at Crown Hill in Indianapolis, where his grave is marked with the following inscription:

William Tinsley
Architect
Born Clonmel Ireland
Feb. 7, 1804
Died Cincinnati O.
June 14, 1885

The greatest tribute to William Tinsley is that so many of his buildings, both in Ireland and America, are still standing and in use to-day. As an architect, Tinsley was not an innovator but a man completely at home in the eclectic mood of his times, borrowing from one style and then another. He found no difficulty in flitting from Italian Renaissance to perpendicular Gothic or Greek Revival styles. In the words of his biographer he was 'a man of his time – a Victorian among Victorians'.

His talent had won him the confidence and respect of the local gentry in Clonmel and its environs and later earned him a place among the foremost architects in his adopted country. A life filled with public recognition and acclaim was all too often marred by ill-health and domestic tragedy. There are many memorials to the members of the Tinsley family, including a stained glass window in Old St. Mary's but, in William's case, the elegant buildings that grace the streets of Clonmel and the additions he made to many a stately home in the surrounding area provide more enduring monuments.

Chapter 17

The Cabinetmaker

While William Tinsley was building and designing houses for members of the nobility and most of the gentry in the neighbourhood of Clonmel, Thomas Graham was making quality furniture for their occupants. He operated a highly successful cabinet-making business at 11 Duncan Street, now Sarsfield Street.

Thomas Graham was the son of Jacob and Joyce Graham who arrived in Clonmel from County Wexford, sometime between 1809 and 1818. Jacob's name first appears in *Pigot's Commercial Directory 1819* where he is listed as a cabinet maker and upholsterer. He died in 1830 at the age of fifty-five, following a protracted illness. An advertisement in 1839 stated that the Graham cabinet and upholstery ware-rooms at 11 Duncan Street sold plate looking glasses imported from England. The mention of 'funerals supplied as usual' leads one to believe that they also sold coffins. The business was trading under the name of J. Graham and Sons, an acknowledgement of the fact that Thomas was not Jacob's only son. Thomas had at least two other brothers, Benjamin born in 1818 and James three years later, both of whom were baptised in Old St. Mary's. There is no further mention of either and it is clear that, on the death of his father, Thomas had become the sole owner of the family business

This is evident from the advertisement placed in the Triennial Commercial Directory of 1843. It said that Thomas Graham 'begged to announce that his Ware-Rooms are always stocked with a very elegant assortment of Articles manufactured with particular care, and of the best and most seasoned materials'. He pointed to the general satisfaction afforded to the gentry of the surrounding country 'in procuring Furniture, not generally attainable in Provincial Towns'. In conclusion, he claimed that 'having directed his attention particularly to Upholstery, he is enabled to execute any orders with which he may be favoured in this line after the most fashionable and approved style'. In addition to his furniture business,

Thomas also became a licensed auctioneer and valuer,[1] but he is best remembered as a craftsman of exceptional skill and as a maker of top class furniture.

Thomas was in business at a time when Clonmel was experiencing an extraordinary period of economic growth. This was reflected in an unprecedented increase in population, rising from ten to twenty thousand in the first four decades of the nineteenth century. This new-found prosperity saw the building of handsome town houses in the suburbs, particularly along the Coleville Road for the town's wealthy merchants. Many of the local gentry were also refurbishing their country homes. These developments provided a ready-made market for first class furniture which, thanks to Graham, could be sourced locally. As Burke put it, this was in stark contrast to the Clonmel of the 1770s when 'it was hardly possible to procure a chair', while now one could purchase 'the magnificent cabinet works of Graham'.[2]

There are a number of houses and institutions in the vicinity of Clonmel where authenticated examples of Thomas Graham's craftsmanship can still be seen. The Graham name is associated with some of the fittings in Clonmel Courthouse, including the decorative woodwork behind the judge's benches. Perhaps, the Graham piece with which the general public is most familiar is the ornate sideboard in the Council Chamber of Clonmel Corporation which was donated by a former mayor, Alderman Denis E. Burke.

Graham made furniture for several Malcomson houses in Clonmel, Dunmore East, Portlaw and Tramore. It is said that his work was exported to St. Peterburg, and installed in the households of wealthy Russians, having been carried on ships owned by the Malcomson shipping line which operated out of Waterford.[3] The Graham firm was also responsible for furnishing the dining room of De La Poer's residence in Gurteen, Kilsheelan. It was described as:

---

[1] *Tipperary Free Press*, 22 December 1847.
[2] Burke, *History of Clonmel*, p. 127.
[3] *Clonmel Nationalist*, 10 March 1979.

one of the most perfect Victorian Baronial interiors in Ireland. The walls are of faded red, above a dado of warm brown oak panelling, elaborately ribbed and moulded, which was supplied by Graham of Clonmel who made the immense carved oak sideboard, dated 1864. The chimney piece, also of carved oak, is the piece de resistance; with its heraldic angels holding shields of the family arms, and its head of St. Hubert's Stag – the family crest – complete with antlers and crucifix, mounted on top of the mantelshelf like a trophy.[4]

Thomas Graham supported the Cork Industrial Exhibition of 1852 which was organised to display Ireland's 'own resources and capabilities'. The promoters, in seeking the co-operation of the whole country, set up a number of local committees. Graham became a member of the Clonmel Committee and also contributed to it financially. The Exhibition attracted exhibits of craftsmanship from all over Ireland, and Graham submitted a number of entries in the furniture competition, but did not win any prizes. At the Dublin Exhibition he was more successful, where his furniture achieved national acclaim. The 'beautiful carved articles' he submitted received 'honourable distinction' and were praised for their 'originality of design and exquisite finish'.[5] He was both a committee member and exhibitor at the Clonmel Art Exhibition of 1858. The three pieces which he submitted give some indication of the variety of woods used. They consisted of a cabriole sofa in rosewood, a library chair carved in oak and a gondola chair in walnut.

He exhibited to wide acclaim at the Royal Agricultural Show which was held in Clonmel in 1880, where his craftsmanship attracted considerable interest from an admiring public. The centrepiece was 'an enclosed cabinet stand fitted up in the most elegant style possible with a beautiful chimney piece, on ponderous pillars and ornamented with a large mirror, set in artistically and elaborate carved framework'. It was positioned so that it could not fail to attract attention and we are told 'that at all hours during each day it was constantly resorted to by pleasure seekers at the show'. The correspondent goes on the state that 'every species of

---

[4] Mark Bence Jones, *A Guide to Irish Country Houses* (London, 1988, p. 148).
[5] *Clonmel Chronicle*, 18 July 1891.

work was a marvel of elegance and artistic taste, reflecting the highest credit on Mr. Graham at whose warerooms they were all manufactured'.

Continuing he stated that:

amongst the superior cabinet work exhibited we found a charming set of dining room furniture in Riga oak, and a sideboard corresponding with the charming piece referred to. This splendid looking sideboard was a curiosity in itself. Exquisitely carved, with living and dead game, singularly realistic; while at the top was another large mirror in its oak frame; it presented an appearance attractive in the extreme. Besides this there was a set of telescope tables, highly polished, and fitted with a powerful screw extender opening twenty feet, by means of which the table could be increased or reduced as the occasion required. The suite of furniture, with chairs to match, being upholstered in crimson Morocco leather, would not be unfitting the most splendid appointed mansion in the county.[6]

Graham's reputation rests on the quality of the furniture he produced. He is regarded as a gifted provincial craftsman who turned out well-made, solid furniture. His work reflected the popular tastes of the age and like most William IV/Early Victorian furniture, Graham's work could be generally described as severely plain, without carving and gilding. Where he used ornamental carving his designs are not innovative in any way but are derivative of contemporary works. However, if the commission demanded it, he could adapt his talents to facilitate the wishes of the customer. Designing furniture to conform to the particular style and architecture of a building seems to have been an inherent part of Graham's business. The oak dining room suite which he supplied to the De la Paor family was made in the Gothic mode to complement the architectural style of Gurteen house in Kilsheelan.

Apart from a few exceptions, it is impossible to identify Graham's work. He had no distinctive style and did not stamp his furniture with a name tag or an identifying number. The provenance of the pieces from

---

[6] *Tipperary Free Press*, 13 August 1880.

Dromana, described below, were supported by entries in the Villiers Stuart papers. However, there are a number of houses in Clonmel and the surrounding area which contain chairs, tables, wardrobes and other pieces said to be examples of Graham's work, but such claims rest on tradition and family lore rather than on any definitive proof.

Some indication of the present value of Graham's work can be got from a catalogue of 1995. In that year an auction of what was described as 'important treasures relating to the Villiers-Stuart family' of Dromana House on the Blackwater, the ancestral home of the Fitzgeralds, Lords of the Decies, was conducted at Ballynaparka, Aglish, Co. Waterford. A number of the items on sale had been originally supplied by Thomas Graham on commission for Henry Villiers Stuart, owner of Dromana from 1809 to 1874. The catalogue also contained a design for a bookcase for the library at Dromana, signed by Thomas Graham, and dated 1856 which might indicate the year in which the commission was executed.

The Graham pieces to be auctioned included what was described as 'a fine rare set of 22 late William IV/Early Victorian mahogany side chairs' and 'an important William IV period mahogany dining table' both of which were expected to fetch between £8,000 and £12,000. A description of the table gives some indication of the technical skill and craftsmanship attained by the Clonmel firm. It had six spare leaves, the top with a moulded edge and rounded corners, raised on a telescopic action, in two sections, with nine reeded tapering legs each with a leaf carved collar, and heavy copes, patent brass cup castors and a panelled mahogany storage cabinet, with six slots for spare leaves. It measured 600 cms. x 168 cms.[7] Also for sale, was a 'rare William IV period Irish mahogany sideboard' valued at £5,000 to £7,000. A photograph of this item featured on the cover of the auction catalogue. A pair of two seater mahogany hall benches and a set of four William IV period mahogany hall chairs were each expected to fetch a £1,000.

Thomas Graham married Rebecca Pepper from Parsons Town in the King's County on 20 May 1835. They had two children, Caroline born in 1838, and Richard, who was born in 1852 but died seven years later. His

---

[7] Auction Catalogue of Mealy's, Castlecomer in relation to Important Fine Art Sale on the Premises at Ballinaparka, Aglish, Co. Waterford., 5 September 1995.

wife died in 1867 and, four years later, he re-married Mary Legge, nee Lawson, widow of Richard Legge, former manager of the Clonmel Savings Bank. It would appear from entries in the commercial directories of the period that Thomas retired sometime between 1886 and 1889. Unfortunately, there was no member of the family left to carry on the business.

Apart from being a successful businessman and a talented craftsman, Graham took a deep in interest in the welfare of his town and its community. His name can be found on various subscription lists to many worthy causes. He was one of the founders of the Clonmel Mechanics' Institute, set up to provide education for the local artisans and, up to his final illness, continued to serve as one of the most energetic members of its executive committee. In 1883 he was elected to the Clonmel Corporation as an alderman for the East Ward, a position he retained until 1887, when ill health obliged him to resign. He was conservative in politics and a supporter of John Bagwell.[8]

He was also appointed a Borough Magistrate, exercising his duties in a kindly and efficient manner. As a member of the Protestant community he contributed to the affairs of his Church, serving for many years either as a select member of the vestry or on the diocesan synod. The Reverend Warren commended his efforts when he said, 'We know, many of us, what his life was in this parish; how by his wise council and help he always sought to advance the interest of the Church in this town of Clonmel'.

In 1891, Thomas Graham, J.P., then in his eighty second year, died at his residence in Sarsfield Street, following a protracted illness. He was buried in Old St. Mary's, under an arch in the medieval walls, close to the grave of his son. His obituary described him as living the life of a Christian gentleman, a good family man and a respected member of the community. He was regarded as gentle and courteous by nature, and upright and honourable in his dealings. In the course of a graveside tribute in Old St. Mary's, the Reverend Canon Warren said 'We know how in his business he was a successful man, and how he raised himself in his work to the highest position in that line of life which he had adopted for himself', a reference to

---

[8] Seán O'Donnell, *Clonmel 1840-1890: Anatomy of an Irish town,* (Dublin, 1999), p. 262.

his reputation as a maker of high-class furniture which he had produced in his Clonmel workshop for over half a century.

Chapter 18

Pioneer Photographer

Dr. William Despard Hemphill was a man of wide-ranging cultural and practical interests. Not alone was he a highly regarded medical practitioner, but also an antiquarian, historian, horticulturalist, geologist and musician. His obituary notice stated that his 'was not an idle existence, but of useful and beneficent purpose … his constant preoccupations seemed never to produce a sense of weariness'.[1] Most of all, he is best remembered as a pioneering Irish photographer and one of the most gifted of his day.

The name Hemphill is said to have derived from a place of that name near Kilmarnock in Scotland, but sometime during the sixteenth or seventeenth century Boyd of Hemphill became the first member of the family to settle in Ireland, when he set up home in Coleraine, county Derry. In 1728, Samuel Hemphill, his great grandson, came to Tipperary, following his appointment as Presbyterian minister in Fethard. He purchased land near Killenaule where he built a house called Springhill.[2]

William Despard Hemphill, who was born in August 1816, was the grandson of that Presbyterian clergyman, and the fourth in a family of six boys and three girls born to Samuel Hemphill, M.D. and Mary Backas. Despard was his grandmother's name. He grew up at 12 Gordon Street, the present Wolfe Tone Street and was educated at the Clonmel Endowed School in the Irishtown. William followed his father into the medical profession. In 1834 he became a licentiate of the Royal College of Surgeons of Ireland, and obtained his fellowship in 1844. In the same year he took his M.D. degree at St. Andrew's University in Scotland and, before returning to Clonmel, he spent some years as House Surgeon of the City of Dublin Hospital.

---

[1] *Clonmel Chronicle*, 16 July 1902.
[2] Pat Holland, *Tipperary Images*, (Cahir, 2003), pp. 82, 83; David Butler, 'Presbyterianism in the Fethard area (1690-1919)' in *Tipperary Historical Journal*, xiii, (2000), p. 67.

During his career in Clonmel, in addition to building up an extensive practice, he served as medical officer to both the District Asylum and Prison. He was also prominent in medical circles at a national level, becoming President of the Irish Medical Association and, as a keen student of forensic medicine, had numerous articles published in the *Dublin Journal of Medical Science*. One of his most important contributions was a series of papers on 'The examination of Minute Blood Stains in medico-legal investigation'.

In January 1849, Dr. Hemphill married Sarah Henrietta Peddar, daughter of a prominent Clonmel family, and took up residence at Brighton Place. In 1871, they moved to nearby Oakville with their four children, Samuel William, Mary Beverly (May), Colyn Alice and Evelyn Alice. This attractive two-storey Georgian villa, which featured regularly in his photographic studies, was built in the 1820s by William's father-in-law, Henry Peddar. It had a typical low-pitched roof and wide eaves, and was so-named because its internal doors, window shutters, staircases etc., were made of polished oak'.[3] It was demolished in 1974 to make way for the Oakville shopping centre.

Photography in Hemphill's day was in its infancy. It was first discovered in France in 1816 by Joseph Niepce and introduced into Ireland in the 1840s. Equipment was heavy and cumbersome and the technique of developing and processing negatives was intricate and complex. It was a hobby that required time and money, as well as a knowledge of science. Hemphill's earliest known photograph, showing a bridge under repair near Lismore Castle, was taken in 1853, but how or when he developed a serious interest in photography is not known.[4]

In 1857 he published a booklet containing eleven images called *Photographic & Stereoscopic Views of St. Mary's Church, Clonmel taken in 1857 before the alterations and dedicated to John Bagwell, J.P. by William D. Hemphill, M.D.* The views of the exterior and interior of the building are of architectural interest, showing the church before the alterations of 1857. Stereoscopic images were to become closely associated with the photography of Hemphill. This technique consisted of photographs

---

[3] James Cusack, 'The Oakville story' in *Clonmel Nationalist*, 31 March 1984.
[4] Holland, p. 12.

taken in pairs from slightly different angles which, when projected together, gave an impression of unity and, when viewed through a viewer, had a three-dimensional effect.

He is best remembered for the book which appeared in 1860 under the title *Stereoscopic Illustrations of Clonmel and the surrounding countryside, including Abbeys, Castles and Scenery* which included eighty of his photographs. They were surrounded by foliated borders and lithographed in gold. This lavish and substantial tome which was priced at five guineas, a considerable sum at the time, is now a valuable collector's item. When it was published, it received what to-day would be regarded as rave notices from many journals and institutions, such as the *London Photographic Society*, which lauded it as containing 'admirable specimens of photographic art'. *The Art Journal* considered many of the photographs 'excellent', while the Dublin Medical Press was impressed by his 'artistic taste'. *The Christian Examiner, Clonmel Chronicle, Kilkenny and South-East of Ireland Archaeological Society* and *Dublin Builder* were equally approving.[5]

The book was dedicated to his friend, Lady Osborne of Newtown Anner, 'for her love of everything beautiful in nature and in art, her warm admiration of photography, or her many private virtues and endearing qualities'. Hemphill's father had attended her ladyship's husband, Sir Thomas Osborne, in his last illness, and William continued to act as family doctor, becoming good friends with Lady Osborne and her children. The house with its furnishings and gardens featured in many of his photographs, while Lady Osborne and her daughters, Grace and Edith, posed for him on numerous occasions.[6]

In his preface to *Stereoscopic Illustrations,* he said that publishing such a book provided him with an agreeable relaxation from his arduous medical duties. His intention was 'to preserve a record of the many beautiful and in some cases little known localities in the neighbourhood' of interest to 'the antiquarian, the artist and the man of taste'. He chose his subjects because of their historical and archaeological value and not

---

[5] *Cork Examiner*, 14 March 1983.

[6] Mark Girouard, 'Miss Smith comes to Tipperary' in *Town and Country,* (London, 1992), p. 129.

because they would make pretty or saleable pictures. His descriptions of the illustrations were based on personal observation and consultation with 'the most authentic sources' which are listed in the bibliography at the end of the book. He claimed to be the first 'to use Stereoscopic Photographs for the purpose of book illustration, and also the first to photograph in detail the antiquities and beauties of this neighbourhood'. Many illustrations were accompanied by detailed descriptions of the history and notable, architectural features of their subjects.

His photographs include the abbeys at Holy Cross, Athassal and the Augustinian foundation at Cahir. Other landmarks of an archaeological and religious interest such as the Rock of Cashel, Donaghmore Church, near Lisronagh, the dolmen at Gurteen, overlooking Kilsheelan were featured. Nearer home, St. Patrick's Well was also included. Almost half of the book was devoted to castellated residences at Lismore, Mitchelstown, Ardfinnan, Cahir, Kilmanahan and Shanbally. Four others, at Marlfield, Knocklofty, Newtown Anner and the Marquis of Waterford's Curraghmore complete the group. Ten photographs are devoted to Clonmel. They include four scenic views of the town and two of Old St. Mary's. The selection is completed by studies of the Scots' Church in Anglesea Street, the Model School, a barge at the Gashouse Bridge and one of the railway station in 1857, showing a steam engine with a number of carriages. This has the distinction of being the first photograph of a train ever taken in Ireland.

Hemphill took his photography very seriously. He was a committee member and exhibitor at the Clonmel Art Exhibition in 1858 and, during the course of the exhibition, he contributed a lecture giving his views on photography. He became a member of the Amateur Photographic Association which was founded in 1859 and he won various prizes for his photography at international exhibitions in Dublin, London and Paris.

Hemphill's photographs illustrate the world with which he was familiar. They record the people he knew and his recreational activities and interests. His membership of the Kilkenny and South-East of Ireland Archaeological Society is reflected in his studies of various historic buildings and archaeological landmarks. He was also a keen orchid grower and became a trustee of the Clonmel Horticultural Society, reflecting his devotion to garden landscapes. He also produced studies of trees, flowers and fruit. His portfolio included intimate studies of his children, formal portraits of friends, records of flora and fauna and items of archaeological or ecclesiastical interest. His celebration of church architecture and a number of tableau depicting biblical themes were inspired by his religious beliefs. Glimpses of the homes and lifestyle of the local landed gentry are valuable sources for the social historian, ranging from the furnishings of the drawing room at Newtown Anner to a game of croquet on the lawn of Marlfield House.

Hemphill has left behind a unique glimpse of life in Clonmel as he knew it. He recorded a number of scenic shots of the town, including one from Merlin House on Coleville Road and another from Heywood Road. Although many landmarks such as the Model School, the Scots' Church and the District Asylum have scarcely changed, others have disappeared forever. It is hard to visualise that the extensive grounds of the Clonmel Horticultural Society were once located on the north side of Queen Street, on a site now occupied by Rink Place and the surrounding houses.

Apart from the town's physical fabric we are also made aware of political and economic changes. Pictures showing a company of British artillery and two gas lighters on the Gashouse Bridge are reminders of a vanished past. While the barges were still plying their trade on the river Suir, the photograph of the steam locomotive is a clear indication that their days were numbered. Others feature local people, the majority of whom cannot be identified. Among the exceptions are the family of Robert Davis, a local Quaker shop-keeper in the grounds of their home at Ashbourne House, and a formal study of Hemphill's friend, the celebrated local furniture-designer, Thomas Graham.

Ivory turning was another of his interests and he exhibited some of his pieces at the Clonmel Art Exhibition of 1858. He was also a talented musician. During a concert held in the Clonmel Parochial Hall, not only did he play two flute solos, but he also conducted the orchestra and the programme included a march which he had composed. His two daughters accompanied him on violin, drum and pianoforte. He was a keen collector of Waterford Glass and a student of geology. His daughter, May, made a provision in her will that his cabinet of geological specimens be given to the National Museum of Ireland.

He was a man of strong, if somewhat bigoted, religious views. His *Stereoscopic Illustrations etc.* contained a section on the progress of Christianity in Ireland and the delight he felt at the Reformation 'when the Irish church gladly threw off the bondage of Rome'. Deeply interested in all matters affecting the Church of Ireland, of which he was a faithful adherent and liberal supporter, he was elected a member of the Select Vestry and of the Diocesan Council and Synod, and became a keen supporter of the Church Missionary Society. During the deliberations of these bodies, his valuable advice was thoroughly appreciated.

In politics he was a committed unionist as was his brother Robert, who was a conservative member of Clonmel Corporation from 1854 to 1858. William's unionist views were illustrated by an incident which took place in 1886 when William Gladstone, the British prime-minister, proposed to introduce Home Rule. In deference to him, the corporation proposed to re-name Johnson Street and call it Gladstone Street. Hemphill, vehemently disapproved of Gladstone and his politics, and in protest at this change, he adopted the name Brighton Place for the block of four houses he owned, adjacent to his home at Oakville. They were named at the suggestion of a friend, Miss Emily Barton, who said that their sunny aspect reminded her of the slogan 'sunny Brighton' which was then being used to promote the tourist potential of that popular English resort.

In his later years he had to suffer his share of upsets and family bereavements. His younger daughter, Evelyn Alice died in 1892 and five years later he had to endure the loss of his beloved wife, Sarah. Her obituary noted that the deepest regret prevailed 'especially among the poorer classes of this district who retain a grateful sense of benevolence, and many acts of kindness on their behalf'. When his son, Samuel, contracted a marriage which his father considered unsuitable, they became estranged. In 1901 Samuel died in London where he gone to work as a music teacher.

Although W. D. Hemphill lived to an advanced age, the last two years of his life were blighted by ill-health. Sadly, while still mentally alert, he was afflicted by blindness. He died at his home in Oakville in 1902. He was highly regarded as a respected member of the community and as a charitable man. It was said that 'the poor without distinction found in him a highly-disposed and generous friend'. He was survived by his daughter May, who lived at Oakville with her niece Eva, Samuel's daughter, until her death in 1925. He is buried, together with his wife and three children, beneath a small Celtic cross on the western side of Old St. Mary's Churchyard, somewhat south of the Anne Street Gate and close to the medieval walls of Clonmel.

Chapter 19

Star-Crossed Lovers

On 26 February 1826 two young lovers met at their customary spot on the Gashouse Bridge and strolled down the towpath by the river Suir. Frederick Close and Ann Grubb set out sometime after eight o'clock in the evening and were never seen alive again. The circumstances surrounding that fateful evening have given rise to much speculation and controversy, which has not been resolved by the passage of time.

Anne was born in 1807 into a Quaker family in the town of Mountmellick. She was the eldest daughter and the second of fourteen children born to John Grubb of Clonmel and Elizabeth Millner of Mountmellick. John Grubb had a bakery in the town but it would appear it was not very successful, for the records of the Mountmellick Quaker meeting indicate that he could not pay his debts. His daughter, Anne, attended the local Quaker school and then, as was customary for all Quaker children, she was placed in an apprenticeship. She was sent to her uncle, Robert George Grubb in Clonmel, who had a millinery shop in the premises now occupied by Maher's pharmacy in O'Connell Street. She arrived there around the end of 1822 and according to accepted Quaker practice a certificate of removal was sent from the Mountmellick Monthly meeting to the Tipperary Monthly meeting, which read:

> Anne Grubb, daughter of John and Elizabeth Grubb, having a considerable time since removed to reside within the company of your meeting, we certify that she is a member of our religious society and from her young tender age when leaving us it seems unnecessary to say more than recommend her to your Christian care and oversight – and remain your friends.
>
> Signed on behalf of the Mountmellick men's and women's meeting held on the 23rd day of first mo. 1823.
> Nathan Beale, Jr. and Anne Beale.

Frederick Close, born in 1804 into a wealthy Manchester merchant family, was the youngest of three sons of John and Mary Close. In 1818 he became a pupil in Manchester Grammar School but left sometime later and enlisted as a private in the army. His father, realising that he was determined to pursue a military career, purchased a commission for him. It was said that he quickly acquired a grasp of military tactics and rapidly rose from ensign to the rank of lieutenant. In 1824 he was assigned to the 86th or Royal County Down regiment of Foot, then stationed in Newry, County Down. The following January he was transferred to Naas and by June he was with his regiment in Clonmel.

The tragic tale of Frederick Close and Anne Grubb has attracted the attention of various writers over the years. In 1860 their story was published under the title *The Clonmel Tragedy – a True Story*. It was reputed to have been the reminiscences of an officer, who had served with Close, but whose name has not come down to us. He described Close as charming and handsome, a universal favourite with his fellow officers and the ladies. In stature he was above middle height, and his frame was both athletic and graceful and he added that few 'could excel him in feats of agility and strength'. Margaret Grubb of Clogheen, a relative of Anne's, says that this was a generally held opinion. In a letter to her sister she wrote that 'all who knew him say he was very handsome and tall with a most pleasing countenance and gentlemanly manners'.[1]

The story of Frederick and Anne also formed the basis of *The Major's Story* which was included in *Bivouac, or the Stories of the Peninsular War*, published in 1830. The author, William Hamilton Maxwell, who had seen Anne Grubb was overcome by her beauty:

Many a year had passed away, but I never shall forget that beauteous girl. She was scarcely nineteen – tall, and notwithstanding the formality of her costume, the roundness of her arm and the symmetry of her waist and bosom could not be concealed. Her eyes were hazel, with an expression of extreme gentleness. Her hair, Madonna-like, was parted on the forehead; but the simple cap could not hide the

---

[1] Margaret Grubb to Mary Leadbeater, 11th day of the third month, 1826.

profusion of its silken tresses. The outline of the face was strictly Grecian – the complexion pale and delicate – while the 'ripe red lip' formed a striking contrast in its hue, and seemed as if 'some bee had stung it newly'. I was perfectly fascinated; and were anything wanted to make her irresistible, her voice was so musical, so modulated, that the listener held his breath to hear.

Apart from her obvious physical attractions, the writer offers no opinion as to her character and personality.

On 25 March, almost a month after the young couple disappeared, *The Times* reported that their subsequent movements were 'wrapped in inexplicable mystery'. As the days went by the townspeople became concerned for their safety, especially after the lieutenant's hat had been discovered on the river bank the night after he left the barracks. Rumours were rife and the town was thrown into 'a state of considerable agitation'.

On the morning of the 15th March, two local boatmen, Edmund Burke and Maurice Davin, saw a shadow in the water about four or five yards from the bank near Kilganey which turned out to be the body of Frederick Close. The deceased lay on his face and hands, with his feet against the current. His boat-cloak, dirk and gloves were missing. Colonel Stuart, who was a boy at the time and the son of an officer in Frederick Close's regiment, recalled in his *Reminiscences of a Soldier* that Frederick's hat and coat were picked up in a field forty yards from the river. However, *The Times* said that neither article was found, a fact confirmed by the inquest. The lieutenant's body was searched by the magistrate, B. B. Bradshaw. He found two bank notes of £1 each and 5s. 6d. in change, a bunch of keys and some papers in his pockets. When his watch was removed from its fob it was found to have stopped at nine o'clock.

His body was brought to town on a barge. It was then removed from the quay and carried to the courthouse. The pantaloons of the deceased were torn about the knees and his face was so thickly covered with river mud, that his features were quite imperceptible. Though he had been in the water for seventeen days, it was reported that 'when washed, his skin appeared fresh as if life flowed in every vein – a half smile was on the countenance, which was quite serene, but the mouth was a little distorted'.[2] The mayor, Thomas Chaytor, had a jury[3] sworn in and then adjourned the inquiry until noon the following day to await the return of the brother of the deceased who had gone to Mitchelstown to meet with some of the officers who had served with his late brother. The inquest was held in a packed courthouse presided over by the mayor and assisted by the following magistrates, W. H. Bradshaw, B. B. Bradshaw, John Bagwell, Robert Constable and Gerald Fitzgerald.

The first witness called was boatman, Edmund Burke, who described the discovery of the body. He said that there was no sign of a boat cloak or a dirk and that he did not see any gloves on the deceased. Next to give evidence was the magistrate, B. B. Bradshaw, who was on his way to Limerick when he heard of the gruesome discovery. He drove down to the spot and, on learning that the lieutenant's clothes had not been searched, felt it was his duty to do so. He also noticed what appeared to be a discolouration on the forehead that could have resulted from a blow. Later, Dr. Fitzgerald, one of three doctors who examined the body, could find no evidence of a fracture. Having consulted with his colleagues, Dr. O'Reilly of the 65th Regiment and Dr. Constable, it was decided to open the skull but no trace of a heavy blow could be detected. Dr. Constable was of the opinion that the mark on the forehead of the deceased was compatible with the imprint of a tight hatband.

Then Private Owen Heffernan of the 86th regiment and servant to Lieutenant Close told the inquiry how his master had come into the room looking at his watch on the Sunday evening he disappeared. He told him that he was going out at eight o'clock and asked to have a glass of punch prepared by ten o'clock when he expected to return. As it was his practice not to wear his uniform on such occasions he called for his white top coat, black pantaloons and his buff waistcoat. On second thoughts he requested his boat-cloak, remarking that 'it would keep her and himself more comfortable'. Heffernan said he clasped the cloak around his master's neck.

---

[2] *Ibid.*

[3] The jury members were Thomas Stokes, James Burke, Simon Prosser, Hugh Daniel, Wm. Thompson, Joseph Higgins, James R. Shee, Charles Achison, Henry Julian, Wm. J. Harvey, Jeremiah Laylor and Thomas Davis.

He said it was tight and could only be opened with difficulty. The lieutenant also told Heffernan to place a twelve inch dirk in the left pocket of his coat which his master had been in the habit of carrying with him since he came to this country, particularly on going fishing, or on any other business which brought him any distance from town.

Heffernan also said the lieutenant had told him how Dominick Harvey, son of the canteen manager in the barracks, and Thomas Taylor, who was on the staff of the Tipperary militia, had followed him several times when he was in the company of Miss Grubb. This was corroborated by Thomas Kettlewell, son of Colonel Kettlewell and a friend of the deceased. Kettlewell said that on one occasion the deceased had told him that he had been two miles from town in the company of Miss Grubb, when he encountered Taylor and Harvey and that he gave Harvey a thrashing. Later, when Close and Kettlewell were on the street they met these youths. Close remarked, 'see they know me, they blush and laugh'. Kettlewell added that Lieutenant Close never felt threatened by Harvey or Taylor. Neither had he experienced or had he complained of being attacked by boatmen or any other inhabitants of the town.

Harvey denied ever having been struck by the deceased or that he had been in company with Taylor on any occasion. He admitted that he saw the deceased with a young woman but that he had not seen the deceased after four o'clock on the day he was last seen alive, nor had he been on the quay that night. However, Harvey did say that one day a companion of his had come up to him in the Main Street and told him that if he went to the bridge near the workhouse he would see something that would please him. From there he saw Frederick Close and Miss Grubb cross the bridge. He concealed himself until they passed but said that he never offered any violence whatsoever. Harvey went on to say they he never sought to be acquainted with Miss Grubb, nor had he made any advances to her.

His companion, Thomas Taylor, made a similar statement and claimed that his name had been introduced into this business without any foundation of any kind. Harvey was also able to provide an alibi to show that he had been in Main Street from eight to half-past nine on the night the deceased had disappeared. Having considered the evidence offered, the court felt that both were no more than callow youths, mere peeping Toms, who were not implicated in the tragedy.

One of the more bizarre incidents connected with the case concerned a mysterious woman who presented herself at the army barracks, two nights after the lieutenant had disappeared. Heffernan said, in evidence, that she claimed to have had a letter for the lieutenant and a bundle which she said contained clothing belonged to Miss Grubb. She stated that the lieutenant intended to take Miss Grubb to Mullinahone that morning. The sentry refused her admission. A scuffle ensued and the woman received a black eye.

When Heffernan was informed of the incident he received the woman in his quarters later that evening. The woman said she was a servant of Mr. Grubb but when Heffernan asked her to produce the note she told him that she had mislaid it. He refused to accept the bundle of clothes as he thought it was a ruse to determine whether or not Miss Grubb was in the barracks. She turned down an offer of a drink with Heffernan in the canteen on account of her black eye. Both of them proceeded to Mrs. Ward's pub in Bridge Street where they had several drinks, after which Heffernan returned to the barracks. Under further questioning the witness stated that he knew all Mr. Grubb's servants and that the woman in question was not one of them. Mrs. Ward said that she did not know her either and that she had only met her that morning. She left a small bundle with her in pledge of a whiskey but she quickly returned to redeem it. She saw the woman open the bundle she had brought from the barracks, and that it only contained a few trifling articles, such as frills, caps etc.. She estimated that the entire collection was not worth 2s. 2d. and that the items were of such inferior quality that no young lady would wear them.

At about four o'clock that afternoon the mayor brought the inquest to a close. He felt it was unnecessary to address the jury as they were fully conversant with the facts. Having retired for a short time, they returned a verdict – 'Found Drowned'. The body of Lieutenant Close was interred with full military honours in the churchyard of Old St. Mary's. The chief mourners were the brother of the deceased, Colonel Johnson of the 86th regiment and the Mayor, William Chaytor, Esq.

The officers of the 65th wore crepe round their arms, and the corpse was followed to the grave by a vast concourse of inhabitants: altogether, we never witnessed more sympathy expressed, nor a more general feeling of regret at the premature dissolution of a young gentleman who promised to add lustre to a profession which he embraced with such ardour and devotion.

The following is inscribed on a horizontal slab close to the south wall of the church:

> Beneath this tomb are deposited the mortal remains of Lieutenant Frederick Close of his Majesty's 86th, Royal County of Down Regiment of Infantry and youngest son of John Close Esq., of Manchester, merchant. He perished in the River Suir near the town, on Sunday evening, the 26th February, 1826, at the early age of 22. Lamented by all who knew him.

Meanwhile, the search continued for the remains of Anne Grubb. On 17 March, her body was found by John Walsh, a crewman on Anthony Whitten's boat, on a weir to which some of her clothes were fastened. She was lying on her back in three feet of water further down the river between Killaloan and Gurteen and was held there by some sand, which had been deposited by the late floods. What struck observers as highly remarkable was the fact that her clothes, including her bonnet and cloak, were still in perfect order. She was placed in an oak coffin and brought to her father's house in Main Street.

The inquest opened at eleven the following day. Mary Nugent, who was a nurse in the house of Anne's uncle, Robert George Grubb, said that she saw Anne on the Sunday she disappeared and did not see her again until her body was brought to town the day before. That fateful Sunday evening Anne gave the witness and another servant their tea at about half-past seven. During tea Anne asked for her cloak. But on hearing that it was upstairs she took her sister's instead. She had her bonnet on and said she was going for a walk and sent one of the servants to see if it was eight o'clock. She said that she was going to Mrs. Bond's and to visit her mother.

Mary spoke to her about being back by ten and Anne told her that she did not intend being out beyond that hour.

Dr. Fitzgerald said that he examined the body on Friday with the assistance of two or three medical men.[4] They found that the strings of the cloak had left a deep mark on the neck. Other than that her body showed no evidence of violence whatsoever, with the exception of a slight abrasion on the skin of the knee which they felt might have occurred when she fell into the river. In Dr. Fitzgerald's opinion the deceased met with no violence, or ill treatment of any description, except from drowning.

At the beginning of the inquest the mayor was handed a note concerning a Mrs. Bagge. It was said that she had a conversation with a man who worked at Capt. Power's, at Gurteeen. The man had been coming in to town on the night of the tragedy and at Dudley's mills (a little below where the body of Lieut. Close was discovered) he heard screams of 'murder' and loud splashing in the water, and shortly after three men passed him, whose names he knew. When Mrs. Bagge was summoned to present herself in court she said that no such conversation took place and that it was just rumour and that she had not spoken to any person who had been on the quay that night.

The jury were unanimous in their verdict – 'Found Drowned'. Anne Grubb was buried nearby in the Friends' Graveyard in O'Neill Street. The funeral was attended by a large gathering including members of every denomination, and most of the officers of the garrison. Her grave remains unmarked in accordance with Quaker practice of the time and the belief that a memorial, no matter how modest, would smack of ostentation. According to local lore their love transcended the grave. On the anniversary of their deaths the ghosts of Anne and Frederick were said to leave their respective graves to conduct a nocturnal tyrst.

The inquests returned a verdict of accidental drowning and this was the opinion of one the noted Quaker historian, Isabel Grubb, from accounts of the tragedy handed down by her family. Circumstances support this.

---

[4] The jury consisted of James Burke, Charles Achinson, William Harvey, John Daniel, George Glascott, Nicholas Fell, John Lawlor, Pat Power, Phil Connell, William O'Neill, Francis Trigg, David Dowling.

Heavy rain had been recorded the previous week and the level of the Suir was higher than normal. It has been suggested that there was a particularly strong north wind that night. A sudden gust blew the lieutenant's hat off. Stooping to retrieve it with his other arm around Miss Grubb, another gust blew them both into the river, and even the lieutenant's reputation as a strong swimmer failed to save them. Heffernan had told the inquest that on one occasion he had seen his master leap out of a boat at place called 'the lake', near Athlone, with a fowling dress on, and swim ashore, a distance of almost two hundred yards. Why they should have chosen to walk along the banks of a swollen river in such conditions no one knows.

Nevertheless, their disappearance and subsequent deaths gave rise to much rumour and speculation. *The Clonmel Advertiser* conceded that 'enough, however, has appeared to justify the conclusion, that the interesting couple had come by their deaths accidentally'. It was also of the opinion that:

> nothing was elicited in this enquiry tending to explain, in any satisfactory manner, the cause of death of this hapless female and her partner in misfortune, nor as yet has any light been thrown on this calamity which probably will remain unexplained to the end of time.[5]

Referring to the findings of the inquest on Lieutenant Close the newspaper commented on 'the undecided way in which the investigation terminated' and that an examination of the evidence shows that the case 'still remains wrapped up in inexplicable mystery'. Although there were many inconsistencies and contradictions in the evidence of various witness, it should be borne in mind that the only question for the jury to determine was the cause of death.

However, the novelist, Maxwell, author of *The Major's Story*, and Colonel Stuart, in his *Reminiscences of a Soldier* were both of the opinion that foul play was involved. The latter stated that Close was putting his life in jeopardy by continuing with these clandestine meetings. He recalled that Owen Heffernan had told the inquest that on the night in question

---

[5] *Clonmel Advertiser*, 22 March 1826.

Lieutenant Close had carried a twelve inch dirk, a weapon that he had been in the habit of keeping about him for some time. When the lieutenant's body was discovered there was no trace of the dirk. On the other hand, there were no marks of violence on the bodies.

Another theory was that the couple had eloped. On the day after their disappearance William Strangman set off for Fethard and the surrounding area seeking knowledge of their whereabouts. It was said that he was also a suitor of the deceased and furthermore, had the approval of her family. Some days later an adjutant in the barracks named Dolman, instructed the drum-major to play *Merrily danced the Quaker's Wife*, an allusion to the supposed elopement. Even the *Limerick Chronicle* went so far as to suggest that the young couple 'had been united in matrimony by the blacksmith of Gretna Green'. Since the contents of the lieutenant's pocket only yielded the sum of £1 5s. 6d. this weakens that argument considerably, as does the fact that they brought no change of clothing with them.

The name of William Strangman and the suggestion of foul play were to occur once more in connection with the case. In 1835, Strangman became the subject of a newspaper article by John Hackett, the editor of the *Tipperary Free Press* claiming that he was responsible for their deaths. Outraged by this accusation Strangman sued for damages. In the course of the trial the defendant was described by his counsel as 'the protector of a mother and two children who run a school for girls in Clonmel'. This was a reference to the Quaker school run by the Misses Strangman in Mary Street. Although he was awarded £750 damages, William Strangman remains an enigma for there is no one of that name in the family pedigree for this period.[6]

There is one more intriguing possibility. Deeply in love and knowing that Anne's Quaker parents would never consent to their daughter marrying a soldier, did they decide on a suicide pact? At the time of their disappearance the young couple had been seeing one another for more than six months but considering their different backgrounds, the relationship was fraught with difficulties. Anne's family were unaware of their

---

[6] Family pedigrees, Friends' Historical Library, Dublin.

attachment and the lovers had to resort to meeting in secret. According to one of his fellow officers, Close, had made no approach to her guardian and studiously timed his calls to the house in his absence. Even Frederick himself was at pains to point out that the difficulty of an arrangement was placing a strain on their relationship.

In the course of a remarkable letter[7] which the lieutenant wrote to Anne some six months previously shows that he was suffering from a great deal of stress. He said that his purpose in writing was to describe the nature of a dream he had. He tells her that he dreamt she was dead and this had made him aware of his strength of feeling towards her. He declared 'I am young. I do not add happy – my heart is sincere. I will be candid and ingenious – I have admired you long with what ardour I know not etc.', Entract states in his article 'The Clonmel Mystery', 'such sentiments seem to be more in keeping with a morbid and introspective poet rather than a young athletic officer of jocund laugh and exuberance of spirit'.

Apart from the official verdict of accidental drowning, other theories surrounding their deaths are no more than speculation. Perhaps, we should heed the words of the Reverend Dr. Bell, who conducted the funeral service of Frederick Close in Old St. Mary's. In the course of his homily he said, 'The voice of mercy cries aloud for the character of the departed, and Christian charity allows us not to whisper a scandal, of which God only knows the truth'.

Following the tragedy, Anne's parents continued to live on in Clonmel, running a small bakery in the Irishtown. Her father died in 1829 and her mother lived on for a further ten years. They were finally interred with their daughter, Anne.

---

[7] Letter dated 12th July 1825 in Friends' Historical Library, Dublin.

Chapter 20

Missionary to China

Alice O'Sullivan dedicated her life to the service of others, educating the poor, caring for orphans and abandoned children and tending to the sick. Her work took her to England, France and finally to China where she died at a tragically early age. Her birthplace is marked by a plaque on the façade of Kavanagh's sports shop, next to the West Gate. Around 1830 her parents, Cornelius O'Sullivan and Mary Waterson with their infant son, Daniel, came from Newry to live in Clonmel, where five more children were to be born. Alice, the second youngest, was the only girl.

She was born on 1 December 1836. Being a delicate child she was baptized almost immediately. In 1840, her mother died at the early age of thirty seven and was buried in St. Stephen's cemetery, near present-day Connolly Park. Alice was left by her father to the care of a devoted nurse by whom she was spoiled, while her older brothers made a great fuss of her and 'made her share in all their games and pleasures'.[1]

Although the O'Sullivans lived in Clonmel for almost thirty years little is known about them. The father, Cornelius, is listed in Shearman's Commercial Directory 1839 as a pawn-broker with an address at the West Gate. He was still in business in 1856 but sometime later, he emigrated to America with one of his sons. Another of Alice's brothers, Daniel, became a Vincentian priest and died in Dublin in 1917.

Alice received her early education from the Presentation sisters in Clonmel who later remembered her with great affection. She was sent to the Dominican Convent of St. Mary's in Dun Laoghaire to complete her studies. A former school friend described Alice as rather older than most of her companions, small, dark in complexion, not particularly good looking, and possessing a keen sense of humour, mature common sense, and

---

[1] Sisters of Charity, Provincial House, Mill Hill, *Pioneer Sisters of Charity of St. Vincent de Paul*, (London, 1955), p. 59.

genuine piety.

From an early age she was attracted to life in the convent. Before she was a teenager she called to the Sisters of Charity in Clonmel asking to be admitted, only to be told that she was too young. The Dominican nuns would gladly have accepted her but, on the advice of her brother Daniel, she entered the Sisters of Charity of St. Vincent de Paul.

She left for France for the convent at Amiens on 31 January 1856. After three months she transferred to the mother house in Paris where she received the grey-blue habit and white cornette of the Vincentian order. Her seminary directress noted that she 'was good and solidly pious, but self-willed with decided views of her own'. She also adds that 'she was sensible, orderly and had good judgement'.[2] She was sent to teach in Boulogne for a short time, where one of her Irish pupils, Miss Cartwright, recalled her as being 'a happy character' and always 'being sweet, patient and even-tempered'.

By 1857, Alice, now Sister Louise, was back in Ireland where she became part of the Vincentian community in Drogheda. She was to spend the next five years teaching the poor children of the town. Conditions were primitive with a converted hayloft serving as a classroom. One of her deepest regrets was that she had not sufficient resources available to meet the demands of all the deserving cases she encountered. In 1925, Mary Byrne, one of her former pupils, paid tribute to 'her generous and self-sacrificing nature', and her devotion to the young girls in her care. In 1862, she moved to the Vincentian convent at Bullingham, near Hereford in England, where she found her work 'was full of struggle and hardships'.[3]

She frequently expressed to her Superiors her desire to serve on the foreign missions. In 1863, Sister Louise's wish was granted when she was asked to go to China where the order was to take charge of a hospital for Europeans. This seemed a remarkable coincidence because when she was a young girl she had told one of her friends that she would go to China one day and die a martyr.

In the latter part of 1863, Sister Louise was one of a group of

---

[2] *Ibid*, p. 60.
[3] Catholic Truth Society of Ireland, *Tipperary's gift to China*, (Dublin, 1919), p. 12.

fourteen Vincentian sisters who sailed from Marseilles. Their voyage took them through the Red Sea, where Alice found the heat and the mosquitoes most trying. When the voyagers reached Shanghai, in October of that year, far more distressing conditions faced her and her companions. For reasons not clear, they were not made welcome by the Protestant hospital administrators and, to add to their woes, the Sisters were lodged in wretched rented quarters that lacked even basic amenities.

Sister Louise, being the only one who could speak English, became the intermediary between her French Superioress and the administrators. It was a task requiring much tact and prudence, but she acquitted herself so well that very soon those who had been most hostile to the employment of the Sisters did everything in their power to assist them. When her Superior expressed her surprise at this change of heart, Sister O'Sullivan told her that she attributed her success to the intercession of Our Lady and her Guardian Angel.[4]

She won the respect of her European and American patients who remembered her as a dedicated and highly competent nurse. She wrote to her brother telling him how, on St. Patrick's Day 1867, thirty Irish soldiers came to visit and presented her with £5 'out of their meagre pay' for the care of the poor. Four years later, in May 1867, she was transferred to Peking, or Beijing, as it is now known, to an orphanage where she dedicated herself to looking after the children.

In spite of all her good work she was deeply unhappy. She had to struggle against bouts of home-sickness, but more distressing to her was her inability to overcome her aversion to Chinese life and customs. Her letters convey some idea of her repugnance. She was dismayed by the ever-present dirt and filth and was appalled by their lack of hygiene and the fact that the Chinese never seemed to change their clothes. She abhorred their practice of killing and eating vermin, but most disturbing was being confronted with the 'corpses you meet in dozens outside the towns' where they were 'thrown out in the fields'.[5]

---

[4] *Ibid*, p. 15.
[5] Quotations for the letters of Alice O'Sullivan. Archives of Vincentian Order, Raheny, Co. Dublin.

Her revulsion became so unbearable that she eventually opened her heart to Father Etienne, the Superior General in Paris. It was a story of effort, service and failure. She told him that 'for six years she tried to adjust herself to China and its people; for six years she had served unselfishly and unflaggingly; for six years she had failed to accommodate herself to the life and ways of the people for whom she had given all'.[6] To her great delight the Superior General authorised her to return to France with her superioress, Sister Azais.

They left for the port of Tien-Tsin, some two hundred kilometres south-east of Peking, on the first leg of their journey home, where they stayed at the Vincentian convent. It had been established in 1862 and included an orphanage, dispensary and a newly built hospital for Europeans. The sisters were all too few in number for their numerous works of mercy and were in urgent need of an English-speaking nun for the hospital, which had many English and American patients. They thought this 'charming Irish sister' was an answer to their prayers, but she would not hear of it and indignantly rejected the suggestion that she might stay.

One day she accompanied Sister Azais and a number of the nuns on a visit to the nearby Church of Our Lady of Victories which had been built in Tien-Tsin by Father Cherier, a Vincentian missionary. One of the nuns recalled that, in the course of the journey, she tried to persuade Sister Louise to change her mind about leaving 'but she was furious at the mere suggestion and made no attempt to hide it'. After her companions left the church Sister Louise remained behind. When she emerged sometime later her companions could see that she had been weeping. When asked what had happened she told them that if she were to tell them they would not believe her. That night she wrote to the Father-General, 'today my heart has been entirely changed and now I fully understand why it will be more perfect for me to remain till death in this country ... The Blessed Virgin herself said to me, *Remain for the rest of your life with these people*'.

She requested Mother Azais to allow her to stay and to take another sister in her place. Mother Azais agreed and when the time came to leave, she said to Sister Louise, 'Good-bye till we meet again' to which Sister

---

[6] Dominic Dowling, 'Alice O'Sullivan. A Tipperary martyr in China' in *Catholic Life*, (June, 2004), p. 29.

O'Sullivan replied 'we will never meet again in this world. You will return but we shall have all gone'. Having decided to remain, she set to work in the hospital with renewed zeal. Sister Marquet wrote of her that she was 'most devoted and does all she possibly can to supply for those Sisters who are ill or convalescing, or unable to fulfil the duties of their office'.[7]

For all their good works the nuns failed to win the affection of the Chinese who referred to them as 'the white devils from the west'. They were seen as part of a resented foreign occupation which can be traced back to the Opium Wars of 1837-1842, a conflict that had ended in humiliation for the Chinese. Among the concessions the western powers and Americans successfully demanded were favourable trading terms as well as missionary access to the interior. Increased intolerance for the meddling of missionaries and merchants in Chinese affairs, led to a series of anti-foreign and anti-Christian riots.

A tense situation was further inflamed by western insensitivity to Chinese customs and beliefs:

> Railways were cut across ancient burial sites. The placing of telegraph poles and lines often greatly upset the peasants who feared that they would disturb the flight of the spirit-dragons who brought good fortune. Church spires soaring higher than the imperial palaces were often located in defiance of the rules of feng shui, the ancient science which governs the proper placing of buildings and household objects so as to ensure harmony in living. In Tientsin the Cathedral of Notre Dame des Victoires (sic) was erected on the site of an ancient mandarin palace, the French Consulate on the ruins of a temple.[8]

In the early months of 1870 there was growing anti-missionary tension in Tien-Tsin. The city was frequented by Chinese warlords who were vehemently anti-Christian and who shared the Chinese contempt for

---

[7] *Pioneer Sisters etc.*, p. 69.

[8] *Illustrated London News*, January 1903, cited in Áine Chadwick, 'Clonmel missionary and martyr (1836-1870) in *Tipperary Historical Journal*, xiv, (2001), p. 84.

all foreigners. During the month of May, the most alarming rumours began to circulate about the missionaries. They were charged with stealing and buying children whose eyes and hearts were being used to make medicine. The sisters received many warnings of their dangerous situation from native Christians and Europeans, but they felt it was their duty to remain and even spoke openly of their impending martyrdom.

Tension was mounting and on 21 June 1870 an angry mob went on a rampage of slaughter directed against the Catholic presence in Tien-Tsin. They gathered in front of the Vincentian mission, massacred Father Chevrier and his colleague, and then set both the mission station and church on fire. A mile away, the flames were clearly visible to the sisters who were gathered in their church preparing for the inevitable. Shortly afterwards, the mob burst into the compound and made their way into the hospital, smashing all before them. Sister Marquet went out and appealed to their leader, who replied by cutting her head open with a sabre, killing her instantly.

While this was going on two sisters escorted the orphans to the crypt for safety. Hoping to divert attention from the children, Sister Louise rushed out of the church in the direction of the kitchen. She was seized by some of the attackers who poured a saucepan of boiling water over her. In her agony, she rushed towards the church only to be knocked down and killed in the courtyard not far from the body of Sister Marquet. Shocking though the death of Sister Louise was, it was merciful compared to the barbarities inflicted on some of her companions. One had her eyes and heart ripped out, while two others were roasted over a fire. Later, their charred bones were collected and buried in a grave on the site of the destroyed mission station on 3 August 1870.

On the morning of the massacre Sister O'Sullivan had discharged the last British subject from the hospital. He was James Mercer, a Scottish Presbyterian and master of the ship *Harwick*, who had unsuccessfully tried to persuade her to seek refuge in the British Consulate. In a letter which he wrote to Cardinal Cullen in Dublin he stated:

> Sister Louise (Alice) was at my bedside day and night, cheering my drooping spirits, broken down with sickness and pain. Often she told

me how delighted she was, although far from old Ireland, to have the pleasure of conversing in her native tongue with a Scotchman (sic) … On the evening before the massacre I received a sign from a Brother Mason that my life was in danger. I however remained all night armed in the hospital and left about nine the next morning. Previous to my leaving, I tried hard to persuade poor Sister Louise to come with me to the British Consulate. Alas, all was to no avail.

When the news of the massacre reached Shanghai, it caused deep distress there, especially among the Europeans. One paper, *The North China News,* wrote of Sister O'Sullivan:

When we call to mind that dear and excellent Sister Louise O'Sullivan, our country woman who nursed so many of our sick at the Shanghai Hospital; when we remember how this guardian angel had been outraged and insulted, our blood boils within us and we burn with indignation to the very marrow of our bones.

A Protestant chaplain, Rev. Charles Butcher, M.A., describing the tragedy in *The Times*, paid the following tribute to Sister O'Sullivan: 'One sister who has been murdered with every circumstance of horror, was an Irish lady whose memory is cherished with affection and gratitude by many of the community here'. After her death, the sister Superior said of her that 'no one could resist the charm of her manners and words which were at once simple and engaging. It was impossible to live with her without loving her'.[9]

Perhaps, the most accurate assessment of Sister O'Sullivan is contained in these lines:

We realize that she was not born a saint, and her efforts after holiness were a constant source of struggle – and often bitter struggle – and that her martyrdom was, as it were, a reward for a well-fought battle to one who had persevered in her daily immolation even unto death;

---

[9] Catholic Truth Society, *Tipperary's gift to China*, p. 16.

that immolation she had taken upon herself fifteen years before and sealed by her first vows in Saint Vincent's, Drogheda in 1861.[10]

To-day her name lives on in Clonmel and is inscribed on the plinth of a statue of St. Joseph erected to her memory in the grounds of the Presentation Convent.

---

[10] *Pioneer Sisters*, p. 72.

Chapter 21

Rebels in the Dock

A tall, handsome man with a cultivated English accent, addressing a meeting of the Clonmel Literary Society on 29 October 1858 said, 'standing within sight of the building in which I was condemned to death ten years ago, I shall be scarcely accused of egotism if I shortly recapitulate the course of events which brought me into that extremity of peril'. These were the words of William Smith O'Brien when he spoke in the Mechanics' Institute, now Mulcahy House, in Anglesea Street. He was referring to his trial in the nearby Clonmel courthouse, where together with his fellow Young Irelanders, Thomas Francis Meagher, Terence Bellew McManus and Patrick O'Donoghue, he had been sentenced to be hanged, drawn and quartered for his part in the 1848 rebellion.

The paths which brought these four men to the Clonmel courthouse were as varied as their backgrounds. Of the four, William Smith O'Brien was the most unlikely revolutionary. Born at Dromoland Castle on 17 October 1803, he was educated at Harrow and later at Trinity College, Cambridge from where he graduated with a B.A. in 1826. His older brother inherited the title, Lord Inchiquin, while William received the estate of his maternal uncle, William Smith, at Cahirmoyle in County Limerick. As well as making it his home, he adopted the name Smith as part of the inheritance, earning the cynical comment of his enemies that there was 'too much Smith and not enough O'Brien'. He married Lucy Gabett, the beautiful daughter of a local landowner, and became the father of five boys and two girls. It proved to be a happy marriage, despite the family tensions that arose from her husband's political activities, imprisonment and subsequent exile.

He was elected as member of parliament for Ennis in 1828. Despite his staunch Protestant background, his keen sense of justice led him to support Daniel O'Connell's demand for Catholic emancipation. He was a hardworking member of parliament who did his utmost to promote the welfare of his country and its people, regardless of class or creed. He held strong independent views and showed a deep concern for the relief of Irish distress. He introduced legislation to relieve the aged and the poor, supported the Municipal Reform Bill and promoted the concept of mixed education to improve Catholic-Protestant relations. He also favoured payment for Catholic clergy and argued for an increase in state aid to Maynooth.

He gradually became convinced that justice could not be attained for Ireland under the Union and in 1843 became a member of the Repeal Association. During O'Connell's imprisonment, O'Brien was elected its deputy leader. The Repeal Association adopted the policy of refusing parliamentary duties irrelevant to Ireland. When O'Brien declined the opportunity to serve on a Scottish Railway Committee set up by parliament, he was jailed in an improvised cell near the clock tower of the Houses of Parliament in April 1846, under the custody of the sergeant of arms. He was the first person so confined for 150 years and also the last. After twenty five days, he was released unconditionally and returned to Ireland to a tumultuous reception.

While confined, he was visited by two of the men who later would share the dock with him in Clonmel courthouse. One was Terence Bellew McManus, a prosperous merchant from Liverpool. Born in county Monaghan in 1823, he was the eldest of three children of Philip McManus, a land agent, and Alice Bellew. After he left school he entered the drapery business. He became a close friend of Charles Gavan Duffy, who regarded him as a 'good-looking, strapping young fellow, full of life and gaiety'.[1]

His biographer states that, 'his early friendship with Duffy and his experiences with the Orangemen probably set the seeds of revolt in his mind'.[2] In 1840 he set off for Liverpool where he became an exporter in the cotton and woollen industry. In a city with a considerable Irish population, he became one of the chief inspirations of the Repeal movement. He attended a number of Daniel O'Connell's monster meetings which were held around the country but O'Connell, fearing military reprisal, called off the proposed meeting for Clontarf, McManus became more identified with the Young Irelanders. These were a group within the Repeal movement who had become increasingly

---

[1] Charles Gavin Duffy, *My life in two Hemispheres*, i (London, 1898), p. 12.
[2] Thomas G. McAllister, *Terence Bellew Mc Manus*, (Maynooth, 1972), p. 4.

disillusioned with O'Connell's pacifist leadership. Among these middle-class intellectuals were the founders of *The Nation* newspaper, John Blake Dillon, Charles Gavan Duffy and Thomas Davis. They believed that repeal would not be secured by moral force alone and that O'Connell's policies would have to be replaced by the threat of military action.

O'Brien's second visitor while in gaol was Thomas Francis Meagher, whose grandfather had emigrated to Newfoundland where he became a prosperous merchant and ship owner. He set up his son, Thomas, in the shipping business in Waterford and his grandson, Thomas Francis, was born in the building now known as the Granville Hotel on 3 August 1823. At the age of eleven, Thomas Francis was sent to Clongowes Wood College, county Kildare and, later, to another Jesuit institution at Stoneyhurst in Lancashire. He showed little aptitude for mathematical or classical studies but excelled at English literature, invariably winning prizes for poetry and composition. Returning to Ireland in 1843 he went to Dublin to study for the bar. However, he became more interested in the politics of repeal, and got involved with the Young Irelanders. Soon he was to reveal the oratorical gifts that were to win the admiration of his fellow countrymen.

On 27 July 1846, six weeks after O'Brien's release, John O'Connell, son of 'The Liberator', introduced a series of Peace Proposals at a meeting of the Repeal Association. They were aimed at purging the organisation of the elements among the Young Irelanders who advocated physical force to secure repeal. The climax came when Meagher, in the course of an impassioned speech said, 'Be it for defence, or be it for the assertion of a nation's liberty, I look upon the sword as a sacred weapon'. It was these famous words that led the English novelist, William Thackeray, to dub him 'Meagher of the Sword'. In the uproar that ensued, the followers of Daniel O'Connell were far from pleased and Meagher was asked to leave the meeting. O'Brien, who was furious at the denial of free speech, accompanied him.

The ensuing split in the Repeal movement led to the 1848 Rising. In January 1847 the Young Irelanders met in the Rotunda in Dublin and set up the Irish Confederation, to further the objects the Repeal Association had in view. The Confederation was supported by a network of clubs throughout the country. At first, O'Brien rejected all overtures to assume leadership of the Young Ireland splinter group, preferring to act as the remote elder statesman. Any hope of reconciliation between the Young Irelanders and O'Connell's supporters was dashed by the death of Daniel O'Connell in Genoa in May 1847.

In February 1848 a revolution in France replaced the monarchy of Louise Phillipe with a republic. This had been achieved without a shot being fired, and O'Brien saw no reason why the same could not happen in Ireland. O'Brien and Meagher travelled to Paris to present the congratulations of the Irish people to the new French Republic. They hoped to gain sympathy for Irish aspirations, but the new French President had no wish to become embroiled in Irish affairs. On his way home, O'Brien addressed the House of Commons for the last time. He was greeted by a hostile parliament who refused to listen as he made a final plea to obtain justice for Ireland. O'Brien and Meagher presented a tricolour to the citizens of Dublin, the same green, white and orange standard which was to become the national flag almost seventy years later.

On 16 July, Meagher accompanied by Michael Doheny, the Fethard-born Young Irelander, addressed a crowd of 50,000 from the summit of Slievenamon. Among that impressive assembly were the members of the Hugh O'Neill and John Mitchell Confederate Clubs of Clonmel. In an impassioned speech Meagher told them, 'I stand here upon the lofty summit of a country which, if we do not win for ourselves we must win for those who come after us' and ended by quoting the *Men of Tipperary*:

> Let Britain brag her motley rag -
> We'll lift the green more proud and airy:
> Be mine the lot to bear that flag
> And head the men of Tipperary!

Alarmed by reports of the Slievenamon meeting, the government suspended the Habeas Corpus Act. The offices of the Young Ireland newspaper, *The Nation,* were raided and a warrant issued for the arrest of the leaders. O'Brien, feeling that armed resistance was the only honourable course of action, reluctantly accepted command of the Young Ireland rebels. Lacking any coherent strategy, in the days leading up to what was to become a military fiasco at Ballingarry, William Smith O'Brien and his followers wandered from one Tipperary town to another in an effort to rouse the people into taking up arms. Faced with a hostile Catholic clergy and the apathy of a famine-starved peasantry, the Young Ireland rebellion was doomed to failure from the outset. O'Brien refused to allow the commandeering of food and, at one stage, told his followers to disperse and come back in the morning with provisions for at least four days, recommending 'oatmeal bread and eggs'.[3] Many probably agreed with Patrick O'Donoghue's assessment of O'Brien that 'a man of such virtues could not and will not succeed in Ireland'.[4]

Patrick O'Donoghue, who was the fourth man in the dock in Clonmel, was sent from Dublin by Gavan Duffy with dispatches for O'Brien. Suspected of being a government spy, he was placed under armed escort and brought to Cashel. Fortunately, he was recognised by O'Brien and released. Of the four Young Ireland leaders, O'Donoghue was the least well known. He was born in Clonegal, a little village on the Carlow-Wexford border. He must have had a reasonable education because he secured a job in Dublin as a solicitor's clerk, despite the fact that it was said of him that 'he lacked the social graces and drank to excess' and that 'his appearance was unprepossessing'. According to Charles Gavan Duffy, his looks made him seem 'the very ideal of a police agent' in that he was 'a big, black scowling fellow'. He did not come to notice until the Young Irelanders broke with O'Connell's Repeal Association. He became a member of the Confederation at their inaugural meeting in January 1847. The following year he became a member of the Grattan Confederate Club in Dublin and later, one of its vice-presidents. It would appear that the authorities considered him a danger because, when the Habeas Corpus Act was suspended, a warrant was immediately issued for his arrest.

On Wednesday 27 July, O'Brien entered Ballingarry at the head of 500 men but the crowds melted away before 'clerical admonition and O'Brien's failure to feed his ragged army'. On the same day, they were joined by Terence Bellew McManus. As one of the two Liverpool

---

[3] Brendan Ó Cathaoir, *John Blake Dillon, Young Irelander,* (Dublin, 1990), p. 86.
[4] Cited in Richard Davis, 'The reluctant rebel' in *Tipperary Historical Journal*, xi, (1998), p. 51.

representatives on the executive of the Irish Confederation, he was fully conversant with developments in Ireland. To aid the revolutionary cause, he had hoped to raise 200 armed men and storm Chester Castle, seize its arsenal and transport it to Wexford in three steamers which he had chartered. These plans were killed in their infancy by his failure to secure adequate support. Determined to redeem himself, in the field of battle if possible, he crossed to Ireland. He was followed by detectives, but succeeded in eluding them.

A council of war, held on the following day, highlighted the indecision of the leaders. Some wanted to go into hiding until after the harvest, but O'Brien, refusing to become a fugitive where his fathers once ruled, persisted in a vague plan of gathering enough support to take the field. It was decided that Meagher and O'Donoghue should set off for Waterford in an attempt to gather support, while McManus remained with O'Brien in Ballingarry. The following day brought the sorry fiasco to an end. A party of forty policemen challenged by O'Brien's depleted forces, barricaded themselves into Widow McCormack's house near Ballingarry, taking her children as hostages. O'Brien refused to allow his subordinates to burn the house down because of the children inside and was almost killed in a parley with the police when stone-throwing by his supporters evoked a volley of fire, killing two men and slightly injuring McManus, who was struck by a splinter from a gatepost. Reluctantly, O'Brien decided to withdraw and the Rising of 1848, derisively referred to as the 'cabbage patch' revolt, was over.

Five hundred pounds was offered for the capture of O'Brien. He remained on the run for a week. Before giving himself up he decided to make one last trip home. Dressed in a black hat, a blue cloak light plaid trousers and carrying a large black stick he walked into the railway station at Thurles. As he approached the ticket office he was recognised by a station guard, an Englishman, called Hume. He told the inspector who escorted him to Kilmainham jail in Dublin that he had played the game and lost and that he was ready to pay the penalty.

On 12 August, Meagher and O'Donoghue, who had aroused the suspicions of a passing police patrol, were arrested on the road between Clonoulty and Holycross and taken to Thurles. Meagher bore his misfortune with indifference and smoked a cigar as he chatted gaily with his companions. Meanwhile, McManus had shaved off his whiskers and made his way to Cork. With freedom within his grasp he was arrested on board the vessel *N.G. Chase* in Cobh harbour. In a letter to Duffy he said that he did not regret any act he had done, but would do it all over again if it would be of any use to Ireland.[5]

On 28 September 1848, William Smith O'Brien, Thomas Francis Meagher, Terence Bellew Mc Manus and Patrick O'Donoghue were brought to Clonmel courthouse. After a trial which lasted ten days, the prisoners were sentenced to be hanged, drawn and quartered. Overnight, all four became national heroes. Such was their popularity that the government took very stringent precautions when they were being moved to Dublin. An eye-witness account of the scene stated that:

> The principal gate of Clonmel gaol was opened and a division of dragoons came out followed by the prisoners' coach. Outside the prison a very large crowd had gathered, and a huge roar of cheering went up at their appearance. Many attempts were made to get close to the carriage, and some tried to thrust their hands through the window, to shake hands with the prisoners. They were prevented from doing so by the second division of dragoons riding alongside the carriage. A third division rode after the carriage, and the rear was brought up by a wagon filled with more military.[6]

There was an outcry throughout the country protesting against the severity of the sentences. Petitions, signed by many dignitaries, flooded into the Viceregal lodge in Dublin. Such was the strength of public feeling that the government decided that the sentence of death should be commuted to transportation for life. But the reaction of the prisoners was not quite what the government expected. They argued that the sentence of transportation was unconstitutional. The government, to allay its embarrassment, had special legislation rushed through the House of Commons which made transportation permissible.

On 29 July 1849, the brig *Swift* sailed from Dun Laoghaire, then known as Kingstown, taking the four leaders into exile. The captain treated them civilly, extending to them what comfort the ship could offer. On their six thousand mile journey to Van Diemen's Land the

---

[5] McAllister, *Terence Bellew McManus*, p. 25.
[6] *Ibid*, p. 29.

prisoners availed of the small library on board. They read their favourite passages from the scriptures or the classics to one another, while they sometimes amused themselves by dancing 'Irish jigs and Scottish reels'. McManus brought with him his backgammon box and fishing rod.

The governor of Van Diemen's Land, Sir William Denison, was not at all sympathetic to the state prisoners whom he regarded as criminals, nor was he in agreement with the directive of the British Home Secretary, Earl Grey, to treat them as gentlemen. His instructions were to offer them tickets-of-leave, on condition that they gave their word not to attempt to escape. They were each to be confined to a particular district and all contact between them was forbidden. Furthermore, they were to report to their local police magistrate once a month.

O'Brien refused to accept his ticket-of-leave believing it was his duty to escape. This resulted in his being confined to Maria Island, while his companions were assigned to various rural districts. This arrangement did not suit O'Donoghue who, unlike the others, suffered acutely from lack of funds. He had a wife and a child in Ireland to support and it was essential that he found employment. Since his only experience was as a law clerk, sending him to a rural district was in effect to 'consign him to starvation'. He requested to be allowed to live in a city. The authorities relented and he was conveyed to Hobart Town.

McManus was sent to New Norfolk where he enjoyed himself shooting and fishing. After some time this aimless life became too much for him. He gave the authorities an ultimatum that he would rescind his parole if he were not transferred to a town where he hoped to employ his commercial skills. He was sent to Launcestown, but his efforts to establish himself in business were continually frustrated by being refused permission to travel.

During his confinement on Maria Island O'Brien's health had suffered. He had not been allowed to talk to anyone and had his letters censored. An attempt was made to rescue him, but failed. Eventually, his friends prevailed on him to accept his ticket-of-leave and he was transferred to New Norfolk. In December 1850, McManus and O'Donoghue left their districts to visit him. This breach of regulations resulted in both of them being sentenced to three months hard labour in the Cascades, a notorious convict prison on the Tasmanian peninsula.

According to Meagher 'they were clothed in the vile yellow dress of the chain gangs – compelled to cut wood, break stones, and do all kinds of servile work in the company of the vilest ruffians that were ever bred upon the earth'. The ordeal, in the words of one observer, left McManus 'worn out in bodily strength, enfeebled in mind'.

After being released, McManus violated regulations once again. On this occasion, he went to Ross to attend the marriage of Meagher to Catherine Bennett, governess to a local doctor. Denison promptly issued a warrant for his arrest. On hearing this, McManus decided to escape. He felt justified in doing so because his ticket-of-leave, which had been revoked after his previous arrest, had not been renewed. A clergyman, Dean Butler, gave him shelter and funds. Helped by friends he made his way to George Town where he boarded a ship bound for California.

The arrival of McManus in San Francisco in June 1851 was marked by a dinner attended by three hundred guests, including senators and generals. Being penniless, the Irish community made a collection to provide him with funds. An attempt to resume his occupation as shipping agent ended in failure. He then tried his hand at real estate but was no more successful. To add to his woes, his health began to fail, making him unfit for work. He deteriorated rapidly during 1860, and he died in January 1861 in St. Mary's Hospital, San Francisco, under the care of the Sisters of Mercy.

A few years later a small group of Irish nationalists felt that his body should be brought home to Ireland. The members of the Fenian Brotherhood turned his funeral into a most impressive propaganda exercise. An estimated 200,000 people lined the route to Glasnevin cemetery. Delegations from many towns throughout Ireland, including Clonmel, were in attendance, all wearing instead of the traditional black, a white ribbon on their left arm, signifying hope for the future. In his graveside oration, James Stephens said of McManus that if the Irish people had failed to honour this man they would be looked upon 'as a doomed race'.

The successful escape of McManus had made a deep impression on Meagher. Although newly-married and living in the lake region of Tasmania, one of the island's renowned beauty spots, he grew restless. In January 1852, having sent his wife to her parents, he unexpectedly presented himself at government headquarters and returned his ticket-of-leave. The constable, who was an Irishman, refused to arrest him and by the time other officers arrived he had ridden off into the bush. Two fishermen took him to a deserted island where he existed for a week on sea bird's eggs and shell fish before making his escape to South America.

Following many adventures he reached New York where he was given a rapturous reception. Shortly afterwards, he was joined by his wife. Restless as ever, he embarked on a nationwide tour, recounting his experiences in Tasmania. His wife, pregnant with their second child, returned to his parents' home in Waterford where she died on 9 May 1854, several weeks after giving birth to a son, also called Thomas Francis. Meanwhile, Meagher took up law and was admitted to the New York bar. While he waited for his legal business to build up, he continued lecturing. One of those who came to listen to him was the daughter of a New York merchant, Elizabeth Townsend, whom he married on 14 November 1855.

Full of boundless energy and always in search of some great adventure, he embarked on an archaeological expedition to Costa Rica. On his return, he launched a newspaper called *The Irish News.* When the American Civil War broke out, he raised and took command of the most famous regiment in the Irish Brigade, which became known as the 'The Fighting 69th'. They fought in some of the great battles of the war, including Bull Run and Fredericksburg, and distinguished themselves for their bravery.

When the war came to an end, Meagher was appointed secretary of the Montana Territory and in September 1866 was appointed Governor. On 1 July 1867, he went to Fort Benton to try to raise a local militia to protect the people from Indian attacks. He took up quarters on the *G.A.Thompson*, an old Mississippi steamer, upon which he died in mysterious circumstances. There is the sinister suggestion that he was murdered in his bunk and that his body was flung into the river. Another opinion is that death resulted from an accident. It is said that during that fatal night he went for a walk on deck, slipped on a coil of rope and fell overboard. His body was never recovered. To-day, he is remembered by a bronze, equestrian statue which stands in the capital city of Montana.

Meanwhile, O'Donoghue unsuccessfully tried to secure employment in a solicitors' office in Hobart. He then started a newspaper called *The Irish Exile* in which he voiced his criticism of British imperialism and the penal system. This brought him to the attention of the governor. His public defence of Meagher's escape which was published in the *Launceston Examiner* on 14 August 1852 resulted in him being sentenced to six months on the chain gangs in the Cascades.

Bishop Wilson obtained his release after three months. O'Donoghue signed a pledge not to escape and returned to Launceston. Believing that his ill treatment justified a breach of parole, he broke his pledge. On 20 December 1852 he boarded a vessel bound for Melbourne and later made his way to Sydney. By February, he reached Tahiti where the American consul afforded him the protection of the American flag. Some months later, he arrived in San Francisco and eventually found his way to New York.

In many respects he was a tragic figure and his new found freedom did not bring him happiness. He was a heavy drinker and subject to bouts of depression. His critical attitude alienated him from other exiles and Irish-Americans. He died in Brooklyn on 22 January 1854. *The Nation* newspaper announced that, 'the immediate cause of his demise was diarrhoea: but his constitution had been previously impaired and his nervous system was considerably shattered'. To compound the tragedy, on the day before he died his wife and daughter had landed in New York, but arrived too late to see him. Mitchel, in writing his obituary notice said that, 'he was of ardent and excitable temperament'.

By this time, O'Brien had become tutor to the children of a Dr. Brock in New Norfolk. In an effort to cultivate Irish good will with the approach of the Crimean War, the British government released him in 1854 on condition that he didn't return to these islands. He went to live in Brussels, where he was joined by his wife and family. There he finished working on his book which he had started in Van Dieman's Land called *Principles of Government, or Meditations in Exile.* In May 1856 his release was made unconditional and he returned to Ireland the following year.

O'Brien played no further part in politics and refused to stand for parliament. He opposed the Fenians, mainly because they were a secret society. Much of his time was spent travelling on the continent and he later paid a visit to the United States, where as a true liberal he spoke out on the evils of slavery. At home, he became active in cultural and agricultural projects, becoming a member of the Gaelic Literary and Antiquarian Society and the Royal Dublin Society. He made a gift of a cup to encourage the growing of flax and presented a medal to the winner of the annual art competition. He died in the Penryyn Arms Hotel, Bangor on the morning of 18 June 1861 in his sixty-first year. Thousands followed his remains from the North Wall to Kingsbridge Station and he was laid to rest in the churchyard of Rathronan, Co. Limerick.

No one could doubt O'Brien's sincerity and concern for the welfare of the Irish people and, in Lecky's view, 'Few politicians have sacrificed more for what they believed in to be right'. He was a monarchist rather than a republican. In a speech which he prepared for his trial in Clonmel, but did not deliver, he declared that 'I harboured no traitorous designs against the life and crown of her Majesty. But I am resolved to risk all I hold most dear for the sake of obtaining for Ireland the power of self-government'. He was primarily a writer and thinker rather than a man of action. He possessed few qualities of leadership or any military ability, but was 'pushed by pride and circumstances into launching a premature and badly organised revolt'.

Despite their failure, the sacrifice of the Young Irelanders was not in vain. They revived Tone's ideal of an Irish Republic and inspired later generations of nationalists to carry on the struggle for independence.

23. John Hackett (1796-1872)

24. William Louis Hackett (1829-1876)

25. Henry O'Connell Hackett (1835-1880)

26. Edward Charles Hackett (1839-1898)

27. Portrait of William Tinsley (1804-1885)

28. Former Methodist church in Gordon Street

29. Adelaide House

30. Thomas Graham (1809-1891)
Photograph by William Despard Hemphill

31. Graham sideboard in the Town Hall, Clonmel

32. William Despard Hemphill (1816-1902)

33. Railway station, Clonmel. Taken by Hemphill in
1857/58 is believed to be the earliest one from
Ireland of a railway engine and train.

34. The grave of Lieutentant Frederick Close (1804-1826)

35. The Quaker burial ground in O'Neill Street, Clonmel. Ann Grubb's grave is in the top right corner

36. Sr. Alice O'Sullivan (1836-1870)

37. William Smith O'Brien (1803-1861)

38. Patrick O'Donoghue (c.1815-1854)

39. Thomas Francis Meagher (1823-1867)

40. Terence Bellew McManus (1823-1867)

Illustrations 37-40: Sketches made by William Tinsley of The Young Irelanders
during their trial in Clonmel Courthouse

41. Charles J. Boland (1874-1918)

42. Frank Drohan (1879-1953)

43. Mary Isabel Leslie (1899-1978)

44. Tommy O'Brien (1905-1988)

45. Pat O'Callaghan (1906-1991)

46. Edel Quinn (1907-1944)

47. Una Troy (1910-1993)

48. Mick Delahunty (1915-1992)

49. Frank Patterson (1938-2000)

Chapter 22

The 'Poet Laureate' of Clonmel

Do the feeble still venture to toddle
To the Quay, and sit down on the balk
And sun their old selves in the even,
With the crows cawing loud in the trees?
That's the spot, I think, outside of Heaven
Where a heart wearied out would find ease.

These lines, which can be seen on a limestone plaque on the Gashouse Bridge, occur in a poem called *The exile from Clonmel* in which a young exile named John in far-away America writes to the girl he left behind asking her for news of home and if she still loves him *'as well as of yore?'* In her reply *From Mary to John in Exile* she gives him all the local gossip and concludes by telling him:

So you mustn't have heard I was married
And am now the proud mother of four!

These poems, which appeared in the pages of *The Clonmel Chronicle* on 27 February 1892, were written by Charles James Boland or Charlie as he was known to his friends. He was born in Clonmel on 25 January 1874 where his parents were master and matron of the workhouse. His mother was Eliza Quirke, daughter of county councillor, Patrick Quirke, from near Tipperary town. His father, who came from county Fermanagh was, at one stage, a member of the Dublin Metropolitan police. On the outbreak of the Crimean war he volunteered for the British army. He was assigned to the Commisariat Department which had charge of food supplies. During the course of the campaign he claimed to have 'had some hair-breath escapes from bullets, cold and starvation'. When peace was established, he returned home and joined the staff of the South Tipperary Artillery militia and served as a quarter master sergeant for several years. In

1878 he was appointed master of the Clonmel workhouse, a position he held for nineteen years until his death in 1897. It was said that he 'possessed literary attainments and a florid style of no ordinary excellence'[1], a talent which his son Charlie clearly inherited.

Charles J. was the eldest in a family of five boys and seven girls. One of his brothers, Henry, was secretary to the Minister of Munitions in Whitehall and was decorated with the Order of the British Empire, while Fred, was agent to the Duke of Norfolk before entering the British army and serving in the First World War. Two of his sisters, Laura and Bessie, became matron and head nurse respectively of the Clonmel Fever Hospital. He was uncle of Frederick H. Boland, the distinguished diplomat, later to become president of the United Nations, whose daughter is the well-known poet, Eavan Boland. Another grandniece, Fanny Feehan, was a violinist, music critic and for a time leader of the Radio Éireann Symphony Orchestra.

The young Charlie received his early education in Clonmel Model School before attending Blackrock College in Co. Dublin. Following a distinguished academic career which included winning several scholarships, he entered the civil service in the Irish Valuation Office, having taken first place in the competitive examination. Serving in Belfast and Dublin, his promotion was rapid and in due course he became chief of the Valuation Office. In after years his alma mater was to pay him the honour of making him President of the College Union, an office he filled with distinction. It was said of him that he was 'unspoilt and unspoilable by success in life'. In a reply to a friend on the occasion of his election as President of Blackrock College Union – he modestly wrote 'and some have honours thrust upon them'.

He was the author of many poems and some prose pieces which appeared over the years in the pages of *The Clonmel Chronicle*. Speaking of his contributions to the local paper a contemporary later stated that his prose and poetry 'were delightful in their fresh, healthy humour, and bore the imprint of unmistakable literary craftsmanship'. A short dramatic sketch called *Napoleon in Clonmel* was published in 1909 in the first

---

[1] *Clonmel Nationalist*, 13 April 1897.

volume of *The Tipperary Annual*. An anthology of his literary efforts was later featured in *My Clonmel Scrapbook* edited by James White. Out of some eighty contributions in that treasury of local reminiscences no fewer than twenty four were penned by Charles J. Boland. This publication, and in particular Boland's offerings, which has won the affection of successive generations of Clonmel people, made a lasting impression on one of his contemporaries, who wrote:

> Many a Christmas since that book was published has the writer taken it down, and, before what is known as a 'comfortable fire', has detached himself into a condition of sentimental abstraction to enjoy the pathos and the gaiety, the wit and humour of Charlie Boland.

Boland found his inspiration in the scenes and memories of childhood. He recalled the days spent trout-fishing in Glenary and learning to swim in well-known bathing spots such as 'Newbolds' where Clonmel schoolboys made their first attempts, before graduating to the 'Thirteenth Hole' and 'Little Hell' in the river Suir. He remembered raiding the gooseberries in the master's garden at the Model School and, on his way home with some of his school pals, playing tricks on some of the local characters. They delighted in placing a stone in the outstretched hand of the Blind Man on Gallows Hill to test his fluency in cursing or in tormenting 'Whistling Joe with the crooked toe'. They took malicious pleasure in miming 'Jack the Rat', as he cobbled shoes on his bench at the West Gate, and later Boland devoted a poem to this 'testy cuss'.

Boland had an abiding love for Clonmel and, for him, the view of the town from the foothills of the Comeraghs with its 'seas of slated roof, with islands of spires and steeples and the turret top of the West Gate to break the monotony' was unequalled:

> The town holds more delight,
> And eloquence more rare
> Than fading light on windswept hill

He wrote about such well known landmarks as the Spa, mundane places like the Potato Market, then located in O'Neill Street, and Blue Anchor Lane, which even in Boland's day was 'a victim to decline'.

The river Suir held a special place in his affections and time and time again he returns to it. Watching the mists which 'gathered on its bosom overnight lazily rolling up the hillside' or leaning over the parapet of the old bridge in the moonlight gave him immense pleasure. He was fascinated by its many moods and textures. Captivated by 'the mournful swish-swish of the water, making its way through the weeds', he enjoyed watching it 'bubbling along happy and careless'. Sometimes it was 'heavy and sluggish' and 'a trifle gloomy' or when swollen by recent rain, it looked 'turgid and sullen'.

In Boland's day the focus of the town's economic activity was on the quays where a fleet of flat-bottomed barges, or lighters as they were sometimes called, were loaded with corn, hides, butter, bacon, timber and other commodities. They floated down-stream to Carrick-on-Suir from where their cargoes were transferred to sea-going vessels. The barges were then re-loaded and hauled by a team of horses along the towpath back to the town of Clonmel. These 'voyages' were not without incident as an article in *The Clonmel Chronicle* which appeared on 4 November 1904 illustrates:

> On Saturday afternoon as two lighters, containing cargoes of coal, were being towed up the river Suir by a team of horses from Carrick to Messrs. Phelan's stores, Clonmel, when passing under Sir Thomas's Bridge, the hind boat stemmed against the archway. As a result of the impact, the boat began to leak rapidly. The boatman, observing this, at once severed the rope connecting her with the other boat, when she drifted some four hundred yards down the river and sank. She happily rests in such a position that traffic can go on the river uninterrupted, and it will not be difficult to have her removed. She contains about thirteen or fourteen tons of coal.

This incident provided the inspiration for *The Wreck of the Avondale*, one of four satirical pieces written about the barges and those who 'sailed' on them. The best known is *The Wreck of the Gwendoline*, which Boland ironically sub-titled 'A tragedy of the Suir'. Adopting a mock heroic tone he tells how a nine year old longs for 'a life on the deep blue sea'. His ambition is fulfilled when he enlists as cabin boy to a Clonmel boatman. He kisses his 'blue-eyed Nell' goodbye and sets sail. Before the barge has left the environs of Clonmel the day grew ominously dark and suddenly:

> the bounding barque
> Was struck with a sudden squall;

Disaster loomed and the panic-stricken Captain grew pale as they were swept helplessly by the gashouse wall. Facing death in the driving gale, the cabin boy tearfully bids farewell to 'his blue-eyed Nell'. When all seemed lost fortune smiled and they ran aground on Dudley's Weir. Struggling ashore 'half dead or more', they hailed a creamery boy and went home by ass and cart. The bargemen, being compared to intrepid mariners risking their lives to brave the perils of the deep, would have been a source of amusement for Boland's readers.

Two such local boatmen, well known to Boland's generation, Captain Jack Flaher and his general factotum Joe Nelligan, occur in a number of his works. Perhaps, his most humorous is the anecdote of *The Soldier's Ghost*. Flaher wagers Nelligan a shilling to walk the church path in the dead of night and face the prospect of meeting the ghost. Nelligan who cannot refuse a bet, accepts. No sooner had he taken a few steps on the flagged footpath than he heard steps behind him. Trembling and perspiring he ran all the way home. Bursting into his kitchen he threw himself on the settle-bed. Having asked his wife to remove his boots, he proceeded to tell her of his encounter with the ghost. Holding one of his boots in her hand, she noticed that the heel and half the sole were hanging loose. As she points to the boot the truth dawns on him and he is overcome with embarrassment. He dreads to think what his colleagues might say if they should come to hear of it.

Apart from the pleasure his reader's got from being able to identify various local characters, there is a strong vein of humour running through Boland's work. Relying on hyperbole and whimsy, a sense of the absurd is to be found in many of his verses, prose pieces and, above all, in his comic sketch which he called *Napoleon in Clonmel*. In his poem *The Battle of Boulick* the flood waters of the Boulick stream, which for so long wrought havoc on many Clonmel people, oblige Brian Boru by sweeping the Danes into the Suir, while *The Fighting Tinkers of Clonmel* describes a faction fight in the streets of the town. Boland rarely departed from the local scene. The exceptions were his poem, *A Departmental Ditty* which describes his experiences in the Valuation office, and two prose pieces which celebrate the fighting prowess of the Carrick dog called *The Dog in the Train* and *The Carrick Dog*.

The yearnings of the exile for his native heath was another theme dear to Boland's heart. Distance cannot dim the emigrant's longing for his beloved Clonmel, whether he be in Kerry or in far off America. For Boland there is nothing to compare with the familiar scenes of home as he points out in his most celebrated poem *The Two Travellers*, sometimes called 'The man that was never in Mullinahone'. It became a local classic and has been recited at numerous concerts down the years. One of the travellers extols the exotic sights and scenes to where his 'peregrinations' have taken him:

> From the land of the ape and the marmozet
> To the tents of the Fellaheen

Not alone that but he has hunted tigers in Turkestan, kangaroos in Australia and sailed the Polar seas. He has lived in such far-flung places as Cashmere, Sierra Leone, Santiago and Del Fuego. He has walked across Panama, served as a medicine man to a tribe of the Katmandoos, stood on the scenes of Olympic games and lunched with the Chersonese. A life filled with wonder and adventure leaves his colleague resolutely unimpressed:

> Don't talk of your hunting in Yucatan,
> Or your fishing off St. Helena;
> I'd rather see young fellas 'hinting the wran'
> In the hedges of Tobberaheena.
> No doubt the scenes of a Swiss canton
> Have a possible sort of charm,

Give me a sunset on Slievenamon
From the road at Hackett's Farm!

And I'd rather be strolling along the Quay,
And watching the river flow;
Than growing tea with the cute Chinese,
Or mining in Mexico.
And I wouldn't much care for Sierra Leone,
If I hadn't seen Killenaule,
And the man that was never in Mullinahone
Shouldn't say he had travelled at all!

Of course, the poem can also be seen as gently mocking the parochialism of those for whom a trip to Thurles by train would have seemed like a journey into darkest Africa. It is interesting that Fethard, Farranalleen, Laffan's Bridge and Horse and Jockey, all stations on the newly opened Clonmel to Thurles railway line, receive a mention. Boland implies that they are places of an exotic and celebrated nature, providing challenging new frontiers for the intrepid explorer.

Much of Boland's sentimental longing may be explained by the fact that all of his adult life was spent in Dublin. Yet, he never lost an opportunity to come back to Clonmel and meet with old friends and see once more his favourite childhood haunts. His last visit took place in June two months before he died. A friend met him at the railway station when he was about to depart for Dublin. Boland told him he had been for a swim at Turn of Abbey or the 'the Turn', as he called it, at six o'clock that morning, and that he had been in the Suir he loved so well three times on the previous day.

His death on the 2 August 1918 at his residence at La Scala, Dalkey, county Dublin at the early age of fifty-four came as a surprise to his family. The previous Thursday night he had come home from a fishing trip and that was the last time he was seen alive. His wife, who had been on holiday, returned to the family home the following Monday. Finding the door locked she climbed in a window to find her husband dead on the floor. In the opinion of the family doctor, death from heart failure had taken place

249

on the previous Thursday night or Friday morning. The father of three children, he was laid to rest in Dean's Grange cemetery.

Boland was immensely popular with friends and colleagues. Regarded as a man of immense charm he was renowned for his 'uprightness, kindness and ability', and was one who would always do a good turn. Described as one of nature's gentlemen he 'never courted or pursued distinction as a deliberate purpose in life, for he was the most retiring of men, and on this account one of the most loveable'.[2] His letters were a delight, as he frequently 'threw in' a few lines of verse according to the inspiration of the moment. One author's opinion is that his writings neither sufficiently represent the true intellectual fecundity nor the versatility of his endeavours. His contributions to local literature are all too few, but none the less highly valued. A contemporary felt that he would have made his mark as a writer had he devoted himself full-time to it.

William Clarke, editor of *The Clonmel Chronicle*, writing of his contributor and friend, said the people of Clonmel would 'mourn the death of one who was deservedly held in the highest regard for his remarkable literary taste, his irrepressible humour, and wonderful power of expression both in poetry and prose, qualities which were widely and most thoroughly appreciated'. Another said of him that he was the one Clonmel man of his time who had something of the spark of genius in him.

A vote of sympathy passed at a meeting of the Clonmel Board of Guardians stated 'that the late Mr. Boland's literary works will preserve his memory in Clonmel long after those of the present generation are all dead and gone'. Nowadays, the humour, sentimentality and nostalgia associated with his stories and verse may seem dated. He was, however, extremely popular and enjoyed a large readership. His presentation of Clonmel life with its well-known landmarks, humorous characters and memorable scenery led one contemporary to describe him as the 'poet laureate of his native town'.

---

[2] *The Clonmel Chronicle*, 14 August 1918.

Chapter 23

The Gentle Revolutionary

The Clonmel Relief Road, which was officially opened on Easter Monday 1998, was named Seachród Ui Dhruacháin in honour of Frank Drohan, who was described as:

> a fearless and outspoken protagonist of patriotic ideals, a sincere lover of the Gaelic tongue and ever ready to lend his wholehearted and willing assistance to the centuries-old struggle for Irish freedom.[1]

Frank Drohan was the eldest of a family of seven boys, born to James Drohan and Mary O'Grady in Carrick-on-Suir on 13 August 1879. The family moved to Clonmel when he was seven and, in 1900, his father set up the firm of James Drohan & Sons at 66-67 Irishtown. Frank attended the Christian Brothers' school until he was twelve and then trained as a painter in his father's coach-making business.

From an early age he took a keen interest in sport, particularly in athletics, swimming and boxing, and also began to develop a love for Irish history, reading everything on which he could lay his hands. He said history 'was a kind of hobby with me, which seemed to have got into my blood because I was always talking about it as well as reading about it'.[2] While his father had a little Irish, his mother was a fluent Irish speaker and it's hardly surprising that when the Gaelic League was founded in Clonmel, Frank Drohan became an enthusiastic member. His love of the Irish language was to last for the rest of his life.

Apart from providing classes in Irish, the local branch of the League promoted a wide range of activities, including debating, drama and classes in Irish music and dance. Frank Drohan was one of the most committed and involved members. He read every manual on Irish grammar

---

[1] *The Nationalist*, 7 March 1953.
[2] Statement made to the Bureau of Military History, p. 1.

that was available and made regular trips to the Ring Gaeltacht in County Waterford. When Séamus Ó hEochaidh, better known as the Fear Mór, founder of Ring College, was sent from Dublin to promote the League in the area, he was accompanied by Frank, who helped to organise feiseanna and céilithe. A contemporary recalled how Frank would frequently cycle to villages such as Ballymacarbry, Newcastle and Kilmanahan to teach Irish without any seeking any fee or reward.

Like many others, Frank Drohan's membership of the Gaelic League was followed by his involvement in other nationalist bodies. Frank O'Meara was a Dublin member of the Irish Republican Brotherhood, the revolutionary organisation which grew out of the Fenian movement of the 1850s. Around 1909, when he came to Clonmel to take up employment as a draper's assistant, he joined the League where he became friendly with Frank Drohan. O'Meara was impressed by Drohan who, at his invitation, agreed to join the movement. It seems that O'Meara had been entrusted with the task of setting up an I.R.B. circle in Clonmel but instead, with the blessing of headquarters in Dublin, he asked Frank to undertake the task.[3]

Drohan was so successful that the leadership appointed him head centre or leader of the I.R.B. for south Tipperary. Through the branches of the League, he set up circles in Cashel, Thurles, Tipperary, Fethard and other towns. Having studied the reasons for the failure of Fenianism, he refused to consider anyone for membership 'who took drink'.[4] He said that the policy he adopted was one 'of picking out good men anywhere', and once he had established contact, left them to recruit further members.

In 1912 the Ulster Volunteers was set up to resist Home Rule. In opposition to them, the National Volunteers, which had the support of nationalists in the rest of the country, was founded under the leadership of Eoin McNeill. The organisation was later taken over by the Waterford M.P., John Redmond. Following a meeting of the I.R.B. circle in Clonmel, it was agreed that they should make every effort to start a volunteer force in Clonmel so that they could manipulate it for their own ends. In 1914 Frank Drohan was appointed company commander of the Clonmel Volunteers. Lieutenant-Colonel Thomas Halpin, another Clonmel man, said that it was

---

[3] *Ibid*, p. 6.
[4] *Ibid.*

252

'Frank's sterling example that inspired a large number of us to go into the Volunteers and other Irish-Ireland activities'.

The Clonmel Volunteers rented a hall at the back of the present O'Connell Mall, got two ex-British Sergeant Majors to train them, and collected two hundred pounds to purchase rifles. When they heard that small quantities of Lee Enfield rifles were being imported through Hearns, a hardware firm in Waterford, Drohan and two others were sent there, where the money was paid over for thirty eight rifles and 3,000 rounds of ammunition. While they were awaiting the shipment of these rifles, World War I broke out and the Volunteer movement split. The majority of the three hundred Clonmel Volunteers answered Redmond's appeal to join the British army. This was hardly surprising, since the British army had one of its biggest garrisons in the south of Ireland in Clonmel which, among other things, conferred considerable economic advantages on the town. Also, up to 1918, local politics were largely dominated by Tom Condon, the Redmondite M.P.

The anti-Redmondite Volunteers consisted of Frank Drohan and some forty others. Their most immediate concern was to secure possession of the rifles that were due in Waterford. When news came through that 'the goods had arrived', Drohan and two of his colleagues set off for Waterford once more, determined that they should not fall into the hands of the pro-Redmondite faction. The journey home was not without incident, as Frank Drohan recalled:

> Having decided to take the arms to Clonmel by road, we hired a motor car. Just outside Carrick-on-Suir we got a puncture. While the driver was mending the puncture two policemen came along. I was armed and it was dark, but nevertheless we did not feel any too comfortable. I was quite determined, no matter what happened, that we would not lose the rifles. But luck was with us. They merely enquired what had happened, said they were sorry for our troubles, cycled off and left us there.

They reached Drohan's yard that night and the following day the rifles and ammunition were distributed. The Redmondites arrived in Waterford the following day and, to their great annoyance, discovered that the weapons had already been taken to Clonmel. When they demanded that they be handed over, Drohan refused and that apparently ended the matter.

Following the departure of Redmond's followers for service overseas, the remaining volunteers, under Drohan's command, began to train openly in preparation for the call to arms, which eventually took place in Easter Week 1916. On Easter Saturday, Frank Drohan, on orders from Dublin, set about mobilising the local volunteers. He told them that the rising was to begin the following day on Easter Sunday and that they should go to confession and be ready with 24 hours rations, rifle and small arms and whatever ammunition they had. Approximately forty Volunteers assembled on Easter Sunday morning when they got word that the rising had been called off and that they were to disband. Drohan went to Carrick, Waterford and New Ross to inform the volunteers in those areas. On his return, he spent the rest of the week waiting for instructions from Dublin. When he received news of the surrender, he gave orders that all arms, ammunition and equipment should be hidden and that any incriminating documentation should be destroyed.

The police raided his house the following Tuesday. He was ordered at gunpoint to get dressed and accompany them downstairs. When told that they intended to search the house he defiantly told them to 'search away'. The six rifles which he still had in his possession and three thousand rounds of ammunition, the latter concealed in empty paint tins in the workshop, remained undetected. He was taken to the army barracks in Clonmel and handed over to the military. From there, Drohan and his fellow prisoners were escorted to Tipperary military barracks and then brought to Cork station, where they received a hostile reception from a crowd which included the wives of men who had enlisted in the British army. This was in marked contrast to the greetings of well-wishers they later received in Patrick Street who offered them cigarettes and words of encouragement. However, an angry crowd surrounded the jail that night and broke some of the prison windows.

After a week of being confined to their cells, they were transferred to the Richmond Barracks in Dublin, where they were given a blanket each and divided into groups of twenty five prisoners who were placed in rooms meant for eleven soldiers. From there they were sent to Glasgow where they were greeted by a hostile mob of dockers. Frank Drohan spent three weeks in Barlinnie prison before being transferred to Frongoch in Wales. Here he found himself in company with many of the future leaders of Ireland's War of Independence, including Michael Collins, Terence Mc Swiney and Sean T. O'Kelly. When the prisoners set up their own military council, Frank Drohan was chosen as one of the camp's officers. He was elected captain of 'G' company in camp no. 2, an indication of his standing among his fellow prisoners. Frongoch was described by the Irish M.P. Tim Healy, as a 'Sinn Féin University',[5] where even the most moderate internee's opposition to English rule was intensified.

After his release in August, Drohan returned home to a changed political climate. Many people were shocked by the executions of the 1916 leaders and there was a rapid shift in public opinion which now became increasingly sympathetic to the Volunteers and the idea of national independence. The returning prisoners were greeted as heroes with bands and processions. The Volunteers had been by now officially banned and consequently I.R.B. activities were carried on under the guise of Sinn Féin, an umbrella organisation for other nationalist groups who were pledged to an independent republic. Frank Drohan was elected President of the Clonmel Sinn Féin Club and set about trying to re-organise the outlawed Volunteer movement.

The proposal by the British government to introduce conscription to Ireland resulted in an upsurge in Volunteer membership, and Drohan estimated that there was an enrolment of 700 in the Clonmel area. Mounting opposition to the proposed measure led the government to issue a proclamation which stated that Sinn Féin had been engaged in a treasonable conspiracy with the Germans. The authorities set about rounding up all its leaders, in what became known as the so-called German Plot.

Drohan's involvement in the anti-conscription campaign brought him to the attention of the authorities once more and, in May 1918, he was arrested and sent to Usk prison, where he said that he devoted his time to teaching Irish to his fellow internees. While there, he fell and wrenched his

---

[5] Seán O'Mahony, *University of Revolution*, (Dublin, 1987), p.58.

255

knee in the prison yard during a game of rounders. The injury was slow to heal and it seriously restricted his participation in the War of Independence which followed. Shortly afterwards, he was transferred to Gloucester where many of the prisoners, himself included, fell victim to the flu pandemic of 1918. No provision was made by the authorities to curtail it and even some of the guards succumbed. With a temperature of 104 degrees, Drohan had to be removed to a nursing home where he remained in a critical condition for some time. When his release was ordered he was so weak that the doctor would not certify him as fit to travel, but he insisted that he should go along with the others.

After eleven months imprisonment, he arrived home to a great welcome. The train on which he was travelling was met at the station by a company of Volunteers and members of Cumann na mBan. Outside, a car was waiting for him. Followed by a large procession of well-wishers he was paraded to his home in Irishtown. He later recalled that he found it most heartening to see among the welcoming party many who previously had not identified themselves with Sinn Féin. In a short address he told the assembled crowd that 'although his health had been broken in an English jail because of his love of Ireland, his spirit was not broken – it was unbreakable'.[6]

While he was in gaol, the political situation in Ireland had altered dramatically. The post war elections in December 1918 saw Sinn Féin secure 71 seats out of the 105 for the whole island. Instead of taking their seats at Westminster, they set up their own republican parliament in Dublin. Dáil Éireann assembled in the Mansion House on 21 January 1919 and ratified the republic which had been proclaimed in 1916. On the very same day, the first armed engagement in the War of Independence took place when eight volunteers killed two policemen in an ambush at Soloheadbeg in County Tipperary.

In the meantime, by the summer of 1918, the Volunteers in County Tipperary had been completely re-organised. The Clonmel Company now became the fourth battalion of the Third Tipperary Brigade, with Frank Drohan as commanding officer. Before his arrest in 1918, he had become

---

[6] *The Nationalist*, 15 March 1918.

engaged to Agnes Davin, daughter of John Davin and Margaret Myles, whose family had a bakery business in Irishtown. Shortly after his release they were married on the 20 August 1919 but she died tragically of a heart infection on 31 January 1920 and was buried in Grange. He never re-married. He said that he 'got into rather bad health following that sad event'.[7] In April 1920, as his condition worsened, he was forced to step down as battalion commander, and was succeeded by William Myles.[8] That Summer he suffered a relapse and was laid up for three months.

Sunday 21 November 1920, afterwards better known as 'Bloody Sunday', was one of the most eventful days in the War of Independence. In the morning, on the orders of Michael Collins, the IRA had killed thirteen British intelligence agents and injured six others. That afternoon, as a reprisal, Auxiliaries opened fire on the crowd in Croke Park, who were watching a football match between Dublin and Tipperary, killing twelve people.

The following day saw further repercussions when the military raided houses in Clonmel looking for republican sympathisers. Luckily, Frank Drohan managed to escape before his own home was searched. This was the start of his days on the run. Recurring bouts of illness and his injured knee impaired his mobility and he became dependent on his colleagues to get him from one safe house to another. Recalling these events he said:

> I was laid up for a good while in Newcastle while I was on the run and they were bringing me from house to house in an old car. If there were any sign of an impending raid, they would get me an old car and bring me away up the hill until it passed. In this way I managed to pull through'.[9]

In the months ahead he narrowly avoided capture on a number of occasions. One Sunday, when his companions were bringing him to Clonmel to attend Mass, they were confronted by a military patrol which

---

[7] Statement to Bureau of Military History, p. 45.
[8] Colm Ó Labhra, *Trodairí na Treas Briogáide* (Nenagh, 1955), p. 307.
[9] Statement to Bureau of Military History, p. 52.

was out searching for them. While his colleagues were about to make a run for it, Drohan realised that there were no police with them and that he would not be recognised. So they drove casually on and no notice was taken of them. On another occasion, when he and a number of his colleagues were helping a farmer thinning turnips some soldiers halted and gazed at them over a wall. They carried on working, and the soldiers eventually moved off. His narrowest escape occurred in his own house. His brother had ferried him across the river Suir by boat at nightfall. The British authorities got word of his presence but, fortunately, in an effort to capture him, they mistakenly raided the house next door. He remained in hiding until daybreak before escaping, and did not return home again until after the Truce.

Although, as has been stated, ill health prevented him from taking a prominent part in the military campaign, he admitted to selecting a spot near Barne for a successful ambush, but most of his energy was spent organising food and shelter for members of the flying columns operating in the area.[10] He had very fixed views on how the war should be conducted. He questioned an order from GHQ which proposed a boycott of the R.I.C by urban traders, realising that the I.R.A. had neither sufficient force to protect those who might try to carry out the boycott from reprisals, or sufficient means to compensate those who would inevitably suffer from implementing it. The order was subsequently rescinded. More controversial was the complaint he made concerning the unauthorised military actions by the more extreme republicans which he felt would expose a defenceless population to the brutality of the Black and Tans. He was supported by Eamon O'Dwyer, Acting Brigade Quartermaster, who realised that such tactics could have detrimental consequences for ordinary citizens.

Drohan's views drew the following rebuke from Ernie O'Malley at the time when Frank was being considered as a candidate for the general election of May 1921:

> Our point of view is that of the IRA. As an officer you are unsuitable. You had not the necessary drive and initiative for

---

[10] *Ibid*, p. 55.

guerrilla warfare. Your area, though possessing good material, was the slackest from the point of view of organisation and offensive action. I did not nor do not doubt your intentions. You are fit for civic honour but as a fighting man I do not respect you. I think that active members of the IRA are the most suitable men at present for the TD position, men whom the youth can look to their fighting record.[11]

This criticism was most unjustified and showed no consideration for Drohan's indifferent health which had severely curtailed his activities.

Frank Drohan's political career had begun in January 1920, when he was elected as an alderman to Clonmel Corporation but, until a truce was called the following June, he was not in a position to attend many meetings. Two years later, he was unanimously elected mayor and remained in office until 1 July 1925, when he was succeeded by Alderman Reidy. During this period he represented the corporation on the Technical Instruction Committee, a forerunner of the Vocational Educational Committee. Unfortunately, it is not possible to evaluate his contribution to the civic affairs of Clonmel, for the minute books of the Corporation are disappointingly lacking in detail for this period. However, they do show that he was one of the first councillors to use the Irish version of his name, a practice soon adopted by his colleagues. His nationalist views were also evident in his opposition to the British government's Education Bill. He argued 'that the education of the people must be designed and approved by the Irish people and not a system designed and maintained by foreigners and in opposition to our views and interests'. On local issues, one of his greatest concerns was growing unemployment in Clonmel.

While Frank Drohan was being held prisoner in Gloucester, one of the fatalities of the flu epidemic had been his friend Pierce McCan, Sinn Féin T.D. for East Tipperary. In the general election of May 1921, Frank was elected to Dáil Éireann for Waterford/Tipperary East to succeed him. A truce was called the following month and in December the Anglo-Irish treaty was signed. The debate on the articles of agreement in the Dáil led to

---

[11] cited in Joost Augusteijn, 'The operations of South Tipperary IRA, 1916-1921' in *Tipperary Historical Journal,* ix, (1996), p. 154

a split in Sinn Fein ranks. Much to Drohan's regret, 'the wonderful movement that had been built up over the years so completely cleft, and men like Griffith, Collins and Cathal Brugha, whom he had learned to love and respect, calling each other names'.[12]

Frank Drohan's unique position in Irish parliamentary history was to be defined by his reaction to the Treaty. His Fenian soul told him to reject it but his democratic principles urged him to obey the wishes of the people. Local bodies, including Clonmel Corporation and the Tipperary S.R. County Council, had voted for its acceptance. Of all the T.D.'s who may have agonised over it, he was the only one to actually resign his Dáil seat. On Tuesday, 5 January 1922, two days before the final vote, the Ceann Comhairle received Frank Drohan's letter of resignation. In it he wrote:

> I regret having to resign my Dáil seat. From the instructions I have received from the people of south Tipperary, it is obvious that they are not satisfied with my opposition to the Treaty that was made with England. Neither my heart nor my mind would allow me to accept it; and the fact that the Sinn Féin clubs had instructed me to accept it, I have no option but to resign because these people were the ones that elected me.

His decision was greeted with widespread surprise. *The Nationalist* announced that:

> a sensation was caused in Clonmel and through the East Tipperary Division when it was learned that our respected T.D., Alderman Frank Drohan had tendered his resignation to the Dáil.

The article went on to state that Drohan was:

> one of Tipperary's most esteemed public men, as the many public offices he holds testifies; he has given of his best for the cause of

---

[12] Statement to Bureau of Military History, p. 60.

Ireland and, while all regret his retirement from the Dáil, his attitude in the great crisis is understood and appreciated'.[13]

His resignation put him into a political wilderness. Following his decision not to contest the Corporation elections of 1925 he dropped out of political life.

Frank Drohan's patriotism was expressed in other ways. Even in the very early years when Irish-manufactured articles were not comparable in standard to imported ones, Frank Drohan would purchase only Irish made goods. When, on his withdrawal from politics, he settled down to running his late wife's grocery shop at 16 Upper Irishtown, he continued to promote the sale of Irish products. Not forgetting his love for the Irish language, he encouraged his customers, especially the school children, to whom he was affectionately known as 'the Irishman', to converse in Irish.

He continued to take an interest in the affairs of the town. When the Clonmel branch of the Gaelic League was revised in 1932, he was elected president and in the same year became a member of the boy scout movement. During the 'Emergency', created by the Second World War, he again answered his country's call and became an officer in the Local Defence Forces and 'despite his years, he played an active part in this organisation, and his hardy figure marching at the head of his Company was an inspiring sight for the younger men of his group'. He was for many years, up to the time of his death, a valued and respected member of the Board of Directors of The Nationalist Newspaper Company.

During the Tercentenary Celebrations of the Siege of Clonmel in 1950 he performed his last public function when he commanded the guard of honour which greeted President Seán T. O'Kelly. He reminded the President that fifty years previously, as vice-president of the Clonmel branch of the Gaelic League, he had greeted O'Kelly, then a young delegate member from the Dublin branch of the Gaelic League. The President remembered the occasion and warmly exchanged reminiscences with him on those stirring days.

---

[13] *The Nationalist*, 8 January 1922.

Frank Drohan died suddenly on 5 March 1953. In his obituary he was described as:

A man of sterling honesty, deeply religious and unwavering in his support of all things Irish, he spoke the native tongue on all possible occasions, especially with members of the younger generation. A keen angler and great walker, he was fond of the outdoor life and was a popular and familiar figure in the countryside around Clonmel, particularly around County Waterford, of which he was especially fond.

A volunteer colleague, Willie Myles, described him as:

A man of deep sincerity and burning patriotism he was ready and willing to sacrifice everything in the cause of a free – and more particularly Gaelic – Ireland for he was one of the most ardent for the revival of the Irish language. He was beyond all doubt the father of the Volunteers in Clonmel. Too gentle and kindly perhaps to make a ruthless man of action he would have accepted any suffering for the cause of liberty.[14]

The Mayor, members and officials of the corporation, as well as leading figures of the old I.R.A. and the Gaelic League, were among the large gathering that attended his funeral. A firing party discharged three volleys and the last post was sounded over his grave in St. Patrick's Cemetery, a final tribute to a kind and compassionate man who loved his town and country.

---

[14] Cluain Meala 1916, (1966), p. 21.

262

Chapter 24

'Temple Lane'

All night around the Thorn Tree
The little people play,
And men and women passing
Will turn their heads away.

But Katie Ryan saw there,
In some sweet dream she had,
The Blessed Son of Mary –
And all his face was sad.

O! if your heart's a child-heart
And if your eyes are clean,
You'll never fear the Thorn Tree
That grows beyond Clogheen!

These are some verses taken from the well-known ballad *The Fairy Tree* written in 1930 by Mary Isabel Leslie, under the penname Temple Lane. She wrote it on a train journey from Dublin to Limerick and the words, she said, came to her effortlessly 'just as long as it took to write them down'. In an interview she admitted that the poem was inspired by a legend her mother told her about a 'fairy' tree that grew in the townland of Kilcaroon, outside the village of Ballyporeen.

She wrote to the Director of Radio Éireann asking if she might recite six of her poems on radio, including *The Fairy Tree,* an offer that was accepted. Dr. Vincent O'Brien, conductor of the station's orchestra, heard the poem and, with her permission, put it to music. It was to become widely popular when it was recorded by his friend, the great tenor, John McCormack. She was present when McCormack sang it in concert at the Cork Opera House. He called on her to take a bow. Seated in the second row of the stalls, she rose to receive the acclaim of the audience. She later regretted that she had not been more business-like because she sold all the concert rights for three guineas.

Reverend John Herbert Leslie, a native of Beaufort in County Kerry, had married Mary Richardson from Waterford in 1898. That same year he was appointed Rector of Clogheen, and Mary Isabel Leslie was born in Dublin a year later. Her childhood days were spent in the little village of Clogheen nestling in the shadow of the Knockmealdowns, where the surrounding landscape with its streams and woodlands made a lasting impression on her. She dearly loved the village with its colourful characters and the intimacy of its community. The Rev. Leslie, like many of his fellow Anglo-Irish Protestants, was firmly unionist in outlook. It was, no doubt, a source of great pride to the family that when King Edward VII paid an official visit to Shanbally Castle in 1908, Mary Isabel presented a bouquet to Queen Alexandria on behalf of the local Protestant community.

In 1910, her father was made rector of Old St. Mary's in Clonmel where the Leslie family were to spend the next twenty years. She obviously found it difficult trying to adjust to living in a big town. She said that she was broken-hearted when she had to leave Clogheen. It was a traumatic experience that damaged her, she said, for she went from being the parish pet to being the opposite. Mary Isabel attended the Model School before being sent to Sherborne Girls' School in England, an experience which she didn't enjoy. She was homesick and looked forward to her summer holidays when she could picnic in the countryside, visit places of local historic interest and take trips to the home of her father's parents in Kerry. She entered Trinity College in 1918 where she secured an M.A. and a Doctorate in Philosophy. An outstanding student, she won the Large Gold Medal in 1922 for academic excellence, becoming scholar of the year. She later became a lecturer in English literature in the college for a short time.

During her Dublin days she met and became friendly with Lady Gregory and frequently accompanied her to productions in the Abbey Theatre. Lady Gregory encouraged her writing and although she showed no talent for drama, she won recognition as a poet and novelist. Fearing that her literary activities would be harmful to her father's career, she decided to use a pseudonym, Temple Lane, which she took from a little street that she passed on her way to visit her Dublin publishers. It is thought that she was also the author of a number of Mills and Boon novels under the pseudonym, Jean Herbert, a combination of the first name of her younger sister, Jean Annette, and the second name of her father, John Herbert Leslie.

From the publication of *Full Tide* in 1923 to *My Bonny's Away* in 1947 she wrote sixteen novels. Her books were widely read and some were highly acclaimed, particularly *The Little Wood* written in 1930, which won the Tailteann Gold Medal. The wood in question was situated near Galtee Castle, a few kilometres from Clogheen. The book traces the story of Hyacinth Comerford, daughter of the local doctor of Ballyliskeen, from childhood to the eve of her marriage. It contains strong biographical elements and has been described as 'her most charming novel' and 'a lovely children's tale set in the Tipperary countryside she knew and loved so well'.

Her novels have been described as 'female fiction before the Liberation'.[1] They could be regarded as popular romances and true to their romantic genre the hero and heroine endure the usual setbacks and complications, but everything comes right for them in the end. While her heroines show a sound moral outlook, their male counterparts are sometimes flawed. Her novel *Friday's Well,* published in 1945, had the distinction of being adapted for the stage by Frank Carney and enjoyed a very long run in the Abbey Theatre.

Her characters are drawn from her own social milieu, that of middle class Irish society and include doctors, bank managers, well-to-do farmers, clergyman's daughters, spiced with one or two members of the landed gentry. The plots are generally predictable and in some cases stretch the bounds of credulity. In *Watch the Wall* we are asked to believe that the heroine does not realize that her lethargic suitor and the daring smuggler were one and the same. She often has to resort to improbable events, unexpected deaths, and characters that undergo a sudden volte-face to bring her stories to a conclusion.

Her work features the landscape of Tipperary and Waterford. In some of her novels current events, including two World Wars and the Irish

---

[1] Tina O'Toole (ed.), *Munster women writers 1800-2000*, (Cork, 2005), p. 114.

Civil War, form a backdrop against which the intricacies of human relationships are played out. Occasionally she departs from the contemporary scene, setting *Watch the Wall* in England, for instance, during the Napoleonic wars, while in *House of my Pilgrimage* there are flashbacks to landlordism in the nineteenth century.

Perhaps the most interesting feature of her novels is her exploration of life in the 'big house' and how its occupants come to terms with an independent Ireland. Regardless of her staunch unionist background her attitude is optimistic and she feels that such people can make a positive contribution to the infant state. In her novel *The Trains Go South* Hugh Devereaux becomes a Free State senator and a model farmer and she fears that 'his type once destroyed, the country would be the poorer'.

As Catholics and Protestants begin to mix in the new Ireland, inter-denominational marriages become more common. The author focuses on the difficulties inherent in such relationships and on the conflicting attitudes to divorce. One of her heroines who finds herself trapped in a loveless marriage can only enjoy the friendship of the man she loves 'and keep it as such, unlit by passion'.

This theme of repressed feeling finds greater expression in her poetry, leading one to wonder whether such emotional repression was reflected in her own life. A thread of loneliness and a yearning for love runs through many of her poems. *Marriage of Convenience* is such a poem where one who rejected love would now willingly trade 'All the dreams of the head for the touch of a hand'.

Leslie admitted that while writing novels was a case of economic necessity, poetry was her first love. She was the author of two books of poetry, *The Fisherman's Wake* and *Curlews,* as well as a number of occasional pieces. She draws heavily on nature and expresses a sentimental hankering for the simple peasant life, which led one critic to refer to her as 'a true poet of her people and of their ways'. At best her poems surprise and delight, and reveal a lyrical gift but much of her work has been dismissed as 'little more than skilful rhyming and merry tinkles'.

She empathised with ordinary people and drew inspiration from simple rural scenes. As in her novels, her poems mainly evoke the countryside of south Tipperary and west Waterford, while a number feature the seascapes and rugged countryside of her father's home in Kerry. Like Patrick Kavanagh, her use of such placenames as Lismore, Melleray and Ardmore help to reinforce a sense of location. Surprisingly, her religious references are drawn from traditional Catholicism. She writes of the lamp before the Sacred Heart as 'the symbol of a faith not mine'.

Leslie's poems made a contribution to the social history of her day. She shows the superstitions of the ordinary people who firmly believed in phookas, haunted fairy raths, wraiths and other eerie manifestations. Superstition is evident in her best known poem, *The Fairy Tree*:

> They'll tell you Cromwell hung them:
> Sure that could never be!
> He'd be in dread, like others,
> To touch the Fairy Tree.

In her poem *Afforestation* she tells how the people would leave 'hen-eggs in the furrow's way' or employ other pishogues in an effort to thwart the efforts of the authorities who endeavoured to change the face of the landscape.

She writes about the poor and the marginalized with sympathy and understanding. *The Lonely Woman,* which has echoes of Pádraic Colum's *Old Woman of the Roads,* longs for 'a settled place' from where she never need 'stir again'. Old Jimmy Ladrigan, *The Anchorite,* who lives in a cave outside Lismore, is reduced to wearing 'an old shirt and a bit of a sack' and cast-off waders on his legs. She prays that God may 'keep Jimmy happy':

> and cancel the day
> When they'll say he's a danger and take him away.

A regular caller to her home was *The Old Brush-Man* who made a living making and repairing brushes. His needs were modest and she recalls giving him milk and tea but 'he wouldn't ask bread or take money'. Isabel regrets not having spoken to him:

> To ask if the things he thinks gracious and fine

On the roads of the world are the same things as mine

On another level, the drudgery and poverty of farming is sketched in *The Poor Farm* on the 'sour coast' where the land is eroded 'grain by grain / To join the sand and foam', and where the 'pale oats is flat'. Love will not be found in the midst of such poverty. Matchmakers advise those with a dowry or fortune to go to the Vale of Aherlow where 'beasts fatten in the grass'. *The Kerry Planters* depicts the struggle to tame and cultivate the land, while *At the Fair* is a commentary on the isolation and loneliness of the 'sad-faced' drovers whose lives are filled with unremitting bleakness and 'hardship'. The sea can be an equally hostile environment. *Fisherman's Wake* captures the desolation that its waters can wreak on human beings with death taking the fisherman 'as the wind the smoke'.

The subject of death is never far from her thoughts, something that may have been prompted by the loss of her only sister, who was tragically drowned in the River Dodder in November 1936. Jean Annette had been missing for almost three weeks before her body was discovered. At the time of her death she was aged thirty-three and was the head of the Students' Training Department and Kindegarten of Alexandra College. The tragic event is recalled in *Poem for Annette*, which was published many years later in 1969 but yet, the memory of her death is still fresh in Isabel's mind:

I hope she knows I know she is not dead

Isabel Leslie was a country girl at heart. City life where 'the sun is only a stranger', is alien to her. Her father felt she was happiest amongst the trees and by the waters, where her real affinities lay. Nothing gave her more pleasure than to spend her holidays walking among 'the scented slopes of Comeragh'. Her images are of the land with its trees, farms and rivers, while the sea is also a sense of inspiration. Word pictures such as 'A moor hen skirts the ice', 'The sliding weir still roars, but all the sedge / Is rigid too with frost' are evocative of Patrick Kavanagh. Memorable nature images are present in that lovely and moving poem *The Last Fishing* where 'all the fragrant clinging light / Drained to the river from the wood' and the 'iris blades were razor grey'. While 'a bat snipped past on stilted wings', she sees fish in the water as 'shapes beneath those winking rings'.

Her writings were very popular and were reviewed in all the leading literary journals and in the national papers. However, for all the success she enjoyed she was unsure of herself. Her sensitivity and her capacity to be hurt is captured in her poem *Rebuff* where she writes:

> I shall never get rid
> Of loneliness and a sneer.

She believed that her literary efforts deserved wider recognition. She was, however, comforted by the knowledge that the Bronte sisters, who were incidentally also daughters of a clergyman, 'were in no contemporary anthology'. Her poem *There may not be Another Summer* finds her in a much darker mood. In referring to it she said that 'the lack of an audience, or even, public appreciation, has driven me to the death wish'.

In addition to her two volumes of poetry, she contributed occasional pieces to The Dublin Opinion, The Cuala Press and other publications, as well as writing verses for greeting cards. She lectured extensively, wrote literary critiques, newspaper articles and frequently read her own poetry on Radio Éireann. In her younger days she travelled widely, spending some time in the Near East, especially in the city then known as Constantinople. She was an accomplished linguist. In her forties she took up the study of Irish, and became an enthusiastic supporter of the language revival movement. A member of PEN, she immersed herself in the literary world of the day and was on intimate terms with some of its leading figures. She was a personal friend of Austin Clarke, who encouraged her poetic efforts, and she frequently visited Bowenscourt, the family home of novelist, Elizabeth Bowen.

In 1930, her father was appointed Dean of Lismore. Following his sudden death four years later, his widow bought a house opposite the R.T.E. headquarters in Montrose and Isabel went to live with her. She never married and her final years were spent in a home for retired people. She died in the Kylemore Clinic in Blackrock on 18 February 1978 and was buried with her parents and sister in the shade of the ancient Cathedral of St. Carthage in Lismore.

Chapter 25

The Voice of Clonmel

The Comeragh mountains form an impressive backdrop to the ruins of the O'Brien ancestral home that stands in the woodlands of Cúleeshal, overlooking Kilsheelan. The family had a substantial holding in the area before being evicted during the Land League days. Martin O'Brien moved to Clonmel and became a clerk in a coal and grain store. In May 1894, he married Brigid Moroney from Ballymacarbry and they set up home in 5 Wolfe Tone Street. She was a very industrious woman and supplemented the family income, serving ninepenny dinners to countrymen who had come to town to transact their business. They raised a large family of six boys and two girls, David, Michael, Jim, Martin, Paddy, Tommy, Alice and Mary.

The O'Brien children were generally regarded as brilliant and talented. David taught oriental languages in an English college, while Martin had a distinguished career in the Irish civil service. Michael was regarded as the outstanding Irish scholar of his generation. He was professor of Celtic Studies in Queens University, Belfast and later at the Institute for Advanced Studies in Dublin. He taught himself German and Russian, while he also studied Hebrew and several mid-European languages. He produced an English/Russian dictionary which became a standard work and was the acknowledged expert on Irish family names and place names.

Tommy, the youngest of the O'Brien brothers, became a celebrated radio broadcaster with a unique and distinctive style and was one of the country's greatest authorities on opera and classical music. He was born on 20 July 1905. He attended St. Mary's C.B.S. before moving to the High School. Of his days in the High School he wrote, 'in the academic sphere I failed to shine with even a dim brightness; athletically, I could be written of as of no account at all'. However, his contemporaries considered him to be one of the best in the class, whatever about his lack of sporting prowess. Like two of his older brothers he had a facility for languages and won a scholarship to Ring College in County Waterford.

He left school at fifteen to join Fianna Éireann, the Irish boy scout movement founded by Countess Markievicz. When she came to Clonmel to accept the freedom of the town he was chosen to deliver an address of welcome. During the War of Independence he became a dispatch rider carrying messages from the Clonmel Battalion to the headquarters of the Third Tipperary Brigade. On one occasion when he had a revolver belonging to Dan Breen in a parcel on the front of his bike, which he was bringing to Clonmel to have repaired, he encountered a lorry load of Black and Tans. He said that when they came around the bend in the road he nearly fell off the bike in sheer terror, 'But there was an RIC Sergeant with them, a man called Sergeant O'Connell who knew my father, and he saw me and gave me a wave, and said ''Hello, Master O'Brien'', and they all went on'.

He once said that had it not been for the Anglo-Irish war he might have gone to university, as had three of his brothers. Instead, after the Treaty, he applied for a job in the *Clonmel Chronicle*. He was told he would need shorthand but he later admitted that he hardly knew what shorthand was but he bought a Pitman Shorthand Manual in a secondhand bookshop in Clonmel for sixpence. 'I went to my grandfather's farm in County Waterford, and spent the whole summer, from morning 'til night, for over three months, studying shorthand'. He got the job as a junior reporter at a weekly salary of 7s. 6d. His employers were obviously impressed by him for they soon offered him a permanent position and raised his salary to 12s. 6d. When the *Clonmel Chronicle* closed in the thirties, he joined *The Nationalist*. In his own modest fashion he said 'they wanted a reporter, and they wanted me because I was bloody good and they insisted that I continue to write a weekly column I had been writing for the *Chronicle*, called Clonmel Notes'.

This column appeared under the name 'Scrutator' and included Tommy's observations on topics as diverse as circuses and court cases or on anything else that took his fancy. It was always written in a witty and colloquial style. A snippet on the efforts of the Corporation to widen Mitchel Street was typical of his weekly offering:

Starting at the Parnell Street end, ten inches are to be added to the pavement at the right hand side, while the opposite side, is to remain untouched. So in order to meet the proposal to widen the street, the Corporation have characteristically decided to narrow it. But the Councillors must be excused. For having wasted so much brea(d)th talking about it, they found they had no width left available for distribution. Yes, I know what you motorists will say. But be a bit broadminded. That narrow outlook will never get you anywhere – least of all through Mitchel Street on a busy day.

Another feature of the column shows Tommy's passion for the cinema. He enjoyed the humour of Laurel and Hardy, the artistry of Fred Astaire and he got particular pleasure from the westerns, especially if they guaranteed him plenty of gun-play.

In the early nineteen forties he became editor of *The Nationalist*, a position he held until 1953. Tomás Ó Duinn, one-time reporter with the paper, who worked under Tommy said that he was the ultimate professional. He stated that he demanded high standards, was a stickler for accuracy and left you in no doubt what he thought of your work. If it was good he praised it, if not he let you know. Tommy was always very much his own man. He took no dictation from anyone, neither from the directors nor from the clergy. At the comparatively young age of forty eight he decided to retire. When asked, 'Tommy are you really serious about retiring?' He replied, 'Sure, what the hell would I be doing editing the Ballyporeen notes when I could be at home playing Mozart!'

For Tommy, music was his abiding passion. He came from a family with a strong musical tradition. His father played the tin whistle, and his mother had a beautiful singing voice. At school, Tommy was a soloist in the choir. As a young reporter he became an avid reader of books on music and, as soon as he had enough to invest in his first gramophone, he paid fifty shillings to have it shipped from England. It came 'complete with needles and six records'. He later bought a better one for £10 from an Englishman who was leaving town and got 50 records thrown in. By the time he died he had an extraordinary record collection. He set up a very elaborate sound system in his house by converting two rooms into one. It was like having his own concert hall, he said. The acoustics were very good and he used four speakers, the two principal ones costing £1,000 each. He admitted that it was 'a lot of money', but, as he said, 'when you're really interested, it's worth it'.

Tommy developed a love of opera attending performances by touring opera companies that visited the town. He saw his first opera when he was still a schoolboy. It was 'Il Trovatore' performed by the Joseph O'Mara Touring Company but he remembers feeling it 'a bit heavy at the time'. Later he heard the Bowyer-Westwood Company performing excerpts from various operas, including Wallace's 'Maritana', an experience which whetted his appetite for more. In the summer of 1925, he read in *The Daily Telegraph* about a forthcoming programme in Covent Garden and decided to spend his holidays attending the operas there. That summer he had the pleasure of hearing Gigli, the great Italian tenor. At the time, it was accepted practice that there was to be no applause until the fall of the curtain. But, according to Tommy, that night all the Italians in London were present and at the end of the big aria in the first act they all got up and cheered 'bravo'. Tommy couldn't restrain himself and 'got up and cheered as well'. Up to the outbreak of the Second World War, his annual holiday was spent at Covent Garden. During that time he attended a total of eighty three operas and had the pleasure of listening to all the greats including John McCormack, Caruso and Margaret Burke Sheridan.

To finance these visits to London, he devised various means to supplement his wages. Apart from his work as a reporter, he secured a job as court stenographer for which he was paid £2 a week. He said that he received a number of compliments from judges and barristers for the accuracy of his reporting. He also sang at the silent films. This came about when the local cinema manager approached him and asked him if he knew 'Mother Machree'. Tommy said:

> of course I did, and he said there was a film being shown the following week in which a live singer had to come on and sing 'Mother Machree'. So I sang it, and do you know how much I got for it? Two pounds. A lot of money then, and I must have been good because I was asked back again'.

charity. He was a generous benefactor to the St. Vincent de Paul Society. Ray Mc Donald, President for the South East Region of the Society spoke of 'the substantial bequest Tommy made 'to the less well off in his beloved Clonmel', saying that it revealed 'a truly Christian and Vincentian concern comparable to his infectious love for classical music'.[3]

Music for his funeral mass was provided by baritone, Peter McBrien, of the Dublin Grand Opera Society and by SS. Peter and Paul's choir. Tommy's final choice was Mozart's Sonata in B for violin and piano which was played as his remains were borne through the streets of Clonmel. 'It was his last choice of music, and the melody which ended each day in his home on the high hill over Clonmel', said his friend Barry O'Donovan, who inherited Tommy's unique collection of 7,000 records, some of them so rare that they were frequently on loan to the B.B.C. and R.T.E.

His death was an occasion of national mourning. Among the many tributes paid to him was one from the Taoiseach of the day, Jack Lynch, who together with his wife, Máirín, had been his fans for over thirty years. He recalled a time in the early fifties when Tommy presented a programme in Cork to raise funds for the recently-built Glen Rovers Hurling Club hall in Blackpool. He expressed the feelings of many when he said that 'he brought love, appreciation and an understanding of opera and good music to homes the length and breath of Ireland. It will be sad that in years to come we will no longer hear over the airways the introduction, 'Good evening, listeners' and that 'in times of turmoil for our country he had been a soothing influence. He found peace and fulfilment in music which he transmitted to us all'.[4]

In the opinion of Vincent Finn, Director General of R.T.E., 'to many radio listeners, he was a friend with whom, over the years, they had developed a close personal relationship. His contribution to an awareness and appreciation of classical music in Ireland was substantial'. Brendan Long said that his outstanding success was due to 'his down-to-earth style which belied his profound musical erudition, a style which won him the ear of thousands who would not have otherwise listened'. Johnny Devlin, who

---

[3] Peter Taylor (compiler), *A Tribute to Tommy* (Clonmel, 1993), unpaginated.
[4] *Irish Times*, 25 February 1982.

had been Tommy's producer for thirteen years said his death 'marked the end of an era. We will never again have anything quite like that. Tommy and his programmes are irreplaceable'. His fellow countyman and Munster M.E.P., T. J. Maher, described him as a unique figure who was really individual in his approach and style as a person and as a broadcaster. He possessed an extraordinary knowledge of classical music and was Co. Tipperary's best known and most popular person.

Tommy had no time for hypocrisy and sham. An early devotee of the Wexford Opera Festival, in latter years he had given up attending. At the beginning, he said, real opera lovers used to go there but he became 'browned off' by the atmosphere and he didn't like the accents. He was always very much his own man. An incident, which marked his independent spirit, concerned a travelling opera company on a visit to Clonmel. A performance scheduled for Sunday night, in the Oisín theatre, incurred opposition from the local clergy. While a number of protestors paraded up and down spying on those who defied the ban, Tommy marched past them defiantly to make sure that he was seen going in.

Tommy was among the most colourful characters Clonmel produced, a man who was larger than life. When asked to compose a fitting epithet for himself he said he would like to be remembered as one 'who gave a little pleasure to a lot of people'.

Chapter 26

Olympic Champion

It had been another successful sports' meeting for Pat O'Callaghan and his brother Conn. They packed their prizes which included an alarm clock, a pen knife, an enamel bucket and a rose bowl and prepared to cycle home. In the course of their journey they came across on a dance in a village hall and decided they needed a break. In the small hours of the morning they set out once more and as dawn approached they were overcome with hunger. With little hope of getting any food they were forced to improvise. Having helped themselves to some blackberries, Pat used the penknife to prepare a turnip, while Conn hopped into a nearby field, rose bowl in hand, and milked an obliging cow. The story may no doubt has been embellished in the telling but the whole affair was one that would scarcely have exhausted two young men whose lives were filled with physical activity.

Pat O'Callaghan was born in the townland of Derrygallon, outside Kanturk, in County Cork on 28 January 1906, the second of three sons of Paddy O'Callaghan and Jane Healy. His father was a farmer and his mother a qualified nurse and midwife for the area. Their uncle, Tim Hayes, was the Irish 880 yards champion and a member of the 1893 Cork/Dromtariffe senior football team that reached the All-Ireland final, only to loose out in acrimonious circumstances when the referee awarded the game to Wexford after Cork walked off in protest over crowd interference.

The O'Callaghan brothers grew up in a district steeped in athletic tradition. One of the annual highlights in the barony of Duhallow was the sports' meeting, an event celebrated in that well known ballad, *The Bould Thady Quill*. At such events it soon became obvious that the O'Callaghan brothers were athletes of exceptional talent. Seán, the eldest, later went on to win an Irish 440 yards Hurdles title, while Con was to represent Ireland in the decathlon in the Los Angeles Olympics, but neither could match the achievements of their brother Pat, the tallest and heaviest of the three. Blessed with a powerful physique, he grew to a height of 6' 2" and was an imposing 17 stone when fully fit. He possessed a surprising agility that enabled him to become an international standard high jumper capable of clearing 6' 3". Combined with a keen intelligence and a confidence in his own ability, these qualities were translated into spectacular success on the athletic field. Pat O'Callaghan became dual Olympic hammer champion and enjoyed all-round acclaim in other events. He was a shot putter, a thrower of the discus and 56 lb. weight, as well as being a more than competent jumper, high, long and triple.

Pat became a pupil in the Derrygallon National School at the tender age of two years and four months. He advanced to the secondary school in Kanturk, and at the age of fifteen won a scholarship to the Patrician Brothers Academy in Mallow. During his year in the Academy he cycled the 32 mile round trip from Derrygallon and never missed a day. According to one biographer, Pat O'Callaghan's youth, was 'spent hunting, poaching and playing football in Cronin's field', while improvised cross-country races over hedges and gates provided a welcome diversion from the chores of the family farm. He had just turned sixteen when he passed the matriculation exam for the Royal College of Surgeons.

Having distinguished himself in the red vest of Banteer Athletic Club as a shot-putter, hurdler and discus thrower it was only when he came to Dublin to start his medical studies that he took up hammer throwing. There are a number of stories told as to how he was introduced to what must have been to him, a strange looking device. One tells that he had seen some of the country's top hammer throwers in action at the UCD grounds in Terenure and, once their training was over, they allowed him to borrow the hammer and try a few swings with it. Another story claims that he had seen a Garda throwing one. However, it appears that this man was very possessive of his hammer and refused to allow anyone near it. It was said that Pat and his friends discovered that it was kept in the gatekeeper's lodge and that they found some means of getting their hands on it for some practice sessions.

Back home he set about making a hammer. He paid a visit to Macroom Castle and picked out an old cannon ball which he felt might be close to the required 16 lb. weight. Later he had it drilled in a foundry in Mallow, fitted a handle and a four foot length of wire snipped from a clothes line, and began practising on the family farm. The Castlemanger Historical Society contained the following account of his first attempts:

> He set out a throwing circle in the front field and with the determination and total concentration that was his trademark he worked up his new technique. It was an exhilarating time for all concerned as the hammer came in for rough handling, frequently breaking to threaten life and limb and involving many tedious searches in the heavy summer undergrowth for the elusive ball.

His first competitive effort with his home-made hammer was in Dublin, at the Garda Sports Meeting in Croke Park in June 1927. He won the event with a modest throw of 136' _", but discovered that his improvised hammer was considerably heavier than the official one.

Two weeks later he took his first Irish title with a throw of 142' 3". The following week he represented Ireland for the first time in a triangular match with England and Scotland in Manchester and was placed second to Malcolm Nokes of England with a throw of 151' 5", a figure which showed rapid improvement in a very short time. O'Callaghan had observed his contemporaries and studied the latest researches into the application of scientific principles to hammer throwing and gradually developed a technique that turned him into a champion:

> Up until that time hammer throwers jumped as they spun in the throwing circle. Working on the principle of the fulcrum O'Callaghan discovered after trial and error that the body generated more power and greater distance was attained if foot contact with the ground was maintained, alternating between heel and toe, as the thrower turned in the circle. He used that technique in Amsterdam and subsequently it was adopted by hammer throwers around the world.[1]

---

[1] *The Irish Times*, 30 July 1988.

The following June at the Irish National track and field championships in Croke Park he retained his National title with a throw of 162' 6" which qualified him for selection on the Irish team for the IX Olympiad in Amsterdam. Few gave him any hope of success as he was not well known at home and unheard of abroad. An exception was the sports' journalist, P. D. Mehigan who had faith in his ability. He wrote in *The Cork Weekly Examiner*:

> Dr. O'Callaghan has not yet perfected his technique with the hammer, but he has all the attributes of mind and body for a record-breaker. Two years ago, he could not swing the missile freely. He has an apt, facile brain, however, and is blessed with delightful optimism and superb physique. Coming from a race of giants in the Duhallow uplands, he is far from being at his best. He is as strong as a bull, active as a cat, and built ideally for hammer throwing.

The favourites for the title were Ossian Skoeld of Sweden and two Americans, Edmund Black and Frank Connor, all of whom had thrown over 170'. Being a relative novice O'Callaghan was not fancied to get beyond the preliminary stage. However, he surprised everybody by qualifying for the final with the third best throw, though he was still not expected to be in the medals. He was almost fifteen feet behind Skoeld, who was the leader with a throw of 168' 3". In the final, the situation remained unchanged until it came to O'Callaghan's turn to take his second throw. According to the report in the *Irish Independent,* he got behind the hammer for the first time and it went soaring out to land fractionally ahead of Skoeld's best throw. Tension mounted for the Irish athlete as the throw was measured and re-measured until it was finally announced that O'Callaghan had taken a lead of four inches over Skoeld. This prodigious effort secured him a personal best with a distance of 168' 7" and it proved to be good enough to give him the Olympic gold medal.

Several Irishmen had won medals before him while competing under the flags of other countries. Seven of the first eight Olympic hammer-throwing champions were born in this country. John Flanagan won three of them but, like Paddy Ryan and Matt McGrath, he had been wearing the American colours. O'Callaghan's victory meant that for the first time in the history of the modern games the Irish national anthem was played in an Olympic stadium. As one journalist remarked, O'Callaghan was the first to win an Olympic title representing Ireland and for this reason his place in sporting history is assured. It was a remarkable achievement from a man who had only seen the hammer for the first time two years earlier and a mere thirteen months since he made his competitive debut in the event

The reporter from Reuter referred to the new champion as a 'great boyish figure of a man, with a mass of golden hair'. When he left the stadium he returned to the ship, *Oranji-Nassau,* at the Ooterdok, the headquarters for the Irish team – the Irish officials being housed in the more comfortable surroundings of the Amstel Hotel. That evening the president of the Irish Olympic team, accompanied by photographers and journalists, went to meet the new champion on board ship. 'I hadn't set eyes on him over the previous ten days', Callaghan wryly remarked. 'Reflected glory was now to be transmitted home'.

O'Callaghan's victory astonished the world of athletics. Many years later, David Guiney, another Olympian from Kanturk, wrote of him in his book, *Ireland's Olympic Heroes:*

> No Irishman had a more fantastic or meteoric rise to glory in sport. In twelve short months he surged from the obscurity of local sports meetings in the south of Ireland into the dazzling limelight of international fame. And there he was to remain for many, many years.[2]

Although he received no state or civic recognition, in his native Kanturk he was treated to a tumultuous hero's welcome in the Market Square. Nagle's Hotel changed its name to Olympic Hotel, a name it has retained to the present day. John D. O'Connor in an address to the local people declared:

---

[2] David Guiney, *Ireland's Olympic Heroes,* (Kilkenny, n.d)

They had read in history the feats of Finn MacCool, of the prowess of the ancient Greeks and Romans, of the wonderful deeds of strength and daring during the misty times of the pre-Christian era. But nothing, either in fiction or reality, had created a more truly noble pride than Dr. Pat's wonderful success in the Olympic Games in Amsterdam.

His feat inspired Ned Buckley, a local bard, to pen the following:

> In Erin's bright band high above all the others
> Stood out those brave lads the O'Callaghan Brothers,
> But the one whose feats shall our history hallow,
> Is young Dr. Paddy that boy from Duhallow.

Less than a fortnight later at the Tailteann games in Croke Park he set up his first Irish record with a throw of 170' 2". He staked claim to another astounding record when he won six national titles in the Irish Championships of 1931. In an all round display of ability he won the hammer, shot, discus, high jump, 56 lb. without follow and 56 lb. over the bar. He cleared 6' 2" for the high jump, remarkable testimony to the athleticism of a man who in his prime weighed seventeen stone. He frequently cleared 22' in the long jump and putt the shot over 49', well within Olympic qualifying standards. His winning discus throw at the 1931 championships was 152' 7" – a fraction of an inch short of the European record.

In the summer of 1930 he was invited to take part in a two-day event in Stockholm where Skoeld was determined to prove O'Callaghan's triumph in Amsterdam was no more than a fluke. A few days before he was due to leave he had injured his heel in a local sports meeting. Although the wound had become infected and he was in considerable pain he decided to go. The journey was horrendous. He cycled to Mallow, took the train to Dublin, travelled across the city to Dún Laoghaire and caught the ferry to Holyhead. From there he journeyed to London, on to Croydon Airport, flew to Copenhagen, took the ferry to Stockholm and arrived on Saturday morning. Having checked into his hotel he sought out the nearest pharmacy bought a packet of razor blades, some antiseptic and dressings. Back in his hotel room he ran a bath as hot as he could endure, used the blade to lance the abscess, dressed the wound and had a few hours sleep.

That afternoon Skoeld broke his own European record with his first throw. O'Callaghan beat this with his second throw and once more the Swede had to settle for second place. In the competition on the following day he set another European record with a throw of 178' 8_" to win. On both days, he won the shot-put and cleared 6' 3" in the high jump to beat the reigning European champion. The young Irishman received a prolonged ovation from the Swedish spectators. It was a truly remarkable achievement and confirmed his reputation as a first-class international athlete.

During this time, his personal and professional life was no less eventful. In 1927, at the age of twenty, after a brilliant scholastic career in the College of Surgeons, which included winning the Carmichael Medal for surgery, he graduated as the country's youngest ever doctor. He was so young that he was not allowed practise medicine in this country. He promptly joined the RAF Medical Corps, serving in Buckinghamshire for almost two years. He came home in 1928 and practised for brief periods in Dublin, Cork and Killarney before being appointed assistant medical officer to the Clonmel District Mental Hospital where he took up duty on 16 February 1931. On 18 December 1934, he married Kitty, only daughter of P. J. O'Reilly, one of Clonmel's leading drapers, at a ceremony in Mount Melleray Abbey. They had five children, a daughter, Moira and four sons.

In the meantime he had been selected to defend his Olympic title at the Los Angeles games, which was to be the scene of one of Ireland's greatest athletic successes. Having paid his own fare to Amsterdam four years earlier, on this occasion sponsorship from Guinness and church gate collections helped to defray the cost of sending the team. General Eoin O'Duffy, President of the Irish Olympic Council, assembled the team at Ballybunion for three weeks of collective training. A financial obstacle to Dr. Pat's departure came from the committee of Clonmel Mental Hospital who demanded that their employee would have to pay the cost of his replacement for the duration of his absence. The authorities later had a change of heart and he was granted three months paid leave.

Early in the afternoon of August Monday 1932, Bob Tisdall won the first of Ireland's gold medals in the four hundred metres hurdles at the Los Angeles Olympics. The hammer throwing competition began one hour later. When O'Callaghan's turn came to throw he knew that he would have to exceed 160' to make the final. After a disappointing first throw of 159' he realised that his spikes were too long for the hard surface. Up to now the hammer circle had always consisted of grass or clay. In Los Angeles this was replaced by a hard cinder surface but for some inexplicable reason the Irish Olympic Council failed to notify Dr. Pat. With half-hour intervals between the throws frantic efforts were made to secure a file so that the spikes could be reduced. One was found in a workman's tool bag and Dr. Pat was still working on the spikes when he was called for his second throw.

By then Villie Porhola of Finland had increased his lead and O'Callaghan's second effort was again short of 160'. He returned to work on the spikes. At three o'clock he was called on to take his final throw in the preliminary round. At this stage there were four in front of him, and three behind any one of whom might deprive him of his place in the concluding stages of the competition. To be certain of qualifying he knew that his effort would have to be a good one. His shortened spikes made all the difference and a throw 171' 6_" guaranteed his place in the final.

He was still not satisfied and Bob Tisdall arrived on the scene, found another file and proceeded to help him. With one throw left only Porhola stood between O'Callaghan and the gold medal. Bill Henry, the American sporting historian, writing in his *History of the Olympic Games* said that the Olympic stadium went quiet and 'the tension spread out into the huge crowd' as the Irishman stepped into the circle for his last throw and 'in a blur of speed and strength', heaved the hammer out far beyond the flag marking Porhola's throw, reaching a distance of 176' 11". For the second time that afternoon the stadium was filled with the strains of the Irish National Anthem. O'Callaghan stepped up on to the winner's podium becoming the only Irishman to win two Olympic gold medals for his native country. Recalling the occasion Tisdall said:

There was pandemonium in the stadium. Speech was impossible for almost five minutes and the few who did not appear to be Irish were shouting, if not for the significance of the achievement, for the manner of its doing. It was indeed a great achievement for Ireland.

In a flight of rhetoric a New York newspaper proclaimed that 'the spirits of Cú Cuchulainn and Oisin and other ancient athletes of Ireland must have hovered over the manly form of Dr. Pat O'Callaghan'. It concluded by stating that 'the powerful Cork doctor upheld the best athletic tradition of his race, rising to wonderful athletic heights for Dark Rosaleen'. It was a remarkable achievement by any standards and even more so for an Irish athlete at the time when, as the new champion stated, 'nobody helped us or taught us' and that 'we learned by our mistakes and by our own endeavours. The people who knew about hammer throwing had their secrets and wanted to keep them. It's hard to realise how we were left on our own'. O'Callaghan also pointed out 'that it was a terrible handicap to participate in sport to the extent that he did, because when you went for a job people believed you had been wasting your time instead of working'.

When O'Callaghan and Tisdall arrived at Dún Laoghaire they received a hero's welcome. Upwards of 250,000 came out to greet them. They were met in Dublin by scenes of extraordinary enthusiasm and the President, Eamon deValera gave them a civic reception in the Mansion House. They were each presented with a silver wreath of laurels, emblematic of the Olympic Games with the designs on both sides taken from the Book of Kells. In Cork, the new champions led the Olympic team through the streets of the city. When they came to Clonmel they were guests of honour at a banquet in Hearns' Hotel attended by the mayor and other civic dignitaries. Also in attendance were former Irish champions, including the great Tom Kiely from Ballyneale.

In the course of an address read on behalf of Clonmel Citizens' Committee, R. J. Long, editor of *The Nationalist*, said that O'Callaghan and Tisdall had covered themselves and Ireland in glory, and certainly deserved the complimentary description given by the American press, as 'Ireland's Magnificent Pair'. Earlier that afternoon O'Callaghan, as captain of the Cork team, was the leading athlete at the Munster Inter-County Athletic and Cycling Contests held in the town. In the course of the competition he set up a world record, in slinging the 56lbs. weight between the legs with a throw of 27' 10_", an improvement of _" on his previous record.

Further successes followed. In 1933 he won the American hammer championship and the British Amateur Athletic Association championship in 1934. In that same year he set up a new European record of 186' 10" for the hammer at the Enniscorthy Sports in County Wexford. It seemed nothing could prevent him from winning at the forthcoming Olympic games in Berlin until he fell victim to the intrigues of athletic politics. In 1935, the International Amateur Athletic Federation had imposed the boundary rule, insisting that Northern Ireland was part of the United Kingdom. The National Athletic and Cycling Association refused to accept this and, as a result, athletes belonging to the association were debarred from competing in the Olympics.

Consequently, O'Callaghan was not able to defend his title in Berlin where it was generally believed that he would have collected a third successive gold medal. The hammer title went to a German, Karl Hein, with a throw several feet short of the Irishman's best at the time. Ironically, O'Callaghan had been brought to Hamburg two years earlier so that his technique and style could be filmed by the Germans. They even x-rayed his shoulders and legs to find out what kind of tendons he had.

He created a world record in Fermoy in August 1937 with a throw of 195' 4_", breaking the world record of 187' 6_" which had been set in 1913 by Paddy Ryan in New York. A native of Limerick, Ryan was later to become Olympic champion throwing for America. O'Callaghan's record was not ratified at the time because he was still a member of the banned N.A.C.A. Since then it has been recognised and included in the I.A.F.F.'s *Progression of World Records*. It remained unequalled until 1950 when it was beaten by Imre Nemeth of Hungary with a throw of 196' 5".

O'Callaghan was once described as the last of what were known as the Irish whales, superb specimens of manhood who dominated weight throwing competitions internationally in the first third of the twentieth century. Between 1927-37, he won twenty-one Irish titles in hammer throwing and other events. O'Callaghan also excelled in a great variety of sports. At home in Derrygallon he starred with the local hurling and football teams. In a football match he shouldered an over aggressive opponent so hard that the airborne recipient crushed a pram well beyond the sideline. Luckily, the pram was unoccupied at the time. The parish priest who was present was not amused. He upbraided Pat for disgracing the parish and chased him off the field with an umbrella. During his student days in Dublin, he played rugby for Blackrock. He also played for Cork Constitution and was a member of the victorious Kanturk team which won the County Rugby Cup Final against Bandon played in the Mardyke in April 1929. On one occasion, legend has it that he kicked a penalty from seventy five yards out on the sideline.

Sadly, while competing in Mallow in 1938, his hammer struck and fatally injured a young boy. Although entirely blameless, the incident deeply affected him and shortly afterwards, he retired from competitive athletics. He went to the United States for a brief period where he flirted with professional wrestling. His celebrity status allowed him to mix with the rich and famous. He was a guest of the Kellys of Philadelphia long before their daughter, Grace, became Princess of Monaco. Kelly senior had himself been an Olympic rowing champion. He also played handball with Bing Crosby, whom he regarded as an excellent player. He turned down an offer from Sam Goldwyn to play the role of Tarzan in a Hollywood film. The threatened outbreak of war cut short his stay in America and he came home to his wife and family in Ireland.

He built up a reputation as an outstanding doctor, serving the people of Clonmel until his retirement many years later. He was particularly kind to the poor and underprivileged, refusing to charge those who could not afford his services. Doctor O'Callaghan or 'The Doc', as he was affectionately known, became an iconic figure in the town. He was closely associated with many sporting bodies, in particular, the Commercials football club. First elected to the committee in 1964, between then and his death in 1991 he served the club as vice-chairman, chairman, president, trainer and selector on a team that won three consecutive county senior championship titles. He was also involved with the Marlfield Hurling Club in an honorary capacity for over forty years. His medical services were always freely available and it was said that the players whose injuries needed stitching were always amazed that a man who was so physically powerful could be so gentle.

He lent assistance and advice to the successful High School athletic teams of the fifties, to which his sons made a notable contribution. All four competed successfully both in the All Ireland College Championships and in the Irish Senior Athletic Championships in a variety of field and track events, breaking numerous records in the process. They also distinguished themselves in other sporting arenas. Pat represented Ireland at clay pigeon shooting, Terry became an accomplished golfer, Brian captained both the Cork and Tipperary senior football teams, while Hughie, the youngest and most versatile, represented Ireland in athletics, boxing, weightlifting and rowing.

Dr. Pat was a countryman at heart and revelled in the outdoor life. In retirement he found more time for two of his favourite pastimes, fishing and shooting, often walking thirty miles a day until well into his seventies. His tough exterior belied a warm and affectionate nature. He was a compelling story-teller, whose yarns were invariably enlivened by numerous asides. He had a simple unpretentious lifestyle and remained unspoiled by the trappings of fame. Lying inside his front door was the brass coloured hammer which he used in Los Angeles, while his Olympic medals were stored in a battered biscuit tin. He had little interest in money, even that to which he was entitled, and refused to apply for his old age pension on the grounds that the country needed it more than he did.

He was regarded as the people's champion, a true sporting legend whose extraordinary achievements were acknowledged by numerous awards. He became the first recipient of the Texaco Hall of Fame Award in 1960 and received the Aer Lingus Hall of Fame award in 1978, while in Clonmel he was presented with the Knocknagow Award by the Tipperary United Sports Panel. Of the many honours 'The Doc' received in his distinguished career the one which gave him the greatest pleasure occurred in his eightieth year when he was made a freeman of Clonmel. Accompanied by the Mayor and members of the corporation, he was led by the Municipal Regalia bearers and Banna Chluain Meala through the streets of Clonmel to the Town Hall. He was a most popular choice and the award reflected the very special affection in which this great man was held by the people.

While he seemed indestructible, time eventually caught up with him. Following a brief illness he died in Ardkeen Hospital on Sunday 1 December 1991. After requiem mass in St. Mary's, the coffin draped in the flag of the Olympic Council of Ireland was placed in the hearse. The funeral cortege moved through the streets of the town led by the Mayor, Vera Hewitt and members of Clonmel Corporation wearing their ceremonial robes. The President and Taoiseach were both represented. The large attendance also included many public figures and sporting personalities, including the great Ronnie Delaney. His remains were brought to Powerstown Cemetery where he was laid to rest beside his wife, Kitty, and son, Brian.

In paying tribute to him, Pádraic Griffen, President of BLE, said 'that he competed during an era when success at sport was seen primarily as an expression of love of community and of country. He continued down the years to take a constructive interest in the development and progress of sport. His achievements and principles stood forth as a shining example for others to imitate'.[3] Pat O'Callaghan is widely regarded as the finest natural athlete Ireland has ever produced. It will be extremely difficult for any other Irish athlete to emulate his all-round achievements.

---

[3] *The Nationalist*, 7 December 1991.

Chapter 27

Envoy to Africa

In the Old Bridge area of Clonmel there is a neatly kept park dedicated to the memory of Edel Quinn whose remains lie in the uplands of Kenya, where her grave has become a place of pilgrimage. What brought a bank manager's daughter to this distant land is a story of commitment and suffering, of courage and perseverance. In 1944, her death went practically unnoticed in Ireland, but she is now recognised as one of the most remarkable Irish women of the twentieth century.

Edel Quinn was born at Greenane, near Kanturk on 14 September 1907. Her father, Charles Quinn, was a Galwayman, while her mother, Louise Burke Brown, came from County Clare. Being the daughter of a bank official her childhood was spent in a succession of Irish towns. A few months after her birth, her father was transferred to Clonmel as assistant manager. The Quinn family lived at Moor Lodge on the Coleville Road for the next six and a half years and Edel went to school in the nearby Loreto Convent.

From Clonmel, Edel's family moved to Cahir and then to Enniscorthy. In the summer of 1921 her father was appointed manager of the National Bank in Tralee. She was a typical teenager, carefree and easy going, bent on fun and mischief.[1] Edel was an all-rounder, an intelligent child, who loved music and excelled in sport. In September 1923, she was sent to school in Upton near Liverpool to the Sisters of the Companions of Jesus. There, she continued to come top of the class and was selected as captain of the school cricket team.

Unexpectedly, word came to the convent that she had to return to Ireland before she could to take her final examinations. The reason given was that her father had suffered a business reverse and could no longer afford to keep her there. The truth of the matter, which the family managed to successfully cover up for many years, was that Mr. Quinn had been using bank money to pay off his gambling debts. He was demoted and

---

[1] Robert Bradshaw, *Edel Quinn, envoy for Mary*, (Dublin 1986), pp. 7, 8.

transferred to the bank's head office in College Green, Dublin, where he now found himself in one of the lowest paid posts in the banking hierarchy. Years of financial strain followed as Mr. Quinn was obliged to pay back the money he had taken.

Edel was the eldest of five children and feeling that she had to contribute to the family budget, she decided to remain at home to help finance the education of the younger members of the family. She completed a secretarial course in Rosse's College and got a job as secretary to a Mr. O'Hanlon, an importer of building materials, with an office in Tara Street. After a year, to her great surprise, her employer entered a seminary for late vocations but assured Edel that his successor would continue to employ her. He turned out to be an attractive young Frenchman by the name of Pierre who became smitten by Edel's good looks and proposed to her. She had to explain that she could not marry him as she intended to become a nun.

Around this time she joined the Sodality of the Children of Mary which was attached to the Loreto Convent in North Great George's Street. The Sodality ran a social club for working girls who lived in the nearby slums, bringing Edel into contact for the first time with the poverty and deprivation that existed in the city. She composed little plays and operettas for the girls, some of which were performed in the A.O.H. Hall in Parnell Square. A family friend, Mona Tierney, who was also a member of the Sodality, persuaded her to join the Legion of Mary, a decision which was to change the course of her life.

The Legion was an organisation for Catholic lay people founded in 1921 by a civil servant, Frank Duff. Although initially treated with suspicion by the hierarchy, it attracted people from all walks of life. It was organised in small groups or praesidia, each one having about a dozen members. They met once a week to pray and, in addition, devoted two hours to various apostolic works such as visiting the poor, the lonely, the sick and imprisoned. Not alone did Edel fulfil these obligations but she soon began to spend more and more of her time calling to hospitals and comforting those who lived in the slums.

It was not long before Edel's zeal came to the notice of Frank Duff. He had a reputation for being a shrewd judge of character and had sufficient confidence in her to ask her to take on the presidency of a praesidium that was involved in the rehabilitation of prostitutes. This was a daunting task, especially for a girl who was barely twenty, and it was hardly surprising that her selection met with opposition from many of the members. They went so far as to express their objections to Frank Duff, who assured them that she would prove equal to the task. Having no option but to accept her they were soon won over by her wholehearted enthusiasm and commitment.

Much of her time was spent talking to the girls on the streets or visiting them in their lodgings. She encouraged those who wished to abandon their way of life to take up residence in the Santa Maria Hostel in Harcourt Street run by the Legion. They were given food and shelter and Edel organised constant diversions and activities for them. The work was difficult and the legionaries were frequently subject to threats and verbal abuse. Edel did not spare herself, never asking her colleagues to do anything that she was not prepared to do herself. However, the confrontational nature of the work and continuous late nights began to tell on her. Friends worried that Edel looked tired. She was losing weight and was subject to bouts of coughing. In an effort to get her to take it easy a friend asked her was she not a worry to her family but Edel told her that her family had given her up as a bad job.

When her sisters and brother were finally settled in employment, she decided to enter the convent, a decision that greatly surprised many of her friends. One of them, Mary Wall, recalled that Edel had prepared herself carefully for her entry into religious life. 'She rose every morning at half past five and Mass, Holy Communion, morning meditation and a very scanty breakfast were her preparation for the day's work'. She was also an avid reader of religious books, one of her favourites being the story of The Little Flower, St. Therese of Lisieux. She had marked many passages which she considered to be of particular importance to her spiritual wellbeing. The day before she was due to join the Poor Clares in Belfast, she suffered a severe haemorrhage. The doctor was called and she was diagnosed with advanced tuberculosis and on 5 February 1932 Edel was admitted to Newcastle sanatorium.

At the time there was no cure for the disease. All the sanatorium had to offer was fresh air from the Wicklow hills, rest and good food and hope that the body's natural powers of recovery would do the rest. Although seriously ill, Edel showed no concern for her own welfare. She was loathe to take advantage of what few comforts the hospital might offer and regardless of how cold she felt, she refused offers of a hot water bottle and extra bedclothes. She helped new arrivals to adapt to the routine of the hospital, and involved herself in social activities such as playing the piano at dances that were organised for the patients. It was no wonder that the matron declared she was the most impressive patient she had met.

Conscious of the financial strain her confinement was imposing on her parents she decided to discharge herself. She was prescribed medication and agreed to moderate the pace of her life. She returned to her secretarial career in a garage on Westland Row and rejoined the Legion. In deference to her mother she abandoned her work with the prostitutes. As a compromise she joined a less demanding praesidium working with young people in Temple Hill Children's Hospital, only five minutes walk from her home.

Although illness may have put an end to her intention of becoming a Poor Clare, her dedication to the spiritual life did not disappear. Having returned from a Legion pilgrimage to Lourdes, in 1934 she agreed to the request from Frank Duff, to accompany Muriel Wailes on a working holiday in Wales in order to promote the work of the Legion there. She returned full of enthusiasm and suggested to Duff that she resign her job and move to Chester with the intention of introducing the Legion into other parts of Wales and England. As Frank Duff was considering this he received a request from Bishop Heffernan of East Africa, who was looking for a volunteer to do missionary work. He approached Edel, who was thrilled to accept.

His choice aroused a storm of protest in the ranks of the Legion. When the proposal came before the Concilium, or general assembly, for ratification, the formidable and respected figure of Dr. Magennis, a former General of the Carmelite Order, who had spent many years in Africa, voiced the fears of many when he said that 'to send Edel Quinn to Africa would be sheer folly, particularly for a woman travelling alone, the deadly climate, the vast distances to be covered in appalling conditions … if someone must be sent, let it be a man of more than average strength, and not a fragile young girl'.

Edel then rose to address the meeting and told the members that 'All those difficulties have been explained to me in detail. I know what is before me. It is exactly what I am looking for … I am going with my eyes open. I don't want to go on any picnic'.[2] Her spirited response disarmed her opponents. Far from being frail and incapable, she was seen as a determined young woman who understood clearly the implications of her decision. The question was put to a vote and Edel won the unanimous support of the meeting.

On 24 October 1936 Edel said goodbye to her family at Dún Laoghaire pier and left Ireland, never to return. She told her friend, Muriel Wailes, that she would not be coming home again despite the expectations of her family, for she felt that she could not put the Legion to such expense. After a voyage lasting almost a month, the *Llangibby Castle* with Edel Quinn on board entered the port of Mombasa on the East Coast of Africa. From there she made an eighteen hour train journey to Nairobi, the civil and ecclesiastical centre of Kenya. She first found accommodation in the Loreto Convent but as it was outside Nairobi, she finally settled at the more central St. Teresa's Convent which belonged to the Sisters of the Precious Blood. This was to be her base for her missionary work and, it was here that she was destined to die eight years later.

Edel found that the Catholic community in Nairobi was deeply divided. The Europeans, mostly English and Irish, who administered the country, considered themselves superior to the Goans who monopolised its commerce. At the bottom of the social scale were the native Africans whose role was to serve their colonial masters. She decided to set up a praesidium of the Europeans and Goans although she was being constantly told 'Ah! you do not know Nairobi', and that it would be impossible to get the two racial groups to co-operate. She also had to contend with the disapproval of the parish priest who felt that there were already too many such organisations in the parish and that, as far as he was concerned, they

---

[2] Desmond Forristal, *Edel Quinn 1907-1944*, (Dublin, 1994), p. 79.

were nothing but trouble. Never one to refuse a challenge she persisted. Her perseverance was rewarded when, on 7 December 1936, a praesidium consisting of four Irish women and two Goans came into being. It was a modest beginning but it made her realise that if she were to establish the Legion in Africa she would have to engage the support of the native Catholics.

When she paid a visit to one of their missions in Nairobi she got an enthusiastic welcome from Fr. Tom Maher, the priest in charge, and throughout her time in Africa he was to remain one of her staunchest supporters. Handicapped by the fact that she had no knowledge of African dialects, she was faced with the difficulty of dealing with members drawn from different tribes speaking different languages and with very little English. Having explained the purpose of the Legion to them, thirteen men and three women expressed a wish to join. It was not long before further groups were set up in and around Nairobi.

The beginning of 1937 saw the start of Edel's travels throughout the mission fields of East Africa. This involved making contact with the local priests, getting their permission to address their congregations and asking for volunteers. The reception she received from the clergy was not always encouraging. While some were enthusiastic and welcomed her eagerly, others felt that there was a surfeit of such lay organisations or that the Legion was unsuited to African needs. One can only imagine how seasoned missionaries viewed the arrival of this frail and sickly young woman coming to work in countries where the inferior status of women was accepted.

Her journeys took her through Kenya, Tanganyika, Uganda, Nyasaland and out to Mauritius in the Indian Ocean, where she set up branches of the Legion. The new recruits were a valuable addition to the Church. They taught catechism to children, instructed catechumens, brought christians to Mass, helped in the school and church and visited the sick and the dying. When a number of praesidia were formed in a particular area and having trained the officers, she would move on to set up another, returning now and again to review progress and offer advice and guidance.

At first, she travelled on foot, bicycle, ox-cart and in uncomfortable lorries until Legion headquarters sent her money to buy a small car. She secured an old dilapidated Ford two-seater for £40 which she referred to as her "Rolls Royce". This enabled her to reach ever more remote areas. Since these bone-shaking journeys would have sapped the energies of a normal person it is difficult to conceive the effect they must have had on her frail physique.

A letter to her family gives some idea of the hectic pace at which she was living:

> Tuesday noon I hit the trail per motor lorry for Nairobi, 200 miles. I am being met about forty miles outside it; a few visits to the outside missions; the Curia on Sunday 14th, a Praesidium meeting, and back 200 miles to Arusha, next 50 miles to Moshi, next 30 miles to three missions, where I have three meetings, one at 6.30, one at 11 o'clock, and the third at 4. p.m. I spend part of the day in the car. Next day back to Arusha, 50 miles; meeting on Monday and Tuesday, motor 200 miles to Nairobi and next day or the day after 200 miles to Kisumu, where I have to meet a new bishop and start in another Vicariate, which is the same as a Diocese at home. So do not blame me if the letters are short and perhaps only postcards.[3]

She had to contend with the difficult climate, dense jungle terrain, and rough earthen roads that were sometimes turned into quagmires by the monsoon rains. One of her reports to Dublin gives some indication of the difficulties she faced:

> The short rains never came so early as this year (they were a month too soon), nor lasted so long, nor were so heavy. The roads churned up into a desperate condition. It was quite an adventurous run for the 50 miles from Arusha to Nairobi. The day after I arrived, no car could get through. It was impossible to ford one of the rivers, it was so swollen'.[4]

---

[3] *Ibid*, p. 137.
[4] Cited in Leon Joseph Suenens, Edel Quinn. *A heroine of the Apostolate (1907-1944), (Dublin, 1954), p. 140.

She cared nothing for her own comfort. At eleven one night she arrived back to the German convent at Kilema at the foot of Mount Kilimanjaro to find the door locked. The lights were out and the nuns asleep. Rather than disturb the whole community she decided to spend the night on the veranda lying on a wooden bench with her coat wrapped around her. No one would have dreamt of sleeping out in the cold at that altitude and when the nuns found her in the morning they were so astonished that soon the story spread from convent to convent.

Apart from recurring bouts of tuberculosis, she was afflicted from time to time with malaria, pleurisy and dysentery. A priest who knew her well referred to her as 'the girl with the graveyard cough'. Yet, she never complained and refused to rest. By April 1941, her condition had worsened and she was forced to enter a sanatorium in Johannesburg, South Africa. She admitted in a letter that the hospital authorities took her for a sixty year old, even though she was only thirty-four at the time. Gradually, she improved and her weight went up from 75 to 88 lbs. Although her condition was still causing alarm she started planning her return to Kenya.

By January 1943, she was back at her base in Nairobi, after an absence of almost four years. Her friends were startled by her emaciated appearance. She was stricken with bouts of coughing, her hair was greying, her voice was weak and she was unable to walk more than a few yards at a time. As her strength improved she resumed her Legion duties, albeit on a more restricted basis. She was acutely aware that she was living on borrowed time and was determined to make the most of it. For the next few months she continued to visit Legion meetings in and around the city.

Her health continued to deteriorate and the following April she placed herself in the care of the Sisters of the Precious Blood. After a series of heart attacks she died on the afternoon of 12 May 1944, facing death with the same fortitude and courage that characterised her missionary work. The bishops and legionaries of Kenya gathered to say farewell. A large Celtic cross of Kenyan marble was erected in her honour. It included the words, 'She fulfilled this mission with such devotion and courage as to stir every heart and to leave the Legion of Mary and Africa itself for ever in her debt'.

Numerous tributes were paid to her and the great service which she had given to the church was acknowledged by the Holy Father himself. Father Lynch who knew her well wrote:

> The work she did and the energy with which she accomplished it in these seven years is out of all proportion to her frail and delicate constitution. No one ever heard her speak of her health. She was always happy, and loved to see others so. No legionary work was beyond her. Anything the Legion needed had to be done, no matter what it cost her.[5]

In a letter to Edel's mother, the superioress of the Franciscan Convent in Nairobi wrote that those present on the day of the funeral felt that they had buried a saint. The cause for her beatification was introduced in 1963 and a total of 258 witnesses gave evidence, covering all aspects of her life. On 15 December 1994, Pope John Paul II who described her as 'an inspiration to youth in this restless world' confirmed her with the title 'Venerable', the first step on the road to canonisation.

---

[5] *Ibid*, p. 259.

Chapter 28

The Judge's Daughter

During the early years of the Irish Free State repressive censorship laws were introduced. Almost all the famous Irish writers whose work had won international acclaim were banned. George Bernard Shaw, Frank O'Connor, Seán Ó Faoláin and James Joyce were among those who achieved literary notoriety. Una Troy also found herself in this illustrious company when a number of her novels fell foul of the censorship board.

Una Troy, eldest daughter of John S. Troy and Bridget Agnes Hayes, found fame as a novelist, dramatist and short story writer. Her sisters were also attracted to the arts. Gráinne (1913-1970), was an accomplished pianist and music lecturer at the Sedgley Park Training School in Manchester. Among Gráinne's musical compositions was a waltz called *Stardust* which formed part of the interval music for a production of Una's play, *Swans and Geese* at the Abbey theatre. Una's youngest sister, Shevaun (1923-1993) ran a ballet school in Clonmel and, writing under the *non de plume*, Gabriel Vand contributed numerous poems to the *Cork Examiner*. She published a volume of poetry called, *Only by the Heron's Flight*. She also won first and second prize at the Doneraile Writers' Weekend in 1981, and the Jameson Prize at the Listowel Writers' Weekend in 1982.[1]

Una was reared in an atmosphere rich in literary and political associations. Her father nurtured her ambitions to become a writer by encouraging her to read and then discussing the books and authors with her. He told stories of a relative whose writings were published under the name 'Bridget' in *The Nation*, the newspaper of the Young Irelanders. Her grandfather was a personal friend of Parnell and her father recalled being bounced on the great man's knee. When Parnell was struggling to maintain control of the Home Rule party following the revelations of his affair with Kitty O'Shea, her grandfather came to his assistance. At a public meeting in Fermoy his eloquence and sheer force of personality won over the

---

[1] Tina O' Toole (ed.), *Munster Women writers 1800-2000*, (Cork, 2005), p. 295.

305

crowd. Although Una grew up in the shadow of the British army barracks in Fermoy, her parents were staunch nationalists. Her father was a committed republican and during the War of Independence he served as a Sinn Féin judge.

Una had been born in Fermoy in 1910 and was educated in the Loreto Convent in Rathfarnam, Dublin. When her father was appointed as a district justice of the Irish Free State, the family came to Clonmel and took up residence at Melbrook on the Coleville Road. In 1943 they moved to Oakville House, one time home to physician and photographer, William Despard Hemphill. Una spent her holidays in the family's summer home in Bonmahon where she met her future husband, Dr. Joseph C. Walsh. He was fourteen years her senior and being the former medical officer to the West Waterford Brigade of the I.R.A., was well known in the area. They married in the Church of the National University, Dublin, in 1931. Dr. Walsh had an extensive practice in Clonmel and was coroner for east Waterford. In 1932, the young couple went to live in Bellview Place on New Quay where, in the same year, Janet, their only child, was born. Una lived in Clonmel until the death of her husband in 1969, and then moved to Bonmahon where she remained until her death in 1993.

Una's literary talents were evident from an early age. As an adolescent, she wrote poems to amuse herself. She later burnt most of them and only a few fragments remain. She 'started scribbling stories at school. They were all sad and full of unrequited love and never got finished'. The first phase of her adult literary career began in 1936 and by 1947 she had written two short stories, *The White Gloves* (1937) and *The Apple* (1942), two novels, and had four plays produced at the Abbey Theatre. All these were written under the non de plume Elizabeth Connor, the name of her grandmother.

Her first novel, *Mount Prospect* (1936), paints a very unpleasant picture of middle class life in provincial Ireland. It is a grim tale of seduction and murder. The central character, Mrs. Comerford, is a domineering and fanatically religious woman who destroys the lives of her children. In the words of one reviewer the novel exposes the snobbery, cruelty, malice, greed and half-hidden lusts of the townsfolk in provincial

Ireland.[2] It also satirises religious hypocrisy, and led her parish priest, Reverend William Byrne, to denounce 'its anti-religious and anti-clerical spirit'.

Dead Stars' Night, like some of her other novels, was inspired by contemporary events. It was based on an incident which had taken place in Stradbally, County Waterford. On Christmas Day 1929, the local postman Larry Griffen went missing after an alleged fracas in a local pub. An exhaustive search of the area failed to discover his body. 'The case of the missing postman', as it became popularly known, aroused widespread interest and made national headlines at the time. It is the most sombre of all her novels, a stark tale of murder, resonant of the work of John McGahern. In Una Troy's version four respectable citizens, a doctor, lawyer, bank manager and bank manager's nephew are driving home from a Christmas Eve night out when their car runs over a tramp, killing him. The lawyer persuades the others to throw the tramp's body down a disused mineshaft. When the accomplices subsequently fall out with one another it leads to blackmail, arson and suicide.

The novel gives a most unflattering portrait of the clergy. The parish priest is seen as being notorious among his parishioners 'for wringing the last penny from the poor' and is 'gross and paunchy with too much food and drink'. While conceding that the Canon was very charitable, his congregation have to endure 'his Jansenistic condemnations of dancing, of cinemas and theatres, and of immoral books'. The novel was viewed as outraging conventional moral and religious sensibilities and was subsequently banned by the Irish Censorship Board.

Una was best known as a playwright during this period. Her first play *Mount Prospect*, written in 1940, was an adaptation of her novel of the same name and it shared a prize of £50 offered by the Abbey Theatre. It was a remarkable achievement for one who admitted to having no knowledge of play writing. She said that she had counted all the words in Sean O'Casey's *Juno and the Paycock* to find out how long a play should be. Described as 'moving and exciting' and 'marvellously constructed', Christina Longford said 'it offered great scope for acting'. *The Irish Times*

---

[2] G. C., 'Review of Mount Prospect, by Una Troy' in *Dublin Magazine*, new series 12.3 (1937), pp. 90-91.

drama critic called it a 'brilliant play', which, he said, 'could lead to the re-birth of the serious play in the Abbey'.

Unfortunately, none of her later plays were as successful. In the opinion of the critics, *Swans and Geese* (1941) 'bristles with dramatic possibilities that were not realised', and was 'hindered by an improbable plot and forgettable characters'. The plot of *An Apple a Day* (1942) was described by the *Dublin Opinion* as 'contrived and weak' and was 'little more than a string of incidents loosely strung together'. Her last play *The Dark Road* (1947), a dramatisation of her novel *Dead Star's Light,* was regarded as a 'play with more promise than performance that unfortunately descends into melodrama'.[3]

In 1955, she resumed writing under the name of Úna Troy and in the next twenty-six years published fifteen novels. Following her death, her daughter Janet Helleris, found an unpublished manuscript *Fly by These Nets* which was translated into German and published under the title *Das Meer ist Music*. It has not yet been published in English. The romantic light-heartedness of these later novels is in marked contrast to the sombre tone of her earlier work.

The first of these, *We Are Seven,* published in 1955, was one of her most popular works. It was based on the trial and execution of Harry Gleeson who was found guilty of the murder of Tipperary woman Moll Carty, who had seven illegitimate children, each by a different father. The crime took place at Marlhill, New Inn on 21 Nov. 1940, and the case initially came before her father, District Justice Troy, at the Cahir District Court.

The author gives the story a romantic twist, far removed from the gory events that inspired it. She sets it in Doon, a County Waterford townland, where the unmarried Bridget Monaghan, with her family of seven children and their multiple paternity, is a subject of village gossip. While Una was praised for her handling of a delicate matter with considerable skill and humour, her parish priest found the theme distasteful. This led to another 'run in' with the author. Her light-hearted, highly

---

[3] *Irish Times*, 23 April 1940; 23 September 1941; 8 September 1942 and 13 May 1947.

entertaining approach led one reviewer to quip that 'due to characters beyond my control Una Troy owes me two hours sleep'.

Later, when the novel was adapted for the screen, Una Troy co-wrote the script. The film appeared under the titillating title *She Didn't Say No!* which she considered 'appalling, vulgar and a misfit'. It became Ireland's official entry in the Brussels World Film Festival in 1958 and among the cast list were some of Ireland's most distinguished actors, including Ray McAnally, Jack McGowran, Joan O'Hara, Hilton Edwards and Anna Manahan. The film was regarded as being so immoral that the Irish film censor banned it. It received generally negative reviews from the UK press. The *Monthly Film Bulletin* said that 'as an entertainment, the film is mediocre as well as mildly offensive', while the *News Chronicle* dismissed it as 'over-fragrant, Blarneyed baloney'.

Almost fifty years later the film was subject to a revival of interest. It was considered lost until a badly decomposed print was discovered in a film distributor's collection in 2002. A successful grant application to the Heritage Council allowed the Irish Film Archive to commission a restored print with re-mastered sound. The finished product was chosen for screening at The Preservation Film Festival which was held at the Museum of Modern Art in New York in May 2005.

Her next two offerings *Maggie* (1958) and *The Workhouse Graces* (1959) were equally popular. The former presented a hilarious picture of Ballybeg, a small fishing village and holiday resort on the coast of Waterford, where a young city-trained doctor comes under the influence of his manipulative house-keeper, Maggie. The village is a thinly disguised picture of her beloved Bonmahon and many of the characters in the novel were readily identifiable to the locals.

The Workhouse Graces (1959) was inspired by the Kilmacthomas workhouse in County Waterford. When it closed in 1920 the few remaining patients continued to be looked after by two Sisters of Mercy from the local convent. In the novel the only inmate in the workhouse of Ballykeen was Sarah Slaney, a sprightly one hundred and four years old, who is looked after by three elderly nuns from the Order of Grace. The prim reverend mother wishes her nuns back inside the convent walls, while a roguish solicitor wants the workhouse building converted into a factory. Although the novel is crammed with diverse and amusing characters, and features the usual mixture of fun and satire, the plot is improbable and the treatment sentimental. One unimpressed reviewer found that, 'everything combines to make Ballykeen as unreal an Irish town as one could imagine'.[4]

Una Troy's literary world reflected what she knew. She married at nineteen and her passport would indicate that her travels outside Ireland were restricted to visits to England, where she presumably went to visit her sister. She confined herself to middle class, provincial Ireland. Her novels are set in small towns or in coastal communities, many of them having a Waterford association. They are crammed with highly entertaining and often eccentric characters, drawn from the professional and mercantile classes, many of them being thinly veiled portraits of people she knew. They include solicitors, doctors, clergymen, writers, factory owners and shop-keepers. She is not blind to their shortcomings and failings, poking fun at their pretensions and foibles in a frank but light-hearted way.

Her plots are sometimes contrived and far-fetched. The most glaring example is perhaps *Caught in the Furze* where two distinct and mutually hostile groups of freedom fighters rob the same bank at the same time. To add to the improbability, both groups seek refuge in the same hotel with their respective hostages. The dangers facing the captives are resolved in a facile way, without any of them coming to harm, and in keeping with the romantic genre, all ends happily.

While on one hand, her novels can be regarded as escapist romances, they also take a critical look at the shortcomings of Irish society. Sometimes, the satire is gentle as she voices her opinions on such diverse subjects as beatniks and women's magazines. On other occasions, she speaks from personal experience, describing censorship as penalising 'some rather outspoken books that are written nowadays'. She castigates the venality of politicians and the avarice of certain members of the medical and legal profession. Social injustice becomes the subject matter of *The Benefactors*. The decision of the wealthy Mrs. Moore of Moore Hall to offer shelter to a harassed group of travelling tinkers has unforeseen

---

[4] Stephen J. Browne & Desmond Clarke, *Ireland in Fiction*, ii, (Cork, 1985), p. 259.

consequences not only for the old lady but for the villagers and tinkers as well. Subsequent events pose questions as to who are the real benefactors.

Una Troy was an intelligent, forthright woman who articulated her views on subjects like divorce and homosexuality without fear of the consequences, at a time when raising such issues was not considered acceptable. Writing from a woman's perspective in a male dominated world, she focuses the reader's attention on the helpless female victim caught up in an unsatisfactory domestic situation. She sympathises with the woman who finds herself trapped in a loveless marriage, understands the bored urban housewife yearning for romance and supports the wife whose husband is tempted to have an affair.

Current events in her life often provide a backdrop for the action. *Dark Stars Night* and *We Are Seven* were based on local events, while *Caught in the Furze* takes its inspiration from the IRA split into Provisional and Official factions. *The Other End of the Bridge* highlights the controversy between Waterford and Cork County Councils as to who should pay for the cost of the new bridge over the river Blackwater, near Youghal.

After the death of her husband she went to live at Osborne Terrace, Bonmahon, where she was able to pursue her interests in swimming and rock climbing. Una became very popular with the locals who were won over by her friendly, unassuming manner. She died in February 1993 and was survived by her only child, Janet, sister, Shevaun, son-in-law, John Helleris and her two grandchildren, Asta and Paul. While her husband's remains lie in his native Kilrossanty, Una was buried with her parents in Kilcrumper cemetery, outside Fermoy.

During a literary career which lasted almost half a century Una enjoyed widespread popularity, although it must be admitted that some of her later novels were less successful than those of her early years. Her work was published in the UK and United States and won recognition on the continent, being translated into several languages including Dutch, Norwegian, Danish, Slovine and German. Literary contemporaries including Austin Clarke, Christine Longford, Seán Ó Faoláin, Ben Kiely and Peadar O'Donnell were among her admirers. Her short stories were published in various magazines including *The Bell, Ireland Today* and *The*

Kilkenny Magazine. While the Ireland of which she wrote is scarcely recognisable to-day, we can still admire her keen intellect, lively imagination, sense of character, narrative gift and witty style that gave pleasure to a wide circle of readers.

Chapter 29

The Music Maestro

Mick Delahunty, or Mick Del as he was more popularly known, celebrated his golden jubilee as a band leader on Easter Sunday night, 5 April 1983, in the Collins Hall, Clonmel. Fans who hadn't tripped the light fantastic for years came out to pay tribute to their own ballroom legend, 'the pied piper of the dance band world'. The management presented him with a Waterford cut glass vase and the capacity audience gave him a standing ovation. In a short address Alderman Seán Lyons said that Mick had been:

> a magnificent ambassador for the town during the past fifty years, as a band leader, a musician and a thorough gentleman and that his name has long since become synonymous with Clonmel, and Clonmel with his.

Mick Delahunty was born in Clonmel in 1915. He grew up at 7 Glenegad Road in the Old Bridge and was educated at the Christian Brothers. He said, 'my father played a mouth organ in the trenches in Italy in World War I and my mother played the gramophone. My grandfather was a great man on the fiddle and that was my musical background'. When friends and neighbours gathered in the Delahunty house for musical evenings, young Mick lay in bed absorbing the music and picking up the tunes effortlessly. At the age of ten he started to play the tin whistle and while he was still at school, Mick joined the Charles J. Kickham Fife and Drum band. He learned the accordion, and an early photograph in his scout's uniform shows him playing the bagpipes. When he was fourteen, his mother bought him a cornet for thirty shillings.

His first public appearance was at a 4d. hop in the Suir Island dance hall. The bandleader, Paddy McCarthy, was far from impressed and after the dance announced to his two colleagues, 'Either he goes or I go'. As Mick recalled, 'It was short and sweet. Not wishing to break up their band, I went'. His next engagement proved to be promising. While working as an assistant in Lipton's grocery shop in O'Connell Street he played a few evenings a week with Johnny Mulcahy and his *Society Five Band.* Recalling his first night with the band which brought him to the Central Hall, Ardfinnan, he said, 'as well as cornet I was entrusted with the vocals, singing through a megaphone. I did alright and stayed on with Johnny and his boys for three years'.

Leading his own band may have seemed a distant prospect but the dream became a reality sooner than expected. One day, two of Mick's friends from Cahir came into the shop and told him they were running an Old IRA Commemorative Dance and that the band they had booked had let them down. Not alone were all the tickets sold but a caterer had been hired. In desperation, they asked Mick if he could get a band together to help them out. He said yes and that was the start of Mick Delahunty as bandleader. On Easter Sunday night 1933, *The Harmony Band,* under the leadership of the eighteen year old Mick Del, took to the bandstand at the Abbey Hall in Cahir. Admission, including supper, was three shillings and the line up included Frank Fennessy on piano, Christy O'Riordan on saxophone, James O'Riordan on trumpet, Willy Power on drums and Mick himself on cornet and accordion.

As his employers refused to allow him to use the phone to take bookings he decided to move to Burke's bacon shop across the road from Liptons. His new employers were only too delighted to facilitate him because, as he said, it meant extra business. His wages amounted to £2 7s. 6d., while his musical pursuits earned him more than £5 weekly. 'I knew this could not last. It didn't make sense. The two jobs were pulling against one another. Giving up one would improve the other'. So in 1942, he abandoned the day job and became a full-time musician. It was a big step to take, as the year before Mick had married Bridie Fitzgerald, his childhood sweetheart. By now, dental problems had forced Mick to abandon the cornet and take up the saxophone. Subsequently, he was joined by his two brothers, Jackie on drums and Paddy who played bass. While his early engagements were confined to a radius of twenty miles of Clonmel soon his music was beginning to find a wider audience.

The war in Europe meant that petrol was rationed, tyres were hard to get and sometimes the band had to travel by train. On one occasion when they went to play at a dance in Killarney they had to stay on there for four days because the trains were only running twice a week. When they arrived they 'were often met by an ass and cart at the other end' to take the instruments to halls, which were often no better than barns. The roads were so primitive that he recalled setting out from Clonmel at 2 p.m., getting to Listowel for a dress dance at midnight, three hours late and grimy all over from fourteen punctures. Sometimes they lost their way as all the signposts had been removed to confuse the predicted German invaders.

They also had to deal with the unexpected. On one occasion, passing through Mallow on their way to Farranfore, their trailer went on fire. Some bystanders flagged them down and assisted in putting out the blaze. Mick remembers turning up 'all black with a skeleton trailer, two jet black trumpets, no music stands, no bass, no guitar, no drum'. They borrowed what they could from the local pipe band and took the bandstand looking, as they said themselves, like the cast of the Black and White Minstrel Show. Yet, they still 'gave their supporters the liveliest night they ever had'.

Mick admitted that 'success came gradually. God, it was hard work and the returns were small. There was little money around in those days and often it was a case of making a deal with some club which hadn't much money'. After the war when normality returned, people wanted colour and excitement and Mick's music, echoing throughout the ballrooms of romance, 'helped to lift young men and women away from the bitter farms of a poor countryside or from the drab streets of towns where the young had one eye on a school book and another on the emigrant boat'.[1]

Mick's big break-through came in 1947 when he was asked to play relief to Teddy Foster at the Kilkenny Lawn Tennis Club Dance. Foster had one of the leading dance orchestras in the world, so Mick decided to put on a particularly good show by hiring extra musicians. Foster's music, though excellent, was more suited to a concert performance but Mick had noticed that the audience were mostly married couples, who were anxious to dance. Mick said afterwards, 'that night in Kilkenny was really the beginning. When the dancers asked for an old time waltz, we played one or two'. The

---

[1] *The Cork Examiner*, 7 March 1992.

reaction was electric. They were greeted with rapturous applause and, instead of the hour-long interval, they had to do a two and a half hour programme. 'Even then', he said, 'it was a reluctant crowd that let us off the stage'.

While Foster had played the music he wished to play, Mick Del gave the patrons what they wanted. His ability to read an audience became one of the hallmarks of his successful career. As he said later, 'I never work to a set programme, as I prefer to bring the audience along with me. Every dance is different and you learn to sense the mood as you go along'. Following his success in Kilkenny, he began to develop his own distinctive big band sound. He engaged top class musicians, and when they couldn't be found in Ireland, he went abroad to hire them and, at one stage he had four Germans playing in the brass section.

He decided to broaden the band's repertoire and give it a more international flavour. The great influences on Mick were the English band-leader, Victor Sylvester, and Glen Millar, who was the most popular American musician at the time. Millar's unique sound and infectious dance rhythms were to have a profound influence on Mick, who adopted *American Patrol* as his signature tune, while other Miller arrangements such as *Moonlight Serenade*, *In the Mood* and *Little Brown Jug* were soon added to his programme.

He claimed that the coursing festival in Clonmel did most to boost his career. People from all over Ireland were in attendance and went home telling their friends what a great band Mick Del had. Soon Mick was the main attraction in ballrooms from the Arcadia in Cork to the Hanger in Galway, from the Olympia in Waterford to the Borderland in Donegal. As he said himself, 'it would be easier to tell you the places we didn't play than the ones we did'. His appearances in the Mansion House in Dublin were one of the highlights in the dedicated dancer's calendar and queues reached halfway down Dawson Street. Mick's name on the bill was the promoter's guarantee of box office success and customer satisfaction.

His name became synonymous with various hunt balls, local festivals and annual functions around the country, which included the West Waterford Hunt in Lismore Castle, the Listowel Races or the Printer's Dance in Clonmel. He was presented with a piece of Waterford cut glass by the nurses at Longford County Hospital, having played at their annual dance for the 21st consecutive year.

Having received the acclaim of the Irish dancing public at home he set out to woo the emigrants. During Lent it was customary for the dance halls in Ireland to remain closed so, in 1951, Mick took the orchestra to England on what turned out to be the first of many sell-out tours of the Irish clubs. The same year saw the beginning of another successful venture when he was booked into The Showboat in Youghal for two weeks. It proved to be such an attraction that for the next ten years Mick and the orchestra spent their entire summer there. Their stay became part of the folklore of Youghal. C.I.E. ran special trains from Cork, each one bringing 700 eager dancers. Tickets sold at Cork station included the return fair and the entrance fee to the dance. On the front of the train was a name plate which read 'The Showboat Express'. To add to the gala atmosphere, Mick and the boys would meet the train at the station and play them the short distance to the ballroom. In 1958, Paddy O'Gorman, on behalf of the Youghal UDC, presented Mick with a silver baton in appreciation of his contribution to the tourism and social life of the East Cork seaside resort.

In 1954 he made the first of three trips to America. Together with his wife he set sail on the SS. America for what was to be an unofficial tour but during his visit he accepted an invitation from the Tipperaryman's Association in New York to play for their annual St. Patrick's Night Ball. One of the highlights of his stay was having the pleasure of meeting two of the greatest bandleaders in the world, Woody Herman and Louis Armstrong, both of whom he greatly admired.

He returned in 1959 when he played to full houses in Toronto, Pittsburgh, Chicago and Boston. He also had the honour of being invited to play in Carnegie Hall. He remembers how nervous he was that night and how his lips dried up with fright as he walked on to the stage. He need not have worried because he stunned a packed audience into appreciative silence with his tender solo rendition of *The Coolin*. To commemorate the occasion he was presented with a large silver salver which bore the inscription, 'Mick Delahunty, the outstanding and consistent man of music'.

His tour two years later was equally successful. Speaking of his experiences, he said, 'I enjoyed touring, especially playing for the Irish in New York and Chicago, but I never wanted to leave Ireland' and although he had opportunities to return to America, he never had any desire to do so.

At home Mick was still the greatest crowd puller in the business. His diary was filled up with bookings stretching two or three years ahead but the dance hall scene was about to be revolutionised by the emergence of a new phenomenon. A band from the north of Ireland, called the *Clipper Carlton*, lit the fuse in the fifties that led to the showband explosion of the sixties. With the Clippers, the emphasis was on spectacle and showmanship. It was not their dance music but their stage routines which became the main attraction. Soon others emerged like Joe Dolan and *The Drifters*, Dickie Rock and *The Miami* and, the most successful of all, *The Royal Showband*, all of whom acquired a devoted following. Dancehalls sprang up in the most unlikely places, from Pontoon to Pallasgreen. At Youghal, Mick's Mecca came under threat when, in 1957, a new ballroom opened at Redbarn, a short distance from the town. Top showbands were booked for the summer and as for *Showboat*, its best days were over.

When asked why he did not respond to the showband challenge he said, 'I didn't feel like jumping around the stage at my age'. He continued to provide his patrons with a beat to which they could dance. The Mick Del tempo did not change and neither did his dance repertoire. His arrangements of Glenn Millar numbers, his rendition of *Cool Clear Water* and other favourites, highlights of any Mick Del performance, were not abandoned. While continuing to provide his faithful followers with the music they had come to expect, he deferred to popular taste by playing some of the current hit tunes. It was a mark of his greatness that Mick was able to adapt to the changing musical taste without sacrificing his high standards, or compromising his own individual style.

Far from resenting the threat posed by this new wave of dance hall entertainers, he extended a helping hand to an unknown group of youngsters from Waterford who later won fame and fortune as *The Royal Showband*, by giving them the opportunity to play 'relief' for him:

I remember them well and they have never forgotten me. They always keep a night free when we're in Waterford for the Hunt Ball. They say they prefer to dance to my kind of music. They presented me with a beautiful piece of Waterford glass some years back. All I ever did for them was spread the word here and there when they were starting out. It was the least I could do. No I didn't think I was cutting my own throat.

The glamour and excitement generated by the showbands put many lesser bands out of business, but Mick Delahunty outlived them all, surviving long after they became relics of a time when the nation danced as if demented. 'He was catering', as he said, 'for people who came to dance and not stand around'.

While the showband frenzy gripped the country, Mick still reigned supreme for dress dances and hunt balls. His most prestigious engagement occurred in 1965 when he was asked to play at a ball in Powerscourt as part of the official visit of Prince Rainier and Princess Grace to Ireland. To celebrate the event he commissioned and played an arrangement of *True Love*, the famous duet from the film *High Society* which had been sung by the future princess, the then Grace Kelly and Bing Crosby. Later, Princess Grace thanked him for 'a lovely evening'.

Mick readily admitted that the band business was never an easy life. It was a relentless and demanding round of one-night-stands that took him and his orchestra to the four corners of Ireland. Sometimes they left home at three in the afternoon, returning in the small hours of the next morning. On one occasion, they faced an eight hour journey with a broken windscreen. While the band members were frozen in the back of the van, Mick's brother Paddy who was driving, was later treated for frostbite. The rigours of travel however, could not be sustained indefinitely and in an interview given in 1969, Mick admitted that he was beginning to scale down operations. Still averaging about 50,000 miles a year, he now confined his engagements to within a hundred miles radius of Clonmel.

As the seventies dawned discos with their flashing lights and loud, pulsating music now became the flavour of the age. The showbands were history and bands downsized to play in smaller and more intimate venues which were being provided by hotel owners and publicans. These were extending their premises to cater for the 'singing pub' phenomenon and the revival of interest in traditional ballads. By then Mick was entering the twilight of his career. His doctor had advised him to take it easy, so he cut back on his commitments. He avoided late night functions and concentrated mainly on playing in large lounge bars, either in Clonmel or in dancehalls within easy striking distance. He was, in a sense, back where he had started. The big band was a thing of the past. He operated with fewer musicians, with the full orchestra only being brought together on special occasions.

He never looked on his talent as a way of making money but rather saw it as a gift. 'It is a gift I have – and that is why I never objected to giving my services for a genuine cause'. Throughout his long career he was always generous with his time, giving freely of his services. When the Franciscan Friary was being re-roofed he prevailed on the O.C. in Kickham barracks to erect a marquee and played there once a week 'on his night off' until the roof was paid for. What should not be overlooked is that when the band was brought together on such occasions, he had to pay the musicians out of his own pocket. The charity event with which he was most closely identified, was undoubtedly the annual Santa Claus Express which for thirty-one years made its way every Christmas from Clonmel to the orphanage in Ferryhouse. Many still remember the sense of anticipation in O'Connell Street with parents holding excited children shoulder high to see Santa passing by as Mick and the band serenaded him with *White Christmas*, *Jingle bells* and other Christmas favourites.

Mick was a most unassuming man, who could be deeply moved by any display of kindness to him. In 1982, prior to playing for the Mayor's Fund dance, a charity with which he had become synonymous, the Mayor, Alderman Sean Lyons invited him to the town hall for 'a cup of tea'. To his great surprise he was presented with an enactment of *This is your Life*. He was greeted by his family and friends, and members of Banna Chluain Meala, the internationally renowned youth band, who played a special arrangement of *Tuxedo Junction*. A camera crew from RTE were also present and when it was shown on television, promoters from all over Ireland once again offered to arrange tours for Mick and his orchestra. One promoter was even willing to put a luxury coach at their disposal but he graciously declined all offers.

One of his proudest moments was being asked to officially open the new Banna Chluain Meala centre on 10 September 1989 in what is now known as Mick Delahunty Square. Since Banna's foundation in 1971, he was one of their biggest fans. Over the years he took great pride in their achievements and growing success, deriving endless pleasure from the fact that the young people of the town had the opportunity to learn an instrument and play music, knowing how much it would enrich their lives.

He had little time for technology and refused to go into a recording studio as he felt that if people wanted to hear his music they should come and listen to him 'live'. However, he did give permission for one professional recording. In 1953, he paid £1 to have the band recorded. It took place while a dance was in progress and a single microphone was used. It was purely for himself and his friends, and was not done as a commercial proposition. In 1994, Tom O'Donnell, the Limerick entertainer of Tom and Pascal fame and a life long admirer of Mick's music, got permission from his family to use the 1953 tape from which he produced a cassette called, 'The Magic of Mick Del', featuring many of the numbers for which Mick is best remembered. It is the only authentic recording of his music available and, if it achieves nothing else, it ensures that the music of Mick Del lives on.

Mick never made a fortune out of his music. He could have earned far more than he did but he played for a straight fee rather than a percentage of the box office takings. He felt that 'they had missed the big money and that they worked for buttons in comparison to the bands that came after them'. He had the reputation of being 'very generous to promoters' and had been known to say 'I don't think the band played too well tonight so I'll reduce the fee'. In the peak days of the fifties they were booked up for two years in advance. Trouble was that by that time inflation had eaten into the original booking fee. When asked would he do it all over again he replied , 'Yes, I would. But I'd hire a manager and work for a percentage'.

In 1992, he was hospitalised and advised to retire. Reluctantly, he agreed. He selected the Greenwood Inn in Ardpatrick in Limerick, a venue that was special to him, to say goodbye to his fans. He did not perform himself but just before the final number Mick took the microphone in his hand for the last time. He thanked the proprietors, John and Mary Quilty, and the dancers for their continued support over the years. He said that the doctors had advised him to retire but added 'Shur, you never know it's in the lap of the Gods. We'll get together again'. A loud cheer greeted these words and he left the bandstand to sustained applause.

Well-wishers were reaching out to say good-bye to him when, without warning, he collapsed and died. The words on the poster outside the Greenwood Inn on that cold February night had proved strangely prophetic:

At Greenwood Inn
Ardpatrick
Saturday 29th February 1992
Mick Delahunty
Last appearance

He was survived by his wife Margaret, his two sons, Michael and Brian, and daughter, Mary, and by his brothers, Jackie and Paddy, who had been performing with the band on that sad evening; He was pre-deceased by his first wife, Bridie, who had died in 1973.

The story of Mick Del's music is part of the social history of Ireland. Former Taoiseach, Albert Reynolds, who at one-time owned and operated a string of dancehalls around the country, said that Mick was a legend of the Irish entertainment world who belonged to the golden age of the dance hall business, and that his name was a by-word for entertainment and romance in every dance hall in the country. Noel Conway, who wrote under the name *Dancelot* in the *Times Pictorial,* said:

> Going to a Delahunty dance was more like going to a party in a house of a very dear friend. He had this gift of making everyone feel welcome. Apart from the music, which was superb, he had an amazing memory for names and faces – and he was always in high good humour. The secret was that he was perfectly sincere. Mick Del really is a nice guy. It isn't a question of someone playing a part.

Employing first class musicians, who played with energy and style, enabled him to produce a polished musical sound. But above all there was the man himself, the sincerity, the warmth, the personal magnetism – that indefinable quality that confers greatness. He was content to find fame and fortune in Ireland, turning down the prospect of an international career and numerous offers from American promoters. Although he was a household name at home and even further afield he was always, at heart, a Clonmel man. For all his success, he was most comfortable amongst his own. He won a special place in the affections of the people of Clonmel who supported him loyally down the years. At his funeral mass in SS Peter and Paul's church, Canon Queally told the large congregation that Mick Delahunty was a distinguished member of the community, and a man of whom Clonmel could be justly proud. Few would disagree.

Chapter 30

The Golden Tenor

Clonmel can boast of a proud musical tradition. It has had more than its share of both musical enthusiasts and performers. While Tommy O'Brien was cultivating a love of good music on the national airways, Mick Del drew enormous crowds to the ballrooms of Ireland. The town had two choral societies, a number of excellent church choirs and a gramophone society. This was the cultural climate in which Frank Patterson grew up.

Frank was born on 5 October 1938 in Clonmel. He had two younger brothers, Maurice and Noel and a sister, Imelda. His father Séamus was a foreman of works in Kickham Army Barracks, while his mother May was a member of the Slator family, who ran a successful printing business in the town. Both parents were talented singers and founder members of St. Mary's Choral Society. It could be said that Frank was born to sing. While attending the Sisters of Charity School, a nun asked the four-year old what he wanted to be and he told her 'a singer'. She promptly stood him up on a desk from where he sang *Killarney*.

As a young boy in the Christian Brothers he took part in the musical and operatic productions of SS Peter and Paul's Primary School, and later in those of the High School. Of his performance in *Maritana,* Tommy O'Brien wrote 'Master Frank Patterson was outstanding'. Frank remembered being brought by his parents to musical recitals of the Clonmel Gramophone Society and later recalled 'I suppose listening to the voices of McCormack and Gigli did fuel my ambition to be one day a professional singer'. While still at school, he was introduced by his parents to St. Mary's Choral Society. His first appearance was as the age of seven as a page boy in *The Gondoliers* and, as he grew older, he joined the chorus and later took the roles of Christophle in *The Bells of Cornville* and Captain of the Guard in *Maritana.*

Having completed his Intermediate Certificate, he left school to serve his time at the printing trade in his uncle's business. He spent much of his money in Belinda Cashin's record shop in Abbey Street, Clonmel's

Mecca for serious music lovers. His mother remembers his delight and infectious enthusiasm as he played his latest purchase on the family gramophone, and how he spent hours on end rehearsing his favourite pieces, accompanied by family friend, Billy O'Brien, on the piano. In 1961, *The Song of Knocknagow* was adapted from Kickham's novel by Brendan Long as the Choral Society's choice for their twenty-first anniversary production, and Frank was cast in the comic role of Barney Wattletoes. Rehearsals had scarcely begun when he was offered an opportunity to take up voice training in Dublin under Dr. Hans Waldermar Rosen.

To leave a secure job in the Ireland of the sixties to embark on a career where the future was anything but certain took courage and self-belief. He was a tenacious competitor, as anyone who played table tennis or golf against him will testify, and he was to show the same determination in furthering his musical career. Mary Cummins, one of his Choral Society colleagues, said that he 'was totally focussed and tireless in pursuit of his goals'. Broadcaster and fellow townsman, Andy O'Mahony, wrote that while Clonmel 'has produced many fine individual singing voices, Frank Patterson was the first to discipline his talent and work with sufficient dedication to make a name for himself'.[1]

For one who freely admitted that he had a burning desire to sing, the choice was simple. The chance to train in Dublin was, he said, an offer which he couldn't refuse. While he was a student of Dr. Rosen, he took a course in acting at the National Academy of Theatre & Allied Arts. To support himself he found a night job at Irish Printers. It didn't take him long to make his mark and in 1964, after only two years of study, he won all four of the major music awards at the Dublin Feis Ceoil. Mr. Hickman, the adjudicator, was effusive in his praise when he said, 'it is seldom we hear a voice of such musical integrity. The singer has such poise that his mind and heart were in close contact with his singing'.

In 1966 Frank was one of twenty two singers, musicians and dancers who toured America under the name Feis Éireann. Among them was Eily O'Grady, who was pianist and musical director. On 27 December 1966, three days before they embarked on another US tour, Frank and Eily

---

[1] *RTE Guide*, 5 March 1971.

were married. Their schedule was physically demanding. They visited 86 cities in Canada and the United States in four months. This involved travelling vast distances, often in temperatures that were far from comfortable and, as Frank said, it was 'no cake walk'.

His performance captured the attention of Emmet Corrigan, music critic for a Californian newspaper, *The Modesto Bee,* who went to see the show and devoted most of his review to Frank. Writing under the heading 'Feis Éireann captivates 800 willing prisoners', he began by quoting one patron who told Frank, 'John McCormack was good but you are great'. Corrigan went on the say, 'he was great, this handsome, gifted native of Clonmel in County Tipperary. When he sang *The Rose of Tralee* and other favourites the McCormack magic swept over the audience'.

Soon after their return to Dublin, Frank was awarded a scholarship from RTE which enabled him to do a course in advanced music study in London. This meant a great deal to him. 'Now, I can study properly', he wrote in a letter home. He added, 'it just goes to show that if you keep trying you will succeed (with the help of a few prayers of course)'. Later that year, a similar scholarship from the Arts Council took him to Holland. While there, Janine Micheau, the famous French soprano, heard him practising and was sufficiently impressed to invite him to Paris, where he was given free singing lessons for the next four years. Perfecting his technique demanded continual effort and total commitment. As he said himself, 'we are working away here trying to improve. It's a slow, painstaking business'. While it was a period of hardship for the young couple, concerts and radio and television performances helped to keep them afloat. A broadcast of Purcell songs on the BBC first brought him to the attention of the Philips Record Company who offered him a contract, leading to six albums in the next three years.

Dr. Rosen's assessment of his talent was proving to be most accurate. While he did not foresee a great career in opera for Frank, he felt that he had a bright future as a concert and oratorio singer. His performances were soon receiving critical acclaim. Speaking of his rendition of Handel, he received the following notice, 'the young tenor, who is a comparative newcomer, has obvious musical ability, a most attractive voice, and boundless enthusiasm for 18th century music'[2], while another felt he performed 'the works of Handel and Schubert effortlessly and faultlessly'. In the opinion of Charles Acton, music critic of the *Irish Times*, his interpretation of the St. Matthew passion by Bach was 'extremely stylish' and 'a performance of real international standard'.

Throughout the seventies, Frank Patterson sang at many landmark events in Irish concert life. These included the visit of Shostakovich to Dublin in 1972 to receive an honorary degree from T.C.D., and five years later, when the 225th anniversary of the first performance of Handel's *Messiah* was celebrated. He was beginning to gain recognition abroad, featuring as guest soloist under the batons of such distinguished conductors as Sir Colin Davis, Karl Richter and Jean Fourmet. He also appeared with many major orchestras, including the London Symphony, Royal Philharmonic, Halle, Liverpool Philharmonic, Orchestre de Paris, Rotterdam Philharmonic Chamber Orchestra, Basel Concert Orchestra, The Academy of St. Martin in the Fields and the R.A.I. Symphony of Rome.

He decided to abandon the world of oratorio for a more lucrative career by turning to the music of his homeland, releasing numerous albums of well-known songs. His preference for popular favourites over classical music did not find favour with musical purists, but there was no doubting their appeal to the public. He was even acclaimed in the world of pop, when the ballad *Tipperary* reached the Irish Top 30 in December 1978. This must have given him particular pleasure since he had learned the words of the song from his father.

When *For Your Pleasure* was first shown on RTE on 16 November 1976 there was little indication that it would prove to be one of the station's most successful light entertainment programmes. It ran for ten years and the main reason for its continued popularity was the choice of Frank as host and performer. As a presenter he exuded an air of relaxed informality, while his choice of music won the hearts of the viewers. Although *For Your Pleasure* helped him to reach a wider audience, his subsequent nationwide appearances on American television won him an even greater following. He appeared in an episode of the *Tracy Ullman Show* entitled

---

[2] *RTE Guide*, 7 April 1967.

'Real Lace', which was subsequently nominated for an Emmy Award. He also starred in three specially commissioned programmes: *Ireland's Golden Tenor – Ireland in Song*; *Frank Patterson – Songs of Inspiration*; and *God Bless America*.

The highlight of his career came when he sang at the Papal Mass in the Phoenix Park, Dublin in 1979. It was celebrated by John Paul II for a congregation of more than a million and an estimated television audience of 500 million. Frank performed for the Pope a second time in 1996 when he sang Schubert's *Ave Maria* during the recitation of the rosary by the Pope at St. Patrick's Cathedral, New York. In 1984 Frank received the knighthood of St. Gregory the Great, the highest honour the Vatican confers on a layman. Frank was also made a Knight of Malta and Knight Commander of the Holy Sepulchre of Jerusalem.

He was awarded various academic honours by several American universities. He received an Honorary Doctorate of Music from Salve Regina University in Newport, Rhode Island in 1990 and an Honorary Doctorate of Fine Arts from Manhattan College in New York in 1996. In 1998 Frank and Eily were presented with the gold medal of the Éire Society of Boston for their contribution to the promotion of Irish culture in the US, joining a distinguished group of past recipients which included John F. Kennedy, Ronald Reagan, and John Huston. The honours continued as Frank was awarded The 2000 Norman Vincent Peale award for Positive Thinking in the Arts. Presented by the Blanton-Peale Institute, this award is given to people 'whose lives clearly and inspirationally exemplify the power of thinking positively, with faith, deep caring for people and dedicated commitment to improving our world'.

On St. Patrick's Day 1982, he was honoured to perform at the White House for Nancy and President Ronald Reagan and their distinguished guests. He made a second appearance at the White House for President and Mrs. Clinton in 1995. On this occasion, he was joined by his wife Eily and his talented son Éanan on violin. Frank and his family had moved to the US in 1987, but they returned each summer to their Irish home in Wicklow. He insisted on making his recordings in Ireland and these visits also gave him the opportunity for a number of nationwide tours on which he was accompanied by his wife and son.

He once recalled that he was among 80,000 people who sang *Faith of our Fathers* at an All-Ireland final. Years later, this hymn was one of twenty religious anthems released in 1999 under the title *Faith of our Fathers*. The album became a recording phenomenon, selling 120,000 copies. Frank sang the title track and four others. One reviewer said that:

> Frank Patterson excelled himself. There was a clarity, a sincerity in his singing of these simple expressions of the faith of his parents that was quite perfect. Like McCormack, he succeeded in raising quite ordinary musical material to the level of high art. That seems to me quite a legacy.

Regarded by many as Ireland's leading tenor, it was perhaps inevitable that he should be compared with the great John McCormack, the artist he most admired. He was just nine years of age when his hero died, but Frank achieved a life long ambition when through the miracle of modern technology he was able to 'accompany' McCormack in a tribute album. 'It was a great honour,' he said in an interview afterwards. 'to think that I've actually sung with John McCormack. I can relax now, that's for sure'. The music critic, John O Donovan, said that:

> many of the characteristics that we think of as idiosyncratically Mc Cormack's are in fact just Irish. But Frank Patterson, although at the beginning of what will certainly be a glorious career, is still no carbon copy of anybody.[3]

Cinemagoers will best remember him for his role as the tenor Bartell D'Arcy in John Huston's film version of James Joyce's short story *The Dead* which starred Donal McCann and Anjelica Huston. *The New Yorker* wrote of his performance, 'The whole world seems still while he sings, and for a few seconds after'. A gramophone recording of him singing *Danny Boy* was used in the Coen brothers production of *Miller's Crossing*

---

[3] *RTE Guide*, 31 October 1969.

and he also appeared as a tenor in Neil Jordan's blockbuster, *Michael Collins*, starring Liam Neeson, Julia Roberts and Stephen Rea.

In January 2000, his hectic schedule was temporarily interrupted when he entered hospital to have a tumour removed from his sinuses. The operation was pronounced one hundred per cent successful and after three weeks he was back on the road. During the next six months he gave some forty concerts and made several T.V. appearances across the United States. The day before he was to sing at the funeral mass of Cardinal O'Connor in New York he got a headache and was rushed to hospital. He was diagnosed with a cancerous brain tumour and he died a week later on 10 June 2000. In accordance with his wishes, he was buried in Clonmel. Friends and admirers turned out in their thousands. The mayor and members of the corporation accompanied the cortege through the streets of Clonmel, while members of Banna Chluain Meala played *Slievenamon* at the graveside.

In a career that spanned four decades, he recorded more than forty albums that featured a broad range of songs in six languages. They ranged from works by Purcell, Handel, Beethoven, Mozart and Berlioz to Broadway hits, popular international favourites and the great songs of Ireland. His numerous albums won him platinum, gold and silver discs. He thrilled audiences around the world, filling such prestigious venues as London's Royal Albert Hall and Washington's Kennedy Center. One of his outstanding American engagements was on the steps of the Capitol in Washington, when he performed with the National Symphony for an audience of 60,000 enthusiastic listeners. As part of the centennial celebration of the inauguration of the Statue of Liberty, Frank joined some of the most prominent American opera stars in a televised performance from St. Patrick's Cathedral. He was the first Irish artist to have his own show in New York's Radio City Music Hall, selling out its 6,000 seats for annual concerts on six consecutive years. He played several times to packed audiences in Carnegie Hall. After his performance there in February 1984, T. Fallon of *Irish World* wrote:

We Irish now have a world-class singer in our midst ..... I'm sure that not only Clonmel, County Tipperary but all Ireland will be proud of this smiling Irishman with the gentle wit and the golden voice.

At the time of his death, among the many tributes paid to him was one from President McAleese who described him as a 'wonderful artist who contributed hugely to the world of music and who proudly promoted Ireland throughout the world. The people of Tipperary, of Ireland and lovers of great musical talent around the world will sorely miss Frank's fantastic personality and generosity which, along with his acclaimed talent, made him one of Ireland's favourite sons'. Taoiseach, Bertie Ahern said 'it is without doubt that Frank Patterson was one of the greatest artists this island has produced. As a world-class tenor he has brought distinction to the Irish musical tradition' and 'though he spent a great deal of time performing abroad, he never lost touch with his roots in his native Tipperary, and the people of Clonmel in particular, who were very proud of his achievements'.

This was certainly a very accurate assessment, for although he enjoyed a glittering international career, he never tried to conceal his Clonmel accent or his deep affection for his native town. Ruairi Quinn, on hearing him sing *Slievenamon,* said that 'afterwards the stunned audience were left in no doubt that, wherever Frank may have travelled, a part of him never left his native county'. A dedicated follower of the fortunes of Tipperary hurling, he never sang 'the county anthem' with more passion and emotion than on the day Tipperary defeated Kilkenny in the 1991 All-Ireland hurling final in Croke Park.

His warm and cheerful personality endeared him to audiences everywhere. This was reflected in articles written about him over the years, under headlines such as 'Ireland's golden tenor', 'the world's jolliest tenor' and 'a happy man'. His brother-in-law, Des Keogh, described Frank's unique relationship with his audiences: 'It was wonderful to see how the audience reacted to him. The love came across. And it was a two-way thing. He just adored his audiences as well'. He was proud of his achievements. In an interview with the Irish Times in 1996 he said 'I love being recognised. I love filling halls. I can fill Radio City in New York and I love it'. His wife Eily said that 'Frank sang for the sheer joy of singing' and not alone did he sing a song well but, in the words of his friend Brendan Long, 'whether is was a lieder by Mahler or a popular song like

The Rose of the Tralee he treated them all with the same respect and reverence and sang them all beautifully'.

Not alone did he enjoy national acclaim but the impact he made abroad was recognised by some of his Canadian and American fans, who subscribed to have a statue of him erected in Clonmel. It depicted Frank in performance mode and was designed by the American sculptor, Jerry McKenna. On 16 June 2002, many American visitors joined the people of Clonmel for the unveiling in Mick Delahunty Square. It was a fitting tribute to one who brought distinction to his native town and joy to all music lovers who were privileged to hear him.

Connolly, S. J., *Religion, law and power: The Making of Protestant Ireland 1660-1760*, (Oxford, 1992).

Coombes, James, 'The beatified martyrs of Ireland (5): Maurice MacKenraghty' in *Irish Theological Quarterly*, lxv, (2000), pp. 57-64.

Corish, P. J., *The Catholic communities in the seventeenth and eighteenth centuries*, (Dublin, 1981).

Corish, P. J., *The Irish Catholic experience*, (Dublin, 1985).

Corish, P. J. & Millett, Benignus, O.F.M. (eds.), *The Irish Martyrs*, (Dublin, 2005).

Cosgrove, Art (ed.), *A new History of Ireland*, ii, (Oxford, 1987).

Curry, John, *An historical and critical review of the Civil Wars in Ireland*, ii, (Dublin, 1786).

Curtis, Edmund, *A history of medieval Ireland*, (London, 1923).

Curtis, Edmund, *A history of Ireland*, (London, 1936).

Dalton, E. A. (Rev.), *History of Ireland*, (London, n.d.).

DeBurgh, U. H. Hussey, *Land owners of Ireland*, (Dublin, 1878).

De Paor, Liam, *The peoples of Ireland*, (London, 1986).

Dickson, David, *New foundations: Ireland 1660-1800*, (Dublin, 1987).

Dowling, P. J., *A history of Irish education*, (Cork, 1971).

Duffy, Charles Gavin, *My life in two hemispheres*, (London, 1898).

Ellis, Peter Beresford, *The Cromwellian colonisation of Ireland*, (London, 1975).

Ellis, Stephen G., *Tudor Ireland. Crown, community and the conflict of cultures 1470-1603*, (London, 1985).

Fitzgerald, Brian, *The Geraldines*, (London, 1951).

Fitzpatrick, Thomas, *Waterford during the Civil War 1641-1653*, (Waterford, 1912).

Flynn, Paul J., *The book of the Galtees*, (Dublin, 1926).

Fraser, Antonia, *Cromwell our chief of men* (Hertfordshire, 1976).

Forbes, J. D., *Victorian architect. The life and work of William Tinsley*, (Indiana University Press, 1953).

Forristal, Desmond, *Seventeen Martyrs*, (Dublin, 1990).

Forristal, Desmond, *Edel Quinn 1907-1944*, (Dublin, 1994).

Foster, Roy, *Modern Ireland 1600-1972*, (London, 1988).

Frame, Robin, *Colonial Ireland 1169-1369*, (Dublin, 1981).

Gaunt, Peter, *Oliver Cromwell*, (Oxford, 1996).

Gilbert, J. T. (ed.), *A contemporary history of affairs in Ireland from 1641 to 1652*, 3 vols. (Dublin, 1879/80).

Glendinning, Victoria, *Trollope*, (London, 1992).

Goodbody, Olive, *Guide to Irish Quaker records*, (Dublin, 1967).

Guiney, David, *Gold, silver, bronze*, (Kilkenny, n. d.).

Guiney, David, *Ireland's Olympic Heroes*, (Kilkenny, n.d.).

Haherin, John (ed.), *Trollope: Centenary essays*, (London, 1982).

Hall, Mr. & Mrs. S. C., *Ireland, its scenery, character etc.*, (London, 1842).

Higgins, Noreen, *Tipperary's Tithe War 1830-1838*, (Midleton, 2002).

Hill, Christopher, *God's Englishman*, (Reading, 1970).

Holland, Pat, *Tipperary Images*, (Cahir, 2003).

Hunt, Tom, 'Portlaw, Co. Waterford. Profile of a model village and its cotton factory', published M.A. thesis (N.U.I. Maynooth, 1999).

Irish, Bill, *Shipbuilding in Waterford 1820-1882*, (Bray, 2001).

Jacob, Robert E., *Quakers in industry and engineering in Ireland in the nineteenth century* (Dublin, 1988).

Johnson, Mary (ed.), *Ireland in the eighteenth century*, (Dublin, 1974).

Jones, Mark Bence, *A guide to Irish country houses*, (London, 1988).

Kelly, James, *That damn'd thing called honour. Duelling in Ireland 1570-1860*, (Cork, 1995).

Kelly, Michael, *Society of St. Vincent de Paul. Conference of S.S. Peter and Paul, Clonmel*, (Clonmel, 1993).

Lewis, Samuel, *Topographical dictionary of Ireland*, 2 vols. (London, 1837).

Liik, Edith Mary Johnson, *History of the Irish Parliament 1692-1800*, (Belfast, 2002).

Lonergan, Eamonn, *St. Luke's Hospital, Clonmel 1834-1994*, (Clonmel, 1994).

Long, Brendan (ed.), *The Nationalist centenary supplement*, (Clonmel, 1990).

Lydon, J. F., *The lordships of Ireland*, (Dublin, 1972).

McAllister, Thomas G., *Terence Bellew McManus*, (Maynooth, 1972).

McConville, Michael, *Ascendancy to oblivion*, (London, 1986).

Mc Redmond, Louis, *To the greater glory. A History of the Irish Jesuits*, (Dublin, 1991).

Madden, R. R., *The literary life and correspondence of the Countess of Blessington*, 3 vols., (London, 1855).

Martin, Francis X., 'The beatified martyrs of Ireland (12): William Tirry, O.S.A., Priest' in *Irish Theological Quarterly* lxvi, (2001), pp. 383-389.

Millett, Benignus, 'The beatified martyrs of Ireland (11): John Kearney, O.F.M., (Priest)' in *Irish Theological Quarterly*, lxvi, (2001), pp. 239-248.

Moody, T.W., Martin, F. X., and Byrne, F. J. (eds.), *A new history of Ireland, Early modern Ireland 1534-1691*, (Oxford, 1976)

Moody, T.W. & Vaughan, W.E. (eds.), *A new history of Ireland. Eighteenth century Ireland 1691-1800*, iv, (Oxford, 1986).

Moran, Gerard, *Radical Irish priests 1660-1970*, (Dublin, 1998).

Murphy, Daniel, *A History of Irish emigration and missionary education*, (Dublin, 2000).

Murphy, Donal A., *The two Tipperarys*, (Nenagh, 1994).

Murphy, J. J. (ed.), *The Delahunty story*, (Clonmel, 1958).

Murphy, Maureen (ed.), Asenath Nicholson, *Ireland's welcome to the stranger*, (Dublin, 2002).

Ní Mhurchú, Máire & Breathnach, Diarmuid, *Beathfhaisnéis*, (Dublin, 2001).

Neill, Desmond G., *Portlaw - a nineteenth century Quaker enterprise based on a model village* (Dublin, 1992).

Nolan, William & Thomas G. McGrath (eds.), *Tipperary: History and society*, (Dublin, 1985).

Otway-Ruthven, A.J., *A History of medieval Ireland*, (London, 1968).

Orpen, Goddard Henry, *Ireland under the Normans*, 3 vols. (Oxford, 1920).

O'Cathaoir, Brendan, *John Blake Dillon, Young Irelander*, (Dublin, 1990).

O'Connell, Patricia, *The Irish College at Lisbon 1590-1834*, (Dublin, 2001).

O'Connell, Philip & Darmody, W. C. (eds.), *Tercentenary Souvenir Record,* (Clonmel, 1950).

O'Connor, John, O.S.A., *A Priest on the Run*, (Dublin, 1992).

O'Faolain, Sean, *The Irish*, (Middlesex, 1947).

Ó Gráda, Cormac, *Ireland: a new economic history 1780-1939*, (Oxford, 1994).

O'Labhra, Colm, *Trodairí na Treas Briogáide*, (Nenagh, 1955).

O'Mahony, Seán, *Frongoch. University of Revolution*, (Dublin, 1987).

Ó Néill, Eoghan, *The Golden Vale of Ivowen*, (Dublin, 2001).

O'Shea, James, *Prince of swindlers. John Sadleir M.P. 1813-1856*, (Dublin, 1999).

Ó Siochrú, Micheál (ed.), *Kingdoms in Crisis: Ireland in the 1640s*, (Dublin, 2001).

O'Sullivan, Donal, *The Irish Free State and its Senate*, (Dublin, 1940).

O'Toole, Tina (ed.), *Munster women writers 1800-2000*, (Cork, 2005.

Power, P. (Rev.), *Waterford Saints and Scholars*, (Waterford, 1920).

Power, P. (Rev.), *Waterford and Lismore: a Compendious History of the United Dioceses*, (Waterford, 1937).

Power, T. P., *Land, politics and society in eighteenth century Tipperary*, (Oxford, 1993).

Sadleir, Michael, *Blessington D'Orsay: A Masquerade*, (London, 1933).

Seoighe, Mainchin, *The story of Kilmallock*, (Kilmallock, 1987).

Smith, Gus, *Tommy O'Brien*, (Dublin, 1987).

Snow, C. P., *Trollope*, (London, 1975).

Suenens, Leon-Joseph (Mgr.), *Edel Quinn: A heroine of the Apostolate (1907-1944)*, (Dublin, 1954).

Tanner, Marcus, *Ireland's holy wars*, (London, 2001).

Walsh, T. J., *The Irish continental college movement*, (Dublin, 1965).

Wakefield, Edward, *An account of Ireland, statistical and political*, 2 vols. (London, 1912).

Watson, S. J., *A dinner of herbs*, (Dublin, 1988).

White, James (ed.), *My Clonmel scrapbook*, (Dundalk, 1923).

Williams, David, *A world of his own. The double life of George Borrow*, (New York, 1982).

Williamson, Arthur P., *Enterprise, industrial development and social planning: Quakers and the emergence of the textile industry in Ireland* (Coleraine, 1992).

Wilson, Catherine Anne, *A new lease of life*, (Mc Gill-University Press, London, 1994.

Articles

Ahern, Michael, 'Clonmel Mechanics' Institute' in *Tipperary Historical Journal*, iv, (1991), pp. 159-162.

Ahern, Michael, 'Clonmel Charter School' in *Tipperary Historical Journal*, v, (1992), pp. 148-152.

Anon., 'An Irish Martyr at Tien Tsin' in *The Irish Ecclesiastical Record*, (December, 1870), pp. 130-139.

Anon., 'Irish colleges since the Reformation' in *The Irish Ecclesiastical Record*, (December, 1872), pp. 137-142.

Anon., 'Students of the Irish college in Salamanca' in *Irish Historical Studies*, iv (1915), pp. 1-58.

Anon., 'Geoffrey Baron (1606-1651) in *Oxford Dictionary of National Biography*, vol. IV (Oxford University Press, 2004), pp. 16-17.

Anon., 'Stephen White (1574-1646)' in *Oxford Dictionary of National Biography*, vol. DVIII (Oxford University Press, 2004). p. 620.

Athanasius, Father, O.F.M., 'Geoffry Baron' in *Tercentenary Commemoration of the Siege of Limerick,* (Limerick, 1951), pp. 51-57.

Augusteijn, Joost, 'The operations of South Tipperary IRA, 1916-1921) in Tipperary Historical Journal, ix (1996), pp. 145-163.

Ball, F. Elrington, 'Robert Marshall of Clonmel, Esq.' in *Cork Historical and Archaeological Society Journal*, iii, second series, (1897), pp. 263-274.

Barry, James Grene, 'The Bourkes of Clanwilliam' in *Journal of the Royal Society of Antiquaries of Ireland,* xix, (1839), pp. 192-200.

Bence-Jones, Mark, 'William Tinsley: Victorian or Georgian?' in *Quarterly Bulletin of the Irish Georgian Society,* Vol. III, no. 2 (April-June, 1960), pp. 13-20.

Blake, Martin J., 'William de Burg' in *Journal of Galway Archaeological and Historical Society,* vii, (1911-12), pp. 83-101.

Brady, Ciarán, 'Faction and the origins of the Desmond Rebellion of 1579' in *Irish Historical Studies*, xxii, no. 88 (September, 1981), pp. 289-312.

Butler, David, 'Presbyterianism in Clonmel' in *Tipperary Historical Journal'*, xvi, (2003), pp. 81-101.

Butler, George, 'The Battle of Affane' in *Butler Society Journal*, i, no. 5, (1973-74), pp. 320-327.

Butler, Theobald Fitzwalter, 'James Butler, first Duke of Ormonde' in *Journal of the Butler Society*, i, (1968), pp. 31-35.

Catholic Truth Society of Ireland, *Tipperary's gift to China*, (Dublin, 1912).

Chadwick, Áine M. 'Alice O'Sullivan, Clonmel missionary and martyr (1836-1870)' in *Tipperary Historical Journal*, xiv, (2001), pp. 83-88.

Corcoran, Timothy, 'Early Irish Jesuit educators' in *Studies*, xxx, (1941), pp. 59-68.

Corish, Patrick J. (ed.), 'Correspondence of the superior of the Jesuit mission in Ireland with John O'Brien, S.J. Rector of Salamanca' in *Archivium Hibernicum*, xxvii (1964), pp. 1-58.

Davis, Richard, 'The Reluctant Rebel' in *Tipperary Historical Journal*, xi (!998), p. 46-55.

Dickson, David, 'Aspects of the rise and decline of the Irish cotton industry' in Louis Cullen and T. C. Smout eds. *Comparative aspects of the Scottish and Irish economic and social history 1600-1900*, (Edinburgh, 1977).,

Dillon, Myles, 'Professor Michael A. O'Brien, 1896-1962' in *Celtica*, vi (1963), pp. v-vi.

Dowling, Dominic, 'Alice O'Sullivan, A Tipperary Martyr in China' in *Catholic Life* (June, 2004), pp. 28-29.

Empey, C. A., 'The Anglo-Norman community in Tipperary and Kilkenny in the middle ages: Change and continuity' in G. Mac Niocaill & P. F. Wallace (eds.), *Keimelia: Studies in medieval archaeology and history in memory of Tom Delaney* (Galway, 1988).

Empey, C. A., 'The Anglo-Norman settlement in the Cantred of Eliogarthy' in John Bradley (ed.), *Settlement and society in medieval Ireland presented to Francis Xavier Martin* (Kilkenny, 1988), pp. 207-228.

Empey, C. A., 'The Butler Lordship' in *The Journal of the Butler Society*, i, (1971), pp. 174-84.

Empey, C. A., 'Medieval Knocktopher: A Study in Manorial Settlement' in *Old Kilkenny Review*, iii (1983), pp. 441-452.

Empey, C. A., 'The Norman Period 1185-1500' in Wm. Nolan (ed.), *Tipperary: History and society,* (Dublin, 1985), pp. 71-91.

Empey, C. A., 'Conquest and settlement: Patterns of Anglo-Norman settlement in north Munster and south Leinster' in *Irish Economic and Social History,* xiii, (1986), pp. 5-31.

Falls, Cyril, 'Black Tom of Ormonde' in *The Irish Sword,* v, (1961-62), pp. 10-26.

Fraser, A. M., 'Marguerite Power – Countess of Blessington' in *Clonmel Historical and Archaeological Society Papaers,* i, no.4, (1955-56), pp. 53-60.

Greene, David, 'Michael O'Brien' in *Lochlann,* iii (1965), pp. 443-44.

Hammerstein, Helga, 'Aspects of the continental education of Irish students in the reign of Queen Elizabeth I' in *Historical Studies,* viii (1971), pp. 137-153.

Hennessy, Mark, 'Manorial organisation in early thirteenth-century Tipperary' in *Irish Geography,* xxix (2), 1996, pp. 116-125.

Hogan, Edmund, 'Life of Father Stephen White, S.J., Theologian and Polyhistor' in *Journal of the Waterford and South-East of Ireland Antiquarian Society,* iii, nos. 12 & 13, (1897), pp. 55-71 & 119-134.

Hunt, Tom, 'The origin and development of the Portlaw cotton industry' in *Decies,* diii, (1997), pp. 17-32.

Kelleher, John V., 'The pre-Norman Irish genealogies' in *Irish Historical Studies,* xvi, (1968-69), pp. 138-153.

Kingsford, C. L., 'Sir Otho de Grandison 1238?-1328' in *Transactions of the Royal Historical Society,* 3rd series, iii (1909), pp. 125-195.

Lanigan, Katherine, 'The Duke of Ormonde's Influence on Irish History' in *Journal of the Butler Society,* ii, (1969), pp. 120-122.

Lonergan, Patrick, Rev., 'The Life and Death of Father Sheehy' in *Irish Ecclesiastical Record,* xvii, (June, 1896), pp. 600-632.

Mac Mórna, Gall, 'The Trial of Father Sheehy' in James White (ed.), *My Clonmel Scrapbook* (Dundalk, 1923), pp. 353-359.

McCarthy, J. F., 'The Story of Sadleir's Bank' in *Clonmel Historical and Archaeological Society Papers,* i, no. 3 (1954-55), pp. 3-7.

Mc Curtain, Sister Margaret, 'The fall of the House of Desmond' in *Journal of the Kerry Archaeological Society,* viii (1976), pp. 28-44.

Millar, Phyllis, 'The Malcomsons of Portlaw and Waterford' in *Journal of the Old Waterford Society*, iii (1972), pp. 126-139.

Murphy, Thomas (Rev.), 'Father Nicholas Sheehy, P.P., Clogheen' in William Darmody (ed.), *Tercentenary Souvenir Record* (Clonmel, 1950), pp. 47-50.

Neely, William, 'The Protestant community of South Tipperary' in *Tipperary Historical Journal*, iv (1991), pp. 132-140.

Orpen, Goddard Henry, 'Richard de Burgh and the conquest of Connaught' in *Journal of Galway Archaeological and Historical Society*, vii, (1911-12), pp. 129-147.

O'Connell, Philip, 'William Tinsley (1804-1885)' in *Clonmel Historical and Archaeological Society Papers*, i, no.3, (1954-55), pp. 51-57.

O'Connell, Philip, 'The plot against Father Nicholas Sheehy: the historical background' in *The Irish Ecclesiastical Record*, cviii, (December, 1967), pp. 372-384.

O'Doherty, D. J., 'Father Thomas White, founder of the Irish college, Salamanca' in *Irish Ecclesiastical Record*, xxix, (1922), pp. 578-97.

O'Higgins, Brian, 'Cloud over Slievenamon' in James Maher (ed.), *Romantic Slievenamon* (Tralee, 1954), pp. 96-101.

Perros, Helen, 'Anglo-Norman settlement in Connacht in the thirteenth century' in *Group for the Study of Irish Historic Settlement*, vii, (Athlone, 1996-7), pp. 1-6.

Power, Rev. P. 'The Portlaw cotton factory' in *Waterford and the South-East of Ireland Archaeological Journal*, xiii (1910), pp. 59-64.

Power, Thomas, 'Father Nicholas Sheehy' in Gerald Moran, *Radical Irish priests*, (Dublin, 1988), pp. 62-78.

Reeves, Rev. Dr., 'Memoir of Stephen White' in *Proceedings of the Royal Irish Academy*, vol. VIII (Dublin, MDCCCLXIV), pp. 29-38.

Sayles, G. O., 'The Rebellious first earl of Desmond' in J. A. Watt, J. B. Morrall & F. X. Martin (eds.) *Medieval Studies presented to Aubrey Gwynn, S. J.*, (Dublin, 1961), pp. 203-229).

Richard Lalor Shiel, 'Glimpses of industrial Clonmel in 1829' in *Catholic Record* (September, 1918), pp. 115-117.

Silke, J. J., 'Irish Scholarship and the Renaissance, 1580-1673' in *Studies in the Renaissance*, xx, (America, 1973), pp. 169-206.

Simms, J. G., 'Hugh Dubh O'Neill's defence of Limerick, 1650-1651' in *The Irish Sword*, iii, (1957-58), p. 115-123).

Sisters of Charity, Provincial House, Mill Hill, *Pioneer Sisters of Charity of St. Vincent de Paul,* (London, 1953).

Vaughan-Arbuckle, Capt. C. L., 'A Tipperary farmer and Waterford tradesman of two centuries Ago' in *Journal of the Waterford and South-East of Ireland Antiquarian Society* ,viii (1902-06), pp. 80-89.

Wall, Thomas, 'A distinguished Irish humanist' in *Irish Ecclesiastical Record*, 5th series, lxvii (1946), pp. 92-102; 317-327.

Wall, Thomas, 'Parnassus in Waterford' in *Irish Ecclesiastical Record*, 5th series, lxix, (August, 1947), pp. 708-716.